MY OCEAN ODYSSEY

John Reginald

To all the lovely people
I met worldwide.

Cover design by

Valerie Fillingham

CONTENTS

INTRODUCTION

I record my life.
Too precious to go untold.
Chequered and unique.

One of my lifelong ambitions has been to write a book. Mission accomplished, here it is, a journal of our 127 night 2016 world voyage shared between P&O's Aurora and Cunard's Queen Elizabeth.

We were hesitant about taking on another world cruise even with many new places to visit but the tipping point came when we learned that Elizabeth's itinerary included six destinations in Japan. The whole voyage was an education of a lifetime, and I thank Val for dealing with all the necessary paperwork which included visas, currencies, communications, house and travel insurance. She also spent three months researching the destinations to enable us to get the best out of them.

I decided to turn my journal into a book mainly for my own gratification rather than for commercial reasons. I imagined holding the finished product and thinking "this is my creation, all my own work". Yes, I have written it mainly for myself as it has enormous personal value. However, you may take whatever you want from it. Be as selective as you wish but of course the honourable thing to do would be to read it from cover to cover!

A cruise ship is a microcosm, a fertile environment for any writer and my enjoyment comes not just from my experiences, but from writing about those experiences I had both on and off the ships. We both enjoy photography, hence the many references to it, but unlike the camera, it's the written word that records thoughts, feelings, comments and observations. Although I have written the book mainly with myself in mind, the thought that others may wish to read it has helped to keep me on my toes in terms of grammar and interest.

SATURDAY 2 JAN 2016.

Luxury coach from Blackpool to Southampton - grey and dismal but optimists see sunshine on grey days!

The voyage hath begun; first the Solent then the English Channel with surprisingly mild weather.

Fifty nights on the Aurora and seventy seven nights on the Queen Elizabeth, a total of one hundred and twenty seven nights world cruise. A huge journey into the unknown. What a prospect!

Encountered a few problems as we passed through security. First I was asked to remove my shoes - maybe they suspected I might be a nail bomber! I was given the ok but someone found my flamboyant socks rather amusing and started laughing. I was frisked and then asked to re-enter the scanner frame as the x-ray machine had picked up my multi gadgetted Swiss penknife which I have affectionately named Edward Scissor Hands! The security officer asked me to remove it from my hand luggage. He measured the longest blade and then told me it was just within the accepted length, otherwise it would have had to be confiscated. The cheek! How can one do a world cruise without such a useful tool?

And so we embarked the magnificent Aurora into a modern but modest square atrium.

Our spacious cabin was at midships with a good picture window and ample wardrobe space. We were well pleased.

The promenade deck soon beckoned. It's fully wrap round with one lap being about a third of a mile. We completed two laps before dusk in surprisingly mild weather. We looked forward to completing many more walks while looking out at the sea in all its moods.

The holiday spirit had taken hold when we popped a bottle of Val's vintage champagne and took it with us to the sail away party on the

2

top deck which was full of excited folk all enjoying a tipple. An extra treat was a firework display from a vessel which was anchored nearby. What a send-off!

Back in the stylish interior was Lynn Frederick in Champion's Bar. Although she sings to backing tracks she's a good performer, has a pleasant voice and plays tasty improvisations on the sax and flute. I had my sights set on jamming with her. I wonder. I'm pretty certain she was part of a duo on the Oceana some years ago. I shall find out.

Table for seven in the palatial Medina restaurant. All bubbly people full of the cruise spirit including a well-spoken guy called James who is travelling solo.

The Curzon theatre gave us Roy Walker, and whilst I admire his dead pan pauses, he's basically a "has been" and I was only able to laugh occasionally. Mick Miller would have been a better choice.

We were two happy cruisers as we read Horizon - the following days' programme before hitting the sheets. An excellent first day!

Cruising to the Azores

SUNDAY 3 JAN. English Channel then the Atlantic Ocean. Mild and sunny.

Slept until 4:00 am after a lovely smooth ride with no engine noise. Just laid there thinking about exploring the ship, but I'm no stranger to navigating cruise ships, its good fun. Part of our routine is checking the daily programme to decide what to do. There's always something for everyone.

Attended the digital camera tutorial called "Get Inspired" which was presented by the paparazzi. I now know how to enlarge a photo in display by using my zoom lever.

Wrote some journal in the luxurious Crow's Nest lounge bar which is situated on the top deck and spans the width of the ship and overlooks the bow with a 180 degree view. It was peaceful with the sun streaming in. Aurora was pitching deeply and gracefully which added to my comfort. Another cruise ship was steaming in the opposite direction and when it was close enough I identified it as the Oceana. It was good to see the old tub again chugging along.

Spent fifteen minutes walking the promenade deck but only horseshoe as the front was taped off. The sun shone on the port side. Very enjoyable. The promenade deck is one the attractions of cruising and I'll have walked a furrow in it by the time we arrive at Sydney. All the while I was thinking about my new year's resolution and the possibility of jamming with Lynn Frederick. Then it was Champions bar to see the great woman. I love her 'Knights in White Satin' with the flute solo. I want her in my band. Then of course I'd be certain of many gigs!

A guy at our lunch table told us that he was stopped by security for carrying a Swiss knife. I then told him my tale with a little more drama of course. Someone else told us they'd cruised round Cape Horn and the Arctic with ice on the decks. I mentioned the Amazon cruise when the decks were covered with insects and the captain saying they well outnumber the passengers!

After I did the dreadful deed of cancelling my gratuities I spoke to a posh guy called Gordon who'd just cancelled his. He's a retired banker from Jersey now living in Lytham. He told me he lived in our street in the sixties just after the houses were built. What a small world. An interesting guy. Meeting people like him is partly why I enjoy cruising.

Lecture, "Happiness-the secret and science of Joy" given by Professor Nigel MacLennan. Told us that some South American countries and Mexico are among the happiest nations but Nigeria is the winner. It seems that happiness is a choice and a belief. See yourself as being happy and you will. It's a habit. A great lecture, he was funny, articulate and entertaining. Spoke to him afterwards about Albert Ellis, the forerunner of cognitive behaviour therapy. Nigel is familiar with Ellis's work.

Talked with a couple who were on our Amazon Cruise. They'll be disembarking at San Francisco then boarding a train for New York. Sounded exciting. They said the average age of passengers on the Marco Polo was 77. They also said the Captain was very friendly with a passenger we nicknamed "Long Tall Sally," nothing like a bit of gossip!

Played my flute, and whilst I produced some very good low notes I felt I could do better. I enjoy playing my flute on sea days, while gazing at the ocean.

More Lynn Frederick in Champions Bar. She's becoming one of our daily doses of good music. We then moved on to Carmens Cabaret Bar where an Asian band called Caravan were playing great smooth western pop standards for dancing.

Six of us on our dinner table in the Medina. We all bonded very quickly. The restaurant however was only half full presumably because of sea sickness.

Aurora was rocking and rolling through rough seas but the shows must go on. We went to the Playhouse to see a brilliant German violin and piano duo called Zeitgeist which means the defining spirit or mood of a particular period of history. Two virtuosos. The violinist became destabilised occasionally through the movement of the ship but her playing was unaffected. The pieces were immaculate but the best was Vivaldi's 'Winter' which was very appropriate. All the while I could feel a tingling sensation. Afterwards we hobbled back to our cabin to be rocked asleep by the huge swells.

Cruising to the Azores

MONDAY 4 JAN. Atlantic Ocean. Cool

A turbulent night with frequent wakefulness. I was tossing and turning like the waves and the wind. But instead of being rocked to sleep I was being rocked awake! It was really quite scary but Aurora had reigned invincible. After the storm comes the calm but the promenade deck was still sealed off.

Another lecture in the Playhouse from the professor of psychology entitled "Relationship Magic" or how to have better relationships. Again he was very funny and entertaining but failed to teach me anything. I happened to be sat next to a retired pharmacist who had verbomania.

Val joined the choir and enjoyed her first session as a warbler in the Aurora singers. She has been put with the sopranos but she said it was early days yet to be making new friends.

The captain made his noon announcement saying last night's weather was exceptional with winds of up to ninety knots and swells between 8 and 10 meters. There were many reports of broken glass in the cabins.

At lunch in the Medina I was sitting next to a retired sister called Beryl who worked for the NHS. She was guns blazing about health tourists and folk who neglect their health who then make demands on the NHS. She is also anti-immigration. An interesting woman.

Port presentation about the Azores. The young female presenter was fluent and knew her subject, but she would have done well to pause more frequently, prune the superlatives and practice painting her picture less vividly to give us an idea of reality.

Two queues formed for the captain's reception. We were told that people in our queue would not be photographed with him. I wasn't too concerned because I wouldn't be buying the photo anyway. Grabbed a couple of gin and tonics and as the officers were not in a hurry to approach us, the passengers with their greetings we approached them but only for a short while as the Italian captain started his speech. He told us that while UK residents made up the vast majority of passengers there were many others from across the globe. Lyn was trying to entertain but was largely being ignored. Shame.

I was pleased to have James on our dinner table again. He has just taken himself off statins after 25 years. He eats porridge and blue berries to try and keep his cholesterol under control.

Roy Walker played to half a house. I think he should retire as he's seen better days. But I did manage a couple of laughs.

Cruising to the Azores.

TUESDAY 5 JAN. Atlantic Ocean. Sunny and cool.

The Atlantic is calmer but the promenade deck remains closed.

Two good books from the Library: "Thinking for the new millennium" and "Silence your mind". Learning never stops when I take a cruise.

Bravo! Deck 7 now open. Completed just over 3 laps, which is about a mile. It was cool but sunny. Felt invigorated.

Exhibition in the atrium called 'Aurora Uncovered'. A behind the scenes insight into life below decks. Generally disappointing and was mainly about getting you to buy wine, and a ships tour for £75.00. However there were a couple of interesting items: the ship produces an enormous amount of waste and we learned how machines deal with it. Metal cans, bottles and other recyclable products have a good commercial value. I was also given some tuition on folding a napkin to look like Sydney Opera House. It's now my party piece.

Lynn Frederick sings and plays some quality numbers that would suit our band. I'm making a note of them. Before she sang 'Baker Street' she told us that it inspired her to learn the sax. Her rendition was excellent.

Lunch in the Medina. We had Gordon for company. He lives in an apartment block called the Shakers in Lytham-St-Annes. Roy Walker also lives there. How unfortunate for Gordon!

Another lecture from the psychologist entitled, "Healthy after Fifty." I always thought that stooping was a symptom of old age but it's usually caused by a lack of suppleness exercises. He talked about the big 5 routes to being fit; don't smoke, don't become obese, have a healthy diet, drink moderately and exercise. We learned that walking for 20 minutes at any speed makes a massive difference to brain activity. The audience contained a few people from the medical profession.

Crow's Nest to listen to David Taylor on the piano. He played "These Foolish Things" and "The Way You Look Tonight" beautifully. Of course I fantasised about jamming with him.

Medina for dinner. We sat with two other couples, Kevin and Denise, she keeps a holiday journal - very wise madam as the journal records things the camera cannot. The other couple, David and Janet were also very friendly and we all got on well.

Ponta Delgada, Azores tomorrow.

WEDNESDAY 6 JAN.

Ponta Delgada Cruise Port, Sao Miguel Island, Azores, Atlantic Ocean. Warm, alternate sun and light rain. Perfect.

The Azores are Portuguese and form an archipelago of nine islands in the mid Atlantic. Dramatic landscapes and crater lakes characterise the islands. Ponta Delgada is the Azores chief port and administrative capital. Oh! and you can enjoy a delicious cheap beer!

We visited previously on the Marco Polo but this time we chose to go walkabout which included an itinerary that Val had prepared. I wasn't too keen at first but I agreed lest we should kill each other. We entered the campus of the University of the Azores, not a tourist attraction but worth a look. The gardens are beautifully kept and there is a small ornamental lake amid well-kept lawns.

Next was a park with an admission charge. We showed our ID and got senior rates at $1.00 each! There were many species of trees from Australia, particularly the Banyan Trees with their huge buttresses sloping downwards and outwards from the trunk. Fascinating. We saw massive bamboos and many other exotic trees and shrubs.

Lastly it was the imposing red and white Governor's House which is set in magnificent gardens, perfect for a stroll and the occasional photo.

We rounded off our morning with a coffee in a pleasant square. Val hitched up to Wi-Fi to try and make contact with Val and Bob to arrange our meeting with them in San Francisco. Alas there was still no contact. We were concerned because we'd set our hearts on seeing them. One or two pigeons swooped down onto the tables in search of morsels. The lady shooed them off but as soon as it was safe they reappeared.

Strolled back to the ship and gluttonised in Horizons before walking back into town by a different route. Had a beer each at $2.00 a pint and we were quite happy to sit and people watch. All was well with the world. The delightful waterfront walk back to the ship is probably the best walk in town. As we were nearing the ship we chanced on David and Janet who invited us to join them for a beer. He's 75 and retired, she's a part time solicitor and a little younger. They're fun loving and enjoy a laugh. Folk are so pleasant when they're in holiday mode. Certainly one of the big attractions in Ponta Delgada is the gorgeous cheap lager.

I love looking at couples and clocking their body language. One such couple were mute and clearly looked unhappy. Were they not enjoying the cruise? Had they fallen out? I don't know, only that there was no communication between them. They had my sympathy.

Finally, Aurora left the Azores and headed off to Barbados.

More David Taylor in the Crow's Nest. It fascinates me that an amazing pianist like him seems to have very little personality. I believe a personality can be developed, it all depends on how much value you put on it.

I usually manage half an hour's flute practice while Val gets ready for the evening. I'm conscious of my neighbours but fortunately no one has been knocking on the walls! I played some nice tones but my pieces need really working at to get the most out of my instrument.

The Playhouse is a small intimate theatre, perfect for minority pursuits. The Zeitgeist duo gave another recital. They played many classics including 'Air in G', 'The Swan' and Vivaldi's 'Summer'. An uplifting experience! The violinist is a perfectionist with an excellent memory. Classical music is certainly a key feature of cruising but sadly we've had no jazz yet.

The Curzon theatre presented a singer called Rebecca Storm with her husband playing bass. She opened up with two great numbers: "Paper Moon" and "I'm beginning to see the light" but it went into decline after that until she sang "The sunshine of your life" which was quite good.

Cruising to Barbados.

THURSDAY 7 JAN. Atlantic Ocean. Windy, grey skies, choppy.

When I talk about a smooth ride I mean we can't hear the engines. Not necessarily conducive to deep sleep as I'm often awake anyway between three and five am. If the mind games fail then I put on the light, make a brew then read.

To get the most from a cruise it helps if you're fit because the venues on the ship are some distance apart, also there can be lots of walking ashore.

A notice board situated in the library or reception would be useful for like-minded people to meet. In my case it would be interesting to get together with other musicians who have brought small instruments aboard.

Another presentation from the paparazzi to learn tips and techniques for taking better photos. It was pretty basic but I learned about the rule of thirds which seems to be the tried and tested formula for producing good compositions.

Another good table of folk at lunch in the Medina. We talked about freedom dining and set dining. Freedom dining means there are no set times for dinner and you have the opportunity to meet different people and sit in different parts of the restaurant. Set dining is just the opposite there are only two sitting times available at the same table with the same people and an obligation to tip. I prefer freedom.

Nigel McClennan had a full house in the Curzon Theatre for his lecture about brain fitness. He claims that crosswords and sudokus contribute very little towards the prevention of dementia but physical exercise and the desire to learn something new are key factors.

As I was clocking out a book from the library, the young female assistant saw my book by the Dalai Lama and said "My friend here is intelligent."

I turned to her friend and asked "How did you become intelligent?" She said, "Because I've met the Dalai Lama" I then asked "Did you speak to him?"
"Yes" she replied "And it was a privilege"
I ended by saying "Well then perhaps it's a privilege for me to speak to someone who has spoken to the Dalai Lama"! Then we all smiled!

It looks like the Crow's Nest has become one of my favourite haunts. David Taylor's flawless piano playing is certainly something to aspire to. I fell asleep, not because I was bored with his piano, I was genuinely tired and I was rather annoyed though when the waiter woke me up at 6:00 pm and kindly asked me to leave because he said I was inappropriately dressed. After that time you're expected to dress as the evening demands. I do agree with these standards. Who would want to see a yob like me in shorts and a tee shirt after 6:00 pm in a public area!!

Progressive flute practice. I'm pulling out all the stops and making every note work. I am aware dear reader that you may feel a little bored with the number of references I make to my flute practice. No apologies because it means so much to me. In any case do skip the references if you wish.

Lyn Frederick plays more sax than flute, pity it's not the other way round.

Carmen's cabaret bar gave us Caravan, the Asian band, who played an Eagles tribute, very polished and though it's not my kind of music the crowd loved it.

The interesting thing about freedom dining in the Medina restaurant is that you never know who you are going to be sitting with. Oh lord let them be interesting and no Melbourne Muppets please. (They were an endurance test on another cruise!). A couple called Jim and Brenda joined our table. He taught engineering at

Blackpool Collage and ended up as principal at Wigan Collage before retiring.

Brilliant finale in the Curzon Theatre - The McDonald Brothers. Two young guys from Scotland who bombed the audience with some rousing traditional music played on the fiddle, whistle, squeeze box, guitar and piano as well as vocal harmonies. We felt a lovely afterglow as we strolled out of the theatre.

Cruising to Barbados

FRIDAY 8 JAN. Atlantic Ocean. Warm, sunny spells and calmer.

Easy night with a smooth sail.

Deck 7 was partially sealed off which prevented a full wrap round walk which was rather frustrating.

Emma gave us a port talk about Barbados. I love her inflections but I can see right through it when she dramatises. Many choices such as snorkelling with turtles, beaches or a sunset cruise and of course there's shopping. Val and I intend to be independent, but whatever happens it will make good journaling.

A sight to behold in the Crow's Nest, a full length rainbow with both ends dipping into the sea, but surprisingly not photogenic.

Another worthwhile lecture from the professor, "Learn faster remember more." You have to make things distinctive even exaggerated to be able to remember them. He demonstrated the Roman Room method for remembering a list of items. I know the formula already but it's still interesting. My son Paul would have enjoyed it because he's a memory freak. As usual it was a packed house.

Played "Surry with the fringe on top" a couple of times to give me some practice with the low D's which are sounding lovely and clear. "Lime house Blues" and "Crush on You" are also taking shape. The question is will I have revolutionised my tone by 10 May to be able to put some fire into my jam sessions back home?

I'm trying to limit myself to one pint a day to keep both my liver and my on board account healthy. Although occasionally no doubt there'll be temptation to grapple with!

An interesting couple from Portsmouth joined our dinner table. Versy, from West Africa who is voluptuously black, and Peter, her husband, is white. He's a retired radio interviewer and presenter. Told me I look like Hank Marvin. For heaven's sake won't someone please tell me I look like Buddy Holly instead!!

The evening theatre gave us "Blame it on the boogie"- 70's singing and dancing. I admire the costumes, colour and energy but little else. Resembles a high energy aerobics class. Not my scene.

Chanced on David and Janet who had just won a bottle of bubbly and have invited us to pop it with them tomorrow night. How kind.

Cruising to Barbados.

SATURDAY 9 JAN. Atlantic Ocean. Sunny.

I'm now about to have a go at the present tense. Let's see what happens.

The sun shines across the ocean and into Horizons as I eat breakfast. It's the best weather to date.

Once again I collect and make a list of lookalikes. I've got Jeremy Corbyn, Philip Larkin, Alice Tinker and Jenny Murry. It's great fun to share these with other passengers who sometimes like to add to my list. I wonder if I can match the list I collected on the Marco Polo. I approach a guy sitting by the pool who is making entries in his journal. He introduces himself as Ken and we immediately

14

started talking about writing and the benefits of journaling. It's the "birds of a feather effect" He must be pretty keen because he writes his journal from a second draught. He's interesting. He disembarks at Sydney, Fly's to Manchester then two weeks later he cruises to the Far East on The Queen Mary. I ask for his views on joining a creative journaling group if one ever became available on a cruise ship, he says it would depend on the weather. I hope to be seeing more of him.

Val loses her temper with me for unthinkingly removing the "do not disturb" card from the door.

A couple in the pool area are writing their journals. Perhaps all the writers could form a group and meet every few days to exchange ideas. It's fascinating how we become sensitised to people with similar interests.

The sea is a gorgeously deep blue and the horizon is razor sharp as I take up a chair on the promenade deck. It's a lovely sunny day for relaxing. As I write I occasionally look up at the various shapes and sizes walking past and then I dispel all notions of my Adonis complex.

The playhouse for another photography lecture about macro photography. Close ups don't appeal to me but at least I learn where the macro button is located.

People zig zag in Horizons self-service because of the impractical way the food dispensers are laid out. The problem would be solved if the food areas were set out in two rows.

I'm having a long relaxing session in the shade with my book and welcome all who stop to talk or just to say hello. I notice yet another woman nearby who writes in her journal. Very sensible madam!

Nigel lectures about body language. He adds fun and interesting descriptions with his cartoon drawings and makes the audience laugh. As a professor of psychology he's also a brilliant showman and has a gift for engaging his audience.

It's 6:00 pm and I start playing my flute - one of the highlights of my day. Val doesn't know how lucky she is to be serenaded every evening! I continue to work on my tone and try to make my playing more sonorous. I have a lot of work to do. I'm not having a brilliant session. So perhaps I should consult with James Galway.

Another life enhancing recital with the Zeitgeist Duo. We're listening to music by Spanish composers, played by virtuosos.

Dinner with Kevin, Denise, Janet and David. David shares his champagne with us but we hope we don't become hitched as we value our freedom. David says I look like Hank Marvin! and Kevin asks if I've got any gossip!

The McDonald Brothers entertain us again. They play some good traditional stuff, but this time some of their songs are a little humdrum.

As is my wont before I go to sleep I make very brief notes about my day to facilitate the next days' writing.

Cruising to Barbados.

SUNDAY 10 JAN. Atlantic Ocean. Sunny.

Much warmer. Time to wear my shorts.

Horizons is busier at 7:30 am because the time change has created lighter mornings.

I always look at what people are putting on their plates. It seems that most people like to eat a lot of saturated fat in the form of sausages and bacon. Overweight folk should know better. Thank you very much but I enjoy my porridge oats and baked beans possibly because I'm neurotic!

It was 8:00 am and I was the only one in the Crow's Nest apart from the people who were setting up the art class. Some folk who have never painted before often join an art class during a cruise because they're in the holiday spirit and have the confidence to try new pursuits. They then get hooked and have a new hobby to take home.

The photographic presentation was about portraiture. We were shown some good examples. The rule of thirds applies to give the best results. Afterwards I was shown how to take bright scenes by using my Pallet mode.

Two lectures today called "Shrink You" which dealt with counselling and psychotherapy. The techniques I've learned on the mental health helpline apply to the letter. An experiment was once carried out where ordinary members of the public posed as counsellors and in a lot of cases people felt more comfortable with them than the real thing.

Deck walk with Val. The ocean resembled a mill pond, beautifully calm. We chanced on Angelina the violinist. I asked her if she'd heard of Stephane Grappelli she said she hadn't. Goodness, he was the world's leading jazz violinist but then Angelina said she doesn't play jazz. I'm not sure if a lot of classical musicians know how to play jazz. Or become frustrated because they can't.

I approached Emma about her port presentations. I told her I love her inflections but she'd do well to pause occasionally just like commas in sentences. She was very nice about it and said she would.

Port presentation, Aruba. As far as possible we travel independently because the ship's excursions can be a bit pricey. There are exceptions of course. We will be seeking some paradise beaches. Alas Emma failed to make the pauses and while she's good at what she does it was a pity a lot of it was all in one breath and overstated. When I spoke to her yesterday it was like "casting pearls before swine".

Part Two of "Shrink You"- the mysteries of the mind. Very little is known about how the brain works despite all the research taking place globally. Nigel discussed sleep and asked questions like "who are we?" which is a difficult question. At the end I personally thanked him for his lectures and the fun and interesting way he delivered them. We shook hands and I felt that he is the second best speaker I have ever heard. Bill Miller is the best.

Table for eight at dinner. One of whom, was a woman with a most dominant tongue which was quite irritating. Her husband simply kept as quiet as a mouse. There's no end to life's psychology lessons!

Final performance from the Zeitgeist duo. It was a packed house with long loud applauses. It didn't matter that they were wearing the same dresses as they had on last night. Salut d'Amour was heavenly.

The epilogue was a bible black walk of deck seven, and then to bed.

Barbados tomorrow.

MONDAY 11 JAN. Bridgetown Cruise Terminal, Barbados, Atlantic Ocean. Hot and sunny.

Barbados is located in the Lesser Antilles Islands in the Caribbean but surprisingly is not actually situated in the Caribbean Sea but surrounded by the Atlantic Ocean. It's a lush island with beautiful beaches.

Aurora was scheduled to stay one day in Barbados but she had encountered problems with her propeller shaft which meant we'd need an extra day there while she was undergoing repairs. Yippee!

Before we disembarked we roamed the upper decks to have a look at three other cruise ships which were in port - good for the local economy.

Aurora was buzzing with excitement as people were preparing to disembark for their adventures. The tourist office in the terminal was packed but we grabbed a map and had one thing on our minds - a paradise beach. The bus station was easy to find. $1.5 each took us to Paynes Bay - two miles towards Holetown. The location was idyllic with a turquoise sea, sunbeds and a big umbrella. We alternated swimming with reading, relaxing and enjoying honing the art of self-indulgence.

Afterwards we headed north about a mile towards Holetown, a tedious walk in the heat but we were rewarded with another beauty spot called Sandy Lane Bay. We decided not to swim there but had a cool beer instead and took many photos.

The ride on a reggae bus back to Bridgetown was the journey from hell, or good fun, depending on your perception. Loud reggae music and clattering windows provided the soundtrack while the women's hairstyles provided the pictures. Often these were piled up high in all directions with many tight thin plaits - very individualistic. The backs of those heads gave me some nice still and video shots. But oh dear, the size of some of the women - rather large to say the least. The journey however, gave us an insight into local bus travel with lovely scenery to boot.

Hunger hit when we boarded the ship and so it was a bee line to Horizons for some early evening nosh.

The fun continued in the Curzon Theatre with a jazz instrumentalist called Michael Grant who played sax, clarinet and piano. He gave us 'Take Five', 'Stranger on the Shore' and many others. His party piece was when he actually played the sax and clarinet simultaneously. I can do that with two Irish whistles! He ended up playing an Irish reel called 'Toss the Feather's, which was hardly jazz! But nevertheless, a great entertainer.

An excellent day but the walk to Sandy Lane Bay was challenging.

TUESDAY 12 JAN Bridgetown Barbados. Day 2. Hot and sunny.

A whirlwind of a day. We prepared a packed lunch and took it off the ship courtesy of P&O! We asked the tourist office about a quiet beach and we were advised to try Mullins Bay. Thirty minutes on a reggae bus towards Speightstown, not a dull moment.

Another paradise beach with big waves and very soon I was dancing with them. It was great fun. I didn't expect Val to cope but she did although she had much difficulty getting out of the sea because of the waves, the back flow and steep incline, until she was rescued by a Canadian man. Again we had a sun bed and canopy and made friends with two slim American women next to us who were probably stunning in their time! Once again we alternated the sea with reading and people watching.

 Back in the sea and disaster struck when a huge wave caught me off guard and ripped off my hat and sunglasses. I was sent tumbling and into a mild panic. I managed to retrieve my hat but my sunglasses were gone forever. I tried not to let it affect me but of course I was slightly upset, after all they are prescription sun glasses. Anyhow we spent a good few hours in paradise before boarding another reggae bus back to town. – I think I've warmed to reggae buses. We tried to find a shop selling clip on sun lenses to no avail.

A well-deserved beer was next. We sat on a balcony bar overlooking the marina and engaged two guys in conversation who we mistook for tourists - they were actually officers on the Aurora. They introduced themselves as Alan, technical stores manager and Pete, environmental officer, who were enjoying a few cold beers.

They're ex Royal Navy and told us the ship's propeller shaft had just been fitted with a new seal, hence the extra day in Barbados. I always say cruising is partially about meeting people and those two guys kept us well and truly connected and seemed to be enjoying our company. I can't remember how many bottles of beer we had but the whole affair was a good experience. We took a taxi back and wouldn't let them pay.

A stay in Barbados would not be complete without a rum punch and so it was to the bar outside the terminal for "two rum punches please" while we raved about the good time we had. Other cruisers were also having a tipple.

At dinner we had two gay men for company, one with the most peculiar hair style which almost stood upright. Was he having an identity crisis?

A ventriloquist called Gareth Oliver was very entertaining, especially after he got a guy to come onto the stage who was given a sort of mask to wear to make him look like a dummy. What followed was hysterical. The audience loved it. A brilliant climax to a brilliant day.

Cruising to Aruba.

WEDNESDAY 13 JAN. Caribbean Sea. Sunny, very warm.

Another nice clear day. Entered into a conversation with a lovely Swedish widow who is doing the whole world cruise. She lives in Northern Sweden where the temperature is minus 19 degrees and gets even colder. She enjoys deck walks with her pedometer which records an average of 11000 steps per day. Her English is good but she seldom gets the chance to practice it at home except through books and sub titles. She does voluntary work with victims of domestic violence.

Emma gave a port presentation about Huatulco Mexico. She used excellent inflections but alas, no pauses! What is wrong with the woman! Anyhow, many passengers will be delighted when they discover that a lovely beach will be awaiting them close to the ship's berth. (But don't attempt to take food off the ship or you'll have the sniffer dogs after you). After a refreshing swim you can have a cool beer under a canopy.

Judging by the number of coughing fits in the theatre I think the cruise cough had taken hold.

I expect "Pros and Cons" to be my main reading book for the entire cruise but it contains some bad grammar making some sentences difficult to understand. How disappointing.

Val jolted me out of the box when she persuaded me to have lunch with her on the Pennant Deck which overlooks the stern. We tried to engage with the couple sitting next to us but they weren't playing -their loss, but they must have had their reasons.

Chanced on Ken who was as exuberant as ever. First we talked about photography and then the laundrette. He is convinced that all the anti-social behaviour you hear about in there is merely exaggeration and rumour. He then said "Ah well I think I'll go and do something useful but I don't know what"!

The classical concert in the play house with the Tranquillo Duo was well worth seeing. The pianist was excellent but although the flautist was good she didn't quite hit the mark. Debussy's 'Clair de Lune' though was special. Two lovely slender young women in long red evening dresses making a nice contrast to the silver flute and the black piano. Afterwards I talked with the flautist. I asked her about jazz but she said she can't play it and has never heard of Miyazawa flutes. She told me that flutes don't need padding very often which I found reassuring.

A guy called Peter Howarth, the new lead singer with the Hollies was hardly Curzon material but we gave him a chance. He sang

Hollies and Roy Orbison but was at his limit with his voice, sometimes straining and killing the high notes. He appeared to be full of himself.

Aruba tomorrow.

THURSDAY 14 JAN. Oranjestad Cruise Terminal, Aruba. Caribbean Sea. Very warm and sunny.

Aruba is a tiny Caribbean island 16 miles north of Venezuela. There are beautiful sandy beaches and coves with landscapes full of colourful cacti.

As there are no paradise beaches back home we always seek them out when we're abroad, and we had the perfect weather for doing so. It was sunny and cloudy but very warm. The tourist desk advised us against swimming at Eagle Beach because of rough seas. Palm Beach was recommended instead. The couple standing next to us at the bus terminal invited us to join them and offered to share their snorkelling equipment so we took the local bus with them.

The return fare on the bus cost $4.00 each and surprise, surprise, the ships' captain was on board. He was standing up and was wearing summer shorts and shirt. He was accompanied by a lady and of course we speculated as to why someone of his status would choose a bus and not a taxi. They got off at a seemingly insignificant stop but Val saw a health centre nearby that perhaps was his destination. But what was wrong with the ship's medical centre?

The bus followed miles of coastline with gorgeous white sandy beaches to look at. We eventually arrived at an idyllic inlet with rocks and palms. The couple had introduced themselves as Paul and Lorraine who were working their passage as bridge instructors. Interesting. They went snorkelling out to sea and told us later that whilst there was no coral there were plentiful species of colourful fish. We declined the use of their gear partly because of the lack of coral.

The pelicans were exciting to watch. These clever creatures appear to spot fish from many meters high then swoop down, entering the water like a spear to make their kill. They use their pouch as a dip net to scoop the fish which they swallow immediately. Val preferred to do some photography while I took a dip. It was difficult entering the sea because of the rocks and stones but once I reached deeper water I felt more relaxed and was able to wallow in luxury! Val refrained because she was afraid of slipping on the rocks and damaging her knee. Later we told Paul and Lorraine we were off to another beach.

After ten minutes, our bus arrived and what fun it was having a laugh with the driver. Soon we stopped at Eagle Beach which looked quite calm and certainly inviting, so we gave it a try. The beach is a long stretch of white sand with three shades of turquoise sea between us and the horizon. Val felt safe here and went in for a long dip. I went in twice. More pelicans again. It was fascinating watching them often hitting the water at 90 degrees.

 Easy bus back to Oranjestad to see something of the town before sail away. It was hot but we enjoyed the walk. We came across some iguanas and huge coloured crabs in a stream. Sparks were coming off our cameras!

After we boarded Aurora we hit Horizons and then ate our food on the Pennant deck. I could not resist a cool pint but I sent mine back and then another because they weren't cold enough. I was then given a pint of Peroni at no extra cost. Delicious!

Val went to see a Sting tribute singer while I went to the Crow's Nest for some David Taylor. The paparazzi persuaded me to have my photograph taken but I had no intentions of buying it.

No tables in the Medina were free for others to join us so it was a table for the two of us. Full marks to the staff for meeting my dietary requirements.

Val went to bed while I went to the theatre and enjoyed the best entertainment to date from an American guy called John Nations, a comedy juggler. A maestro with a mesmerising act which was almost surreal. Watching him juggle five tennis rackets was an eye opener. The finale though, was the massive cherry on the cake. The lights went out and he juggled five coloured illuminated balls in complete darkness with the trajectories looking absolutely magical. It could have been something out of the Tate Gallery. The audience loved him. The show was a perfect climax to another wonderful day.

Cruising to Panama Canal.

FRIDAY 15 JAN. Caribbean Sea. Sunny and choppy.

Breakfast at 7:30 am in Horizons with the sun pouring in. I often feel like a journalist reporting what I see with people never ceasing to amaze me. I was about to serve myself some baked beans when I noticed an Asian guy standing next to me who was definitely thinking outside the box. His plate contained fair helpings of raspberries, prunes, and large green seeds; I then felt like commending him for originality when he topped the lot with baked beans and a fried egg!

Found a nice shady spot on the promenade deck for some diary and Dalai Lama when James stopped by for a chat. He reaffirmed his new regime after ending twenty five years of statins because of adverse side effects. He's now trying to control his cholesterol with diet and exercise. He also told me he's had two unsuccessful marriages and has worked all over the world.

As I walked round the deck I thought about the Dalai Lama's take on many subjects and felt I could do the same. There might be a book in me yet.

The photography presentation was mainly about light sensitivity. In the days of roll film this was all about film speeds. The higher the speed the more the film was sensitive to light but the grainier the image and vice versa. I lost count of the number of times the young presenter, God bless her said "Oaky dokes." I could predict when she was about to say it, it was really funny.

A retired guy called Captain Keith Pearson gave a lecture in the theatre about the Panama Canal. He was telling so many stories about his personal life that I wondered if he'd ever get started. However we learned that the "Mules" operate to keep ships in a centralised position to stop them scraping the sides. They guide the ships through the locks but don't tow them through. A reasonable talk but he was driven by his ego! I'd like to hear Bill Miller give a similar lecture.

Once again we took our lunch out onto the Pennant Deck. An elderly couple were sitting at the next table. She was in a wheel chair and he was holding her hand while Val took their picture. They then kissed. How touching, other people thought so too.

Better flute practice especially after Val told me I sounded a bit breathy.

Bible black deck walk. We chanced on John Nations the juggler who just happened to be singing his head off. We stopped to chat and he gave us a private recital of some funny songs he'd written. He comes from South Carolina but lives in Germany. He was manic but he has a huge personality, just as though he was still on the stage. He could give lessons to David Taylor!

We gave Paul Emanuel a chance in the theatre, but he's just another standard singer howling his head off as though he was stranded in the woods, and there was nothing original about his announcements either. Fortunately I was able to divert my mind by concentrating on the orchestra.

Panama Canal tomorrow.

SATURDAY 16 JAN. Panama Canal. Sunny, hot.

Today would be D Day for many passengers because of the Panama Canal transit. One of the highlights of the cruise. We christened it in 2013 but today we decided to experience it in a bit more depth! (no pun intended)

While Aurora was cruising the channel approaching the Gaton Locks, the passengers were vying for photos. We eased ourselves under the handrail to secure some deck to ourselves to capture some great pictures. The ship entered the staircase of three locks which is a massive feat of engineering, and a sight to behold. The operation took about two hours. We then entered Gaton Lake which is man-made and twenty three and a half miles long. The searing temperatures forced us to crash out for a while in our cabin before having a swift breakfast.

We had two easy chairs on deck seven and enjoyed the sights and sounds of the lake. Three container vessels passed by and we saw a container train with sixty trucks. The lake is also used for pleasure craft. After a delicious barbeque on the pool deck which was a nice change from the Lido we resumed our sightseeing. Aurora then cruised through the Galliard cut which is nine miles long and terminates at a single lock that drops down to the Miraflores Lake which is one mile long. It is also man-made or to be more precise "dammed up" and flooded. Finally we took up our positions to photograph the final two locks called the Miraflores Locks to drop us down into the Pacific Ocean. And that was it, the eighth modern wonder of the world. The transit took from 7:30 am until 3:00 pm and covered 48 miles. We were left with an unforgettable experience, not forgetting the superb views of the Panama City skyscrapers.

Completed two laps of deck seven and then some reading and writing.

What is happening to my flute practice? My tone was rubbish. After trying every which way and where, I put it in its case out of sheer frustration. My mood lifted however in the playhouse where Tranquillo played 'The Arrival of the Queen of Sheba' as well as some Bach and Vivaldi. Beautiful uplifting music.

We sat with two other couples at dinner, the ones from Accrington were ordinary but the other couple, especially him, looked as smarmy as he sounded. He made sneering remarks about the volume and contents of women's luggage. Val wasted no time in giving him a hand bagging by saying men's suits and shoes are heavy and occupy a lot of space - he immediately went into mute mode.

Took a bible black deck walk before the show which featured Fogwell Flax (of Sting tribute). He sang impressions of others singers. Very talented but not for me. The theatre was only a third full presumably because folk were tired from of an early start with Panama.

Cruising to Huatulco Mexico.

SUNDAY 17 JAN. Pacific Ocean.

Lovely and sunny in the Pacific with thunder forecast which would have been a new experience for us on a cruise ship but it didn't happen.

June and Rod seemed impatient to give me the news that their daughter had just had a baby girl by water birth.

During my promenade walk I revelled in the sunshine and calm sea. I'm no longer counting the number of laps, instead I'm now clocking it by time and aiming to walk twenty minutes both in morning and the afternoon. The warm wind on the starboard side was gorgeous.

The daily program failed to grab me. Nothing of interest but fortunately I'm resourceful and don't always have to rely on being entertained.

Val has just added a lookalike to my list "Moses" I said that he certainly looked like a character out of a biblical film. My list now totals nine.

Val introduced me to a guy called Ron Kemp aged eighty eight. He's an artist. He showed me a photo album of a selection of his paintings which included many subjects including landscapes and seascapes. He paints mainly in acrylic. He is a professional and sells most of his work and donates the money to charity and his church. He let me borrow his album to browse through in my spare time. Meeting him was a privilege.

Secured a comfy position on the promenade deck for reading and people watching, and once again I could advise anyone who is uncomfortable with their build to spend a few minutes watching the walkers going past then you'll love your body, and your self-esteem might even take a boost.

My Waldorf salad was made up of apple, grapes, walnuts and lettuce and was so tasty I went back for seconds.

I didn't have to look I could hear Capt. Pearson's voice resonating loudly round Horizons. He was airing his ego yet again. When I looked in his direction there he was in his captain's uniform holding court with just one person!

When I chanced on Peter Howarth, lead singer with the Hollies I decided to engage, as cruising is my only opportunity to meet celebrities. I asked what has happened to Alan Clark. I was told he'd got voice problems and can no longer sing. Actually Peter is a very nice guy. He liked talking with me and said "Thanks John I'll include a blues number in tonight's show."

Poor James, he's distraught about his impending divorce and even on a cruise ship he's in touch with his lawyers. He said he was about to go to the cinema to take his mind off things.

I believe the best way to write is to speak it then write it. This is controversial but it seems to me lots of writing appears to be rather stilted.

The stopper on my flute has worked loose, some sellotape did the trick which seemed to improve my tone which always makes me feel good.

Discovered the sounds of Kool Blue in Campions bar who comprise keyboard, bass and drums. They were playing some nice American song book which may bore some people but I don't think it's ever been bettered.

Val and I fantasised about working a world cruise through me running a creative journal group. She liked the idea and made some good suggestions about content and structure. Very interesting.

Bible black deck walk and then to the show to see Peter Howarth. He performed better than he did the other night and gave us some guitar playing and sang a blues number. A very reasonable act.

Felt some sympathy for David Taylor as he was playing his lovely piano music to empty chairs and tables in the Atrium.

Cruising to Huatulco, Mexico.

MONDAY 18 JAN. Pacific Ocean. Sunny and warm.

Lovely warm breeze with a slight choppy sea. Rain was forecast but didn't happen.

I was enjoying a nice quiet breakfast in Horizons and before I even looked round I knew it was her. I could tell by her voice, it was the ship's tongue, a frightful woman with the most uncontrollable urge to babble loudly. My escape was to change tables immediately.

I've noticed that some folk like their breakfast as late as 11:00 am. Not for me thank you, it's a complete waste of the morning.

Sat with Ron Kemp when I returned his album and showed him the video I made of his pictures. A lovely guy. He worked for the world's second largest oil drilling company as head of human resources with a work force of 8000 which included many nationalities with Holland being the most troublesome because of their laws. I discovered he's married to the lady in the wheelchair He's very devoted to her.

My next encounter was with the lovely pianist from the Tranquillo Duo. She said they get lots of work on cruise ships. I then told her I'd been playing the piano for 4 years. I then mentioned my two keyboard friends and the difference between them that one plays from her head the other from her heart. It was an enjoyable conversation which ended with her advice about the importance of playing scales.

During the captain's noon announcement he informed us that Aurora would not be visiting Huatulco because of prolonged rough seas and that an alternative destination is on the cards but nothing concrete yet.

Pigged out at lunch time with two Waldorf salads - and they were only starters!

Port talk with Emma. Instead of Huatulco we will be going to Cabo San Lucas which is on the tip of the Mexican peninsula. We arrive on Thursday. Sounds good. Her presentation was about San Francisco and was trying to tempt us with trips to Alcatraz before introducing other options. More superlatives but I won't mention pauses again because I don't think she has any intention of using them.

Delighted in the company of the Tranquillo Duo in Carmens. 'Meditation' and 'The Swan' were particularly nice. It was the only real culture on the ship today.

Decided to enter the photographic competition with 3 entries: COUPLE WALKING PAST A PALM TREE; RED TELEPHONE BOX; and FRANTIC CAMERAS ON THE PANAMA CANAL. I was charged £3.00 entry fee, the cheek!

A great show from Fogwell Flax. He gave us impressions and comedy. The audience were tumultuous when he did impressions not only of people but of everyday appliances including a washing machine, a spin dryer and a flushing toilet. He's one of the best acts to date.

A small world. A retired police officer on our dinner table told us he frequently visited Blackpool when he was young. He used to stay at 14 Dean Street, Val lived at No 16 - what a coincidence!

We decided to give Paul Emmanuel another chance because he would be singing Nat King Cole songs. Sorry, but he failed to grab us. Just another boring ten a penny singer.

Finally a pint and Kool Blue in the Crow's Nest. Excellent music but the bass player experiments too much. Peter Howarth was there and we chatted and I can report another small world. As a youngster he lived on Hardhorn Road Poulton - not far from where we live.

Cruising to Cabo San Lucas.

TUESDAY JAN 19. Pacific Ocean. Hot and Sunny.

Aurora was shaking during the night. I had no concerns but Val felt a little distraught.

Captain James Pearson was sat on his own at breakfast and I couldn't help sympathising with him because there was no one on whom he could inflict his ego.

Oh dear! The port side of the promenade deck was drenched through from waves raging in during the night. The deck assistants were busy with mops and some were towelling the recliners but the hot sunshine dried everything out in 30 minutes.

During my promenade walk I see the same couple every morning sitting in their customary positions. They're probably in their 80's. She reads while it looks like he's a prolific writer. I'd like to say hello to him and create the birds of a feather effect without being intrusive.

Many people must be afraid of losing their security cards and so they wear them around their necks, and some may also see the cards as fashion accessories. Odd!

The merchandise in the shops are grossly overpriced but because they are advertised as tax free, passengers think they are getting real bargains.

Interesting talk about Cabo San Lucas. The tall peaks in the sea look inviting but we have decided to go it alone and find our own way round.

The Pacific resembled a mill pond. Felt calm and relaxed. A far cry from last night's rough seas.

As we were pigging out in Horizons, I felt irrationally, that some folk clock how much I eat, but when I see how many cakes some folk put on their plates, my guilt disappears.

I was mulling on the brilliant but slightly unsettling paintings hanging on the walls around the ship. They depict people doing seemingly happy things with unhappy looks on their faces. There is something uneasy about them but it's only my speculation.

I've had no complaints from either side of the cabin about my flute practice. Perhaps they're on the early dinner sitting or maybe they revel in my playing and should feel privileged that there is a master flautist in their midst!

I'm rather disillusioned with Kool Blue. While the keyboard player is faultless, the drummer overuses his brushes and the excellent bass player prefers to be on another planet! I wonder how they'd react if I was to have words with them?

I was trying to engage Val in a discussion about the sinister paintings I spoke about earlier. She seemed to want to turn it into an argument because I didn't agree with her interpretation. I kept telling her I love the pictures but I felt there was something disturbing about them. And then she tried to belittle me in front of one of the staff and then I let my feelings show in no uncertain terms.

Crow's nest. I asked the waitress to kindly go back to the bar and fill my glass to the top. I sometimes wonder if the staff think I'm a problem, and yes I can be if things clash with my standards.

Lynn Frederick was in good voice but she looked a little isolated. She'd project much better with a spotlight.

Bible black deck walk with many folk doing the same thing.

The show in the Curzon Theatre was called "My Generation" and centred on Carnaby Street. The Headliners song and dance group were in high energy mode and sang 60's songs often very badly. The main character was moving round the stage in all directions as camp as candy floss which I found quite irritating. I was swearing at him, under my breath of course!

Cruising to Cabo San Lucas.

WEDNESDAY JAN 20. Pacific Ocean. Sunny, hot.

At 7:30 am, a little silence is as welcome as the food but there is always the occasional loud person or persons, which is my cue to move tables.

Just as yesterday the ocean was lovely and calm with a pleasant luke warm breeze as I sat drinking my tea on the Pennant Deck. The sun was casting silver light between the clouds. The heat came later.

We arranged a dinner date for the evening with David and Janet as there may not be another chance before they disembark at San Francisco.

My strategy to get near the prolific writer was simple. I grabbed the seat next to his wife and as expected I soon got into conversation with her. She is called Iris. Her husband is called Tom who spends a lot of time on the cruise writing children's adventure stories. Over the years he has written sixty four stories, two of which have been published. He also wrote a poem and sent it to the Queen which resulted in an invitation to Buckingham Palace. They are the second top cruisers on the Aurora. Apparently the '98' year old man is the top!

Iris loves Jeffry Archer and is currently reading Prison Diaries Book two. She recommended an author called James Patterson, a crime writer who writes very short chapters. I said I'd look him up. She owned the Osbourne Hotel in Blackpool for 11 years but gave it up because of drug addicts who squatted in her garage. Iris and Tom are seasoned travellers and have driven all over America. We talked for about 2 hours and enjoyed each other's company.

As I relaxed in the shade I gazed at the ocean - a glorious sight - calm and sparkling under blue skies with a razor sharp horizon. Perfect for reading my book of verse. James joined me for his daily chat. We discussed the difficulties of understanding modern poetry. Afterwards I carried on writing my journal.

Once again to the Playhouse to be wooed by those good looking sleek girls who know their instruments well. They gave a recital of film music but the pianist was a little heavy handed at times.

David and Janet were 20 minutes late for our dinner date, shame on them! But they're a really nice couple. I'm surprised that Janet never talks about her work as a solicitor but we do know she does child protection work.

Bible black deck walk to kill some time before the show started. I would love to have played some jigs and reels on my whistle out on deck because of the good acoustics but alas there were too many people about!

The show was called "We'll meet again" comprising popular music of the war years. It was more enjoyable than the previous evenings show and as expected the dancers were good but all the female singers could do was shriek. I find the camp guy quite irritating but fortunately he was less camp. The finale consisted of the audience rising to their feet waving their flags while singing Land Of Hope and Glory. I was half hearted about it.

Cabo San Lucas early tomorrow morning.

THURSDAY JAN 21. Cabo San Lucas. San Lucas Bay. Sea of Cortez, Mexico. Hot and sunny. Ship at anchor.

Cabo San Lucas is situated on the southern tip of the Baja Peninsula, boasts near perfect weather, stunning scenery, beautiful beaches, under water nature reserves and whale watching. What more could one want.

I was in Masquerades at 7:30 am and secured our tickets for the first tender.

The views from our anchorage position on the starboard side showed a long stretch of beach that looked inviting and from the port side dramatic rock formations. The decks were awash with people taking photographs.

We were ashore by 9:00 am and soon booked a boat trip. "Land's End" is actually the extreme tip of the Baja Peninsular with rock formations and pinnacles towering up out of the sea, and with a profusion of seals and pelicans the scene was set for our cameras. Another couple shared the experience. He was calm and quiet but she was over excited and had a loud squeaky voice and laugh - the grit in the morning's Vaseline! I could have happily thrown her overboard. Anyhow they soon got off to go snorkelling while we photographed everything in our midst including: the arched rock, Lovers Beach, Neptune's Finger and at one point there was a gap in the rocks through which you could see the Pacific. All very educational and certainly exciting. We told the boat man to drop us off at a beach and that we'd make our own way back to the tender.

Medano Beach is stunning and so we remained there for 4 hours with sun beds and a big umbrella. The highlight of our stay were the beach hawkers. At first they were a little irritating but we soon began to embrace them. They looked like human rainbows as they paraded past almost in a continuous procession bearing their colourful wears. They were loaded up to capacity which comprised hats, sun glasses, jewellery, ceramic plates, mangos, carvings, clothing, sheets and henna! Yes we were pestered a bit but they would easily take no for an answer. Val actually bought some earrings. We were lucky having so many hawkers around because they provided us with some brilliant pictures which are quite unique. We took to the sea a few times and although the water was cold, we quickly adjusted to the temperature, and then it was exhilaratingly enjoyable.

The walk back was longer that we expected but it was pleasant even in the hot sunshine. We arrived at a marina with tavernas and a few shops. A cold beer each in the heat cooled us down before we settled on a nice eatery overlooking the marina. It was tapas and another beer each which totalled $12.00. Not bad. We were well received and as we were leaving I shook hands with a few people.

As we made our way back to the tender we reflected on the day's adventures and concluded that Caba San Lucas was as good as Huatulco.

The photographic exhibition of competition entries was rather uninspiring but I felt No 124, my best entry, "Couple walking past a palm tree" could be in with a chance. One woman told me I could expect her vote!

Analisa Ching played violin for us in Carmens. What an entertainer! 5 ft. tall with a big personality and killer heels almost as long as her legs! She played fast furious, hyped up classics on her amplified violin sweeping round the floor with her long hair swirling in all directions. Her performance was full of energy, but the 6 piece band were a little loud. Nevertheless, this was super entertainment.

Table for 6. The two other couples had difficulty engaging with us. Val said it was because we're Northerners, you know, where they wear cloth caps!

Finally it was the Beatles Experience. Two of the original band members had changed. The new Paul in particular wasn't as good as the old Paul. But nevertheless they were fantastic and played to a packed house. Everyone stood up for their last number which was Twist and Shout. Heard some reviews on the way out which were not favourable nor were they for Angelina Ching. But I thought both acts were excellent.

Cruising to San Francisco.

FRIDAY JAN 22. Pacific Ocean. Sunny with a cool wind.

Laid long in bed thinking about relaxation and my aim to apply it to everything I do.

Saw the beautiful sunrise from the cabin window and later when I was having my breakfast I watched the sun streaming across the gentle swell. The Swedish lady told me it was minus 21 degrees in her country and minus 40 two days ago.

The winning picture in the photo competition was pretty ordinary, a cluttered sunset scene taken from the ship in Barbados and the runner up was a container ship with large shadows of passengers from the Aurora. Really! Val thought my entries were far superior. People don't seem to have any taste!

After just 3 weeks of rehearsals the passenger choir gave a magical performance and proved that Gareth Malone does not have the monopoly on coaching choirs. The Aurora singers presented a good choice of songs with harmony and the odd counter melody that blitzed the audience. Val was manic. Some of the taller women who stood at the front should have stood behind to balance people's heights but they refused because they wanted to be noticed. Shame on them.

As I was writing up my journal in the Crow's Nest I was asked to leave at six o' clock again because I was inappropriately dressed. Really!

An information note was delivered to the cabin advising us that on arrival at San Francisco we would be required to attend a face to face immigration inspection that would take place deck by deck.

As we are deck F we could expect to be interviewed between 11:00 am and 11:45 am. Shock Horror! That means we would lose almost a morning in San Francisco. Totally unacceptable. So off I went to the reception desk to request an earlier interview on the pretext we would be meeting Bob and Val at 10:15 am. Actually we would be meeting them the following day! I was told a decision in writing would be delivered to our room. If we get rejected then I would be seeking out the manager. It's the rebel in me!

And so to the Playhouse for Tranquillo's final concert. As expected those lovely girls gave their very best of music of the British Isles - virtuoso piano and flute. A flawless performance of heartfelt music. I particularly enjoyed Elgar's 'Salut d'Amour'. Their appearances matched the quality of their playing. We shall miss them.

When I took my seat in the Curzon I suspected I wouldn't enjoy the show and I was right. Forty five minutes of persecution to a half full theatre. Gwawr Edwards, Welsh soprano was the anti-climax of my day. She gave us naff songs in a painfully piercing voice mainly to backing tracks. But occasionally she had live piano accompaniment which was good. Even so she should be sent to the medical centre to have her vocal chords surgically removed to stop her from inflicting pain onto the world.

Cruising to San Francisco.

SATURDAY JAN 23. Pacific Ocean. Eventually sunny but cool.

It wasn't a pretty sight at breakfast time because guest speaker Captain Pearson was binge sneezing into his blue napkin, it was really quite disgusting. The woman on the next table also thought so, and moved elsewhere.

Chanced on Tranquillo and thanked them for their wonderful concerts. They perform on two cruise ships a year and have lots of work at home. I told them I play piano and flute and can feel quite low sometimes if I can't achieve good flute tone. She said she feels the same and that perfection can never be reached. They appeared to appreciate my company.

The passenger art exhibition was pretty ordinary except for "Yacht under the cliffs"

Analiza, and the soprano, Gwawr Edwards were due to share the stage for the matinee in the Curzon but the soprano was indisposed because she had lost her voice. While she has my sympathy I'd still ban sopranos from cruise ships. So we were treated to a full forty five minutes of the fire ball fiddler, bowing like the devil with her hair in a frenzy. Her high octane performance had the audience reeling. Once again though the band were a little heavy on her.

Back to the Crow's Nest but this time the bow was pitching so deeply it was like being on a see saw.

Bravo! We have been granted priority disembarkation at 8:00 am tomorrow morning which means we can expect a long day in San Francisco.

Finally it was another performance from the Beatles Experience. Paul had voice problems so they brought on the bassist from Kool Blue. Although he didn't sing, the overall sound was good, but there was too much twelve bar rock. The theatre was only a third full.

San Francisco tomorrow

SUNDAY 24 JAN. Pier 35. San Francisco Bay. San Francisco, California. Occasional sun, cool.

San Francisco is a beautiful hilly city on the North Californian coast. Famous for its cable cars, the Golden Gate Bridge and Alcatraz.

Normally Val would have wanted to murder me for waking her up at 5:30 am but she was forgiving when I told her we would shortly be cruising under the Golden Gate Bridge. It was a spectacle indeed as were the city lights.

The sun shone on the deck but it was quite cool. Alcatraz was nicely framed by one of the openings at the stern, but alas I left my camera behind.

Chanced on one of my next door neighbours. He introduced himself as Alan. I asked if he could hear my flute he said yes and so I apologised, but he said there was no need to because he enjoys listening to it. Bravo. Now I only have the people on the other side to worry about.

We were able to complete our face to face inspection by 8:50 am, but five minutes later our names were called out on the P. A. system to report to reception. There was a problem with our immigration papers. Although we felt like VIP'S as we were being escorted back to the border police and jumping the massive queues, we were in the dark as to what to expect but it was a relief when it was only a case of handing back some forms we were wrongly given.

We strolled past Fisherman's Wharf to pick up a street car to experience a long ride along the hilly streets to the terminus. We sat on the outside facing sideways which was quite thrilling. The clanking, clattering coach resembled something out of a museum while cameras were clicking non-stop throughout the whole journey. At the terminus we watched the car swing round on a turn table to prepare for its return journey.

I took Val's photo as she posed with three policemen. She also posed with a lovely black guy called Wayne. He's an ambassador, and wore a bright red suit. We had a laugh with him before he "spoke a souvenir" into my camcorder.

We headed off to China Town for some photos after we looked in St Mary's old cathedral where Val was greeted with a hug from one of the officials. Seems like it's one of many catholic churches in the city. China Town is big, and colourful with occasional locals playing traditional instruments. We then decided to sample Union Square which meant we had to double back. No problem because there was plenty of sights to occupy us. The Square is surrounded by famous shops including Tiffany's, Saks, 5th Avenue and Macy's. The weather was sunny with blue skies but slightly cool. Perfect. It was two large coffees al fresco with trees and sky scrapers for company, all was well with the world! An interesting area. We found the 'rest rooms' in Macy's before marvelling at the beautiful displays.

Back to China town for lunch. Val and I never do posh eateries while abroad, we prefer being down to earth and eating with the locals. We found a rough and ready basement restaurant and had delicious chicken, vegetables and rice with China tea.

Coit Tower was built in the late twenties to honour the city's voluntary fire fighters. A huge land mark with a 360 degree view from the top. Unfortunately there was a forty minute wait so we decided to explore some of the immediate area instead. The huge murals on the ground floor depicts different trades and technology of the 1930's.

We took various photos of the bay and marvelled at the beauty surrounding us but all the while we were concerned that we were unable to make contact with Val and Bob because of a connection problem on Val's phone. We were quite anxious and wondered if our meeting with them would ever go ahead.

Our next objective was the Crooked Street, with a long and undulating walk to reach it. The street is a tourist attraction, a steep zig zag narrow descent for cars with exclusive houses and large shrubs on either side.

By that time we were craving a beer and after walking downhill we found a bar. A little down market with American football on the screen. We had a pint of beer each which was tasty and inexpensive. We might have stayed for seconds but felt slightly uncomfortable so we drank up and moved on past Fisherman's Wharf and eventually found another bar near where Aurora was berthed. A well-mannered doorman, possibly seven foot tall, greeted us and let us in. The inside is quite small, and not for the claustrophobic. It was busy with a band rocking it out but we managed a couple of bar stools. It didn't take Val long to get into the swing as she started dancing with some of the local women who seemed quite friendly. I managed to capture the atmosphere on my camcorder. It was all hugs when we were leaving and the woman next to me told us not to forget her as she was from Louisiana!

It was 8:15 pm and after a long day we walked back to the ship while reflecting on the lovely vibrant city and the nice people we met.

The cherry was on the cake later with Dixieland Jazz from a local band. They were elderly and had a female vocalist. A guy played the Sousaphone. What a "mission accomplished" day we had!

MONDAY JAN 25. San Francisco. Day 2. Sunny and mild.

Once again at breakfast I looked out across the bay to Alcatraz and feared the ghosts of Al Capone and others might be looking out at me!

Good news! At last I made contact with Val and Bob. They have arranged to meet us at pier 35 at 11:00 am. Of course Val was overjoyed. Last year when we e-mailed them to tell them we would be in San Francisco for two days they said "It will be our joy to show you round our beautiful city" Little did we know what would be in store for us. It was no ordinary Aladdin's cave it was something much bigger.

It was two minutes past eleven when they picked us up in their shiny 4 w d Lexus. We made our first stop at the Aquatic Park. Then it was emotional hugs and greetings. The views of the Golden Gate Bridge and Alcatraz were superb. We then took the city by the throat and covered everything imaginable. How lucky we were that not only were we in the company of two nice people but they were about to give us their lovely city on a plate!

We saw Fort Mason which are ex-army barracks and are now let out for astronomic sums. Next was a beach with more magnificent views of the Golden Gate Bridge. Another photographic gem was the Palace of Fine Arts fronted by a huge rotunda surrounded by tall columns. A small lake captured the reflections of the buildings and trees and you could see the odd swan drifting by.

You don't realise the scale of the Golden Gate Bridge until you cross it - a massive feat of engineering with six lanes of traffic and at the other end more views especially of the city. It's interesting to look at the Bridge and Alcatraz from different viewpoints.

We motored on along winding roads and hills and passed through a millionaire's neighbourhood called Sea Cliff. These mansions face the Golden Gate inlet. Our cameras were clicking now and then and it was difficult taking it all in. Val's super commentaries were almost non-stop and her knowledge is amazing.

The house boats at Sausalito are interesting but rather grim looking and perhaps a little oversize.

Although we were taken to Land's End, Point Lobos and Ocean Beach I cannot place them because everything at that particular time was like a whirlwind.

Back across the GGB then onto one of the best stops of the day - Twin Peaks for a panoramic view of the city. This was indeed a sight to marvel at especially when you gaze at the long wide avenue with trees at its centre that goes up hill and seems to split the city in to two. The views of the GGB, the bay and the distant hills were equally impressive.

The next gem to visit was St Mary's Cathedral - the principle Catholic Church in San Francisco. The interior is a spectacle of coloured light that floods in from the many stained glass windows. Particularly interesting is the huge long square conical chandelier of glass rods with more stained glass windows behind - the crème de la crème of modern art! and space age churches.

Bob and Val refer to their apartment as the "Loft". It's big on security and once inside the building you enter a concrete corridor to access their entrance.

We were made very welcome with hor's d'ouves, wine and beer. Their loft is quite cluttered which I don't mind because some rooms in our house are just the same, it's far more homely than somewhere clinical. They have oversized furniture and big mirrors, one in particular is about eight feet high with a frame about fourteen inches wide. It's not hanging on the wall yet. The patio has decking and is cluttered with pots of flowers and shrubs. All very welcoming.

Bob has had back surgery and decided to rest while Val took us on a walkabout round Yerba-Buena gardens which has an ice rink, waterfalls dedicated to Martin Luther King, metal sculptures and an entertainment area. As it was evening in down town San Francisco we managed some good shots of the night scenery which included streets and sky scrapers which were all colourfully lit up.

Back to the Loft where I showed them some of my u-tube clips which they enjoyed. The four of us then went out for a meal to the Chaat Café which is a couple of blocks away. Our dinner consisted of Indian Street food. It was delicious and they were happy for us to share the cost.

We took a further short tour this time with Bob at the wheel. Val's knowledge of the city is extensive and as well as being a human dynamo she is a volunteer guide.

They dropped us off at the ship at 10:15 pm after many hugs and goodbyes. They're two lovely people as lovely as San Francisco and we felt very fortunate indeed to be treated like VIP'S.

There were only seven more passengers to board for the deadline of 11:00pm.

How strange it felt being in the atrium as we'd been away from it for so long, and when we got into bed our heads were still spinning with all the fantastic images we'd collected.

Cruising to La Haina, Hawaii.

TUESDAY JAN 26, Pacific Ocean. Sunny.

Still reeling from yesterday. Felt that a few days at sea would ground us.

The newbies have hit horizons for breakfast. A new batch of body shapes and behaviour to satisfy the most extreme people watching cravings.

Emma continues to bewitch me with her adorable voice although the hype sometimes irritates me. She gave a good presentation of the Hawaiian Island of Maui. Sorry Emma we won't be buying any trips. It's independent for us.

The deed hath been done. I have cancelled my gratuity charge for the next leg of the voyage. I sympathise with those newbies who probably don't realise the gratuities can be cancelled.

As I was relaxing on deck seven, James plonked himself next to me while we discussed the subject of sleep. He seemed interested in the mind games I play that keep me occupied during my long periods of wakefulness.

The ocean was another mill pond - calm and relaxing.

As we were having lunch on the Crystal Pool Deck we gazed at a row of huge women on recliners - bursting out of their swim suits - uninhibited and undignified - not a pleasant sight!

The entertainment in Carmen's comprised an American pianist called Craig Dahn with fingers like a hurricane. He played classics and rock and wore a sparkling blue jacket and sequinned shoes. He has worked with Liberace. The band were so loud that they prompted Val to proceed to the sound box to complain, but to no avail.

Shared the dinner table with a couple called Carol and Vic from Guernsey. She told us she does all the housework while he has it cushy! But they enjoy cliff walking together.

Mike Doyle comedian. Fairly good but most of his jokes are a bit retro and are about cruise ships. He sings as well, but some of his high pitched notes are irritatingly piercing.

I'm still imagining a duet with Lynn Fredrick. But it probably won't happen.

Cruising to La Haina, Hawaii.

WEDNESDAY 27 JAN. Pacific Ocean. Sunny

7:50 am. A few circuits of the promenade deck in the warm sunshine. The sea was deep blue but choppy.

Val showed me a note she was about to take to the reception desk to invite Ann Widdecombe to join us for pre-dinner drinks as Ann was friendly with Val's daughter and son in law. If we do meet up it will make a good journal entry!

Port talk Honolulu. We have pre booked Pearl harbour and a coach trip for the morning and then Waikiki Beach on our own in the afternoon.

I have two dreams; to play my flute on board with other musicians and to do a port presentation. I'm confident of doing both.

Took up a nice shady position on the promenade deck while the sun flooded across the ocean. I imagined the weather to be pretty cold back home.

Ann Widdecombe had a packed house with many people standing in the aisles. She talked about life after Westminster and her time on Strictly Come Dancing. She's a gifted speaker and very funny. She's positive, assertive, slightly patronising, school marmish but very entertaining. She's little with a large chest and little dress sense, but nevertheless she's a darling. Afterwards it was book sales and signing.

Who would have thought I'd be sat in the Crow's nest with an Adrian Mole book. But my method was to glean some ideas from it!

The play house is a small state of the art theatre with lovely orange seating - an ideal setting for classical music simply because classical music is in a minority pursuit. We had Martin Jacoby on piano and Jennifer Watson on the saxophone with "An introduction to the classical saxophone." I think it should have been rephrased to "An introduction to classical music played on the saxophone "The Swan' was nice and so was the Bach. She's right, her sax does sound a little like the cello. The piano accompaniment was excellent. They also played some modern pieces but sadly no American song book which to me is synonymous with the sax.

Table for eight in the medina. I think we allowed ourselves to be slightly marginalised because one guy talked that much I thought his tongue would seize up.

The 4 Tunes in the Curzon. Good voices, good falsetto's but failed to grab me because of their minimal harmonies. Fortunately I was able to focus on the band.

We Chanced on June and Rod, and then we were hopping round the atrium taking photographs of each other. Afterward Rod and I had a rant about immigration

Cruising to La Haina, Hawaii

THURSDAY 28 JAN. Pacific Ocean

I looked out of the cabin window over the great swell. Aurora was pitching and rolling quite dramatically. It must feel like confinement for people with inside cabins. I think I'd go over the edge if I had an inside cabin on a world cruise.

The fashionista was sauntering almost dream like round the food dispensers in Horizons. Her massively dyed red hair was her main feature. She was draped in a bright orange top, a long flimsy rainbow skirt and shiny grey high heel shoes. I thought "Wow! You are certainly entertaining me, but madam this is a cruise ship not a cat walk"

I hit the promenade deck with a twenty five minute walk. The ship was a big see saw on a big choppy ocean. It was windy but warmer.

As I was having my customary coffee with Val and a brief episode of people watching I concluded that a lot of women should go in for liposuction!

Back to the promenade deck for some peaceful writing with the gorgeous Pacific ocean within easy sight. It's the life indeed. I prefer to see myself as an amateur writer rather than someone who keeps a journal.

James joined me for a tete-a-tete. Our conversation moved from keeping fit on a cruise ship, to obesity and then to people who are boring.

We chanced on Allen, technical stores manager who we met in Barbados. He was friendly, willing to chat and gave Val a hug. Meeting people like him are always feel good occasions.

John Clitheroe's lecture about the lives and works of Rogers and Hammerstein was excellent. Rodgers's previous lyricist Lorenz Hart was only five foot tall and suffered from alcoholism and depression and hated his body image but what a gifted writer. Sadly Hammerstein died shortly after The Sound of Music opened on Broadway. Occasionally we sang along to some of their songs which was great fun.

Bigger flute practice than normal because Val went off to Carmens to see a band singing Bee Gee numbers. Not for me. The American song book is much more intelligent. My investment with tone is paying off.

Val has not had a reply from Ann Widdecombe.

Cruising to La Haina, Hawaii

FRIDAY JAN 29. Pacific Ocean. Warmer with less pitching.

Its little wonder the NHS are concerned about the diabetes epidemic when one looks round the ship at all the obesity cases. It seems that diabetes is often a choice.

At breakfast time once again the fashionista could be seen weaving her way around the food dispensers wearing a cardigan with mock fur back and front. She was also wearing a short white pleated skirt and the same shoes, huge blue eye make-up and Gypsy Rose earrings. She certainly likes standing out from the crowd. So go on girl, you're a people watcher's gem and I love writing about you.

Another packed house for Ann Widdecombe who talked about her life in Parliament. She made an analogy between Noah's Ark and the EU. Again she was interesting and funny. Afterwards she invited questions from the audience. Some serious some frivolous, but Ann being an ex-politician shrewdly knew all the answers before the questions had even been asked, yet I felt she was being honest.

Tom and Iris were in their customary positions on the promenade deck as I sidled over to say hello. Like lots of people on the ship they are very welcoming. We discussed folk who like to do Sudoku, word search and crosswords and how Tom and I enjoy creative writing. We also touched on experience v intelligence. Interesting. I thought I was bringing them news about the fashionista but they've seen her on previous cruise ships and have nicknamed her "Daisy May."

Another saxophone and piano concert. I felt sympathy for the duo because the Playhouse was only a quarter full but I began seeing it as an elite audience enjoying quality music. She played part of one of Bach's unaccompanied cello suites, some obscure pieces and Gershwin. They're very accomplished musicians. After their performance I approached her, with a few questions. I asked how often she has her saxophone keys repadded. She said she's been playing it for fifteen years with no sign of wear. She said the sax is easier to play than the flute but both have the same fingering. She also told me not to think in terms of biting the mouthpiece on the sax. She was so happy to answer my questions and said I could see her any time and would put me right about the sax. What a lovely woman.

Table for eight at dinner. We had the Guernsey couple, the babbler and his nice quiet wife. But by far the most interesting couple were the Australians. He told us that Bondi beach is a tourist attraction and that there are much nicer beaches within easy distance. And the babbling man delighted in babbling while his wife sat there so serenely. I imagine at home she takes anti-depressants to ease her mental agony! Val and I certainly have folk weighed up and categorised. Anyhow, I thought, "Where's the waiter with my dietary requests? Has he overlooked my neurotic choices?"

Now over to Mike Doyle. I've completely gone off him. I refuse to go to any more of his performances so he can f*** off. Not as funny as he was previously, besides he's discriminatory and likes making fun of disadvantaged old people. Politically incorrect. Also we have him well and truly clocked. At the end of his act he gets everyone to stand up, sway about and clap in time to his singing; this is to delude people into thinking his show has been brilliant. We think it's his way of rigging a standing ovation.

Still no reply from Ann Widdecombe.

Hawaiian Island of Maui, La Haina tomorrow.

SATURDAY 30 JAN. At anchor Hawaiian Island of Maui. Pacific Ocean. Sunny

Hawaii is the 50ᵗʰ US State comprising an archipelago of eight major islands situated in the mid Pacific. The scenery is beautifully diverse and has paradise beaches.

Maui is the second largest island and we spent a day in the capital La Haina.

Aloha!

A glorious day as we looked out from the promenade deck. We chanced on Ken and I think I've got him clocked. He's probably a stock phrase man meaning that some of his communication comprises stock comments, stock responses and stock observations rather like Peter from the Marco Polo. I do enjoy Ken's company though.

Daisy May was on our tender. There was something unnatural about her facial cosmetics which did not seem to gel with her heavy blue eye make-up. She was dressed like a celeb and would probably regret wearing semi high heels in La Haina.

As we stepped onto the main street we were greeted by The La Haina Senior Citizens Choir which comprised five women and a man with ukuleles and a guitar. They were draped in garland or "leis" while they sang catchy Hawaiian songs - a perfect start to our visit.

As we strolled along Front Street en route to Baby Beach we had the Aurora for company while she was anchored out at sea. Baby Beach is a paradise but we refrained from a dip because the sea looked rather shallow.

Val's heart leapt up when we came across a huge Buddha with a backdrop of mountains and palms. The beautiful temple nearby was also an interesting site which we briefly explored.

Back on the beach we heard two guys playing guitar and blues harmonica I sidled up to them and was made welcome to sit in. One guy, Derek, was bending the notes almost double while the other guy, John played the guitar and sang. He did most of the talking. He does a lot of composing and keeps the songs in his head. They are very talented. I asked if they'd let me play the guitar and John willingly handed it to me. And there we were banging out the blues on Baby Beach with Derek giving his all on the harmonica. Two nice American guys who liked my playing and enjoyed having me around. Already I was feeling it was the highlight of my day. If I'd have had my flute we could have had a trio.

We talked with some friendly locals as we headed back to look for somewhere to eat. The weather was gorgeous. We found an al fresco setting overlooking the beautiful sea - perfect for lunch and coffee.

Later we chanced on Ann Widdecombe gazing at a menu outside a café and we stopped to talk. She's received Val's invitation but no firm arrangements have been made yet for a get together. She told us that her lectures are paying for her cruise.

Banyan Tree Square resembled an open air art gallery containing mainly surrealistic paintings. It seemed like the hub of Lahaina.

After wandering around for some time we decided to take the local bus to another beach but we were given confusing directions as to where the bus stop was situated and of course we missed our bus and because they run every hour we aborted our mission.

More tramping round, more sights and sounds and more photos.

Inevitably we'd worked up a thirst for a cool beer. One bar invited you to open a tab and when you come to pay, a spin of a coin determines whether you pay half the bill! We refrained because we thought there might be a catch. Eventually we ended up in a sort of balcony bar overlooking the hustle and bustle of the street. We were surprised to see the Guernsey couple, Carol and Vic, who beckoned us to join them. No regrets. It was high spirits all round as we sipped two very large beers each. We revelled in each other's company and exchanged notes about Lahaina. Carol and Vic were a far cry from when we first met them on our dinner table when they looked so prim and proper! We let our hair down in an ideal setting with occasional glances at the colourful street below. A great day. Thank you Lahaina.

On the tender back to the ship we were ragging Mike Doyle and the 4 Tunes. I feel so comfortable when other folk agree with me.

Val was zonked but I went to the Curzon. Craig Dahn was good but the 4 Tunes again failed to move me. Fortunately it was their last performance.

Honolulu tomorrow.

SUNDAY JAN 31 Honolulu Harbour, Oahu Island, Hawaii. Pacific Ocean. Sunny.

Oahu is another stunning island. Its two major attractions are Pearl Harbour and Waikiki Beach.

Aloha!

Another glorious day. We had a good driver on our coach to Pearl Harbour but I think he had verbomania.

In 1941 Japan bombed Pearl Harbour Naval Base because they feared the USA would wage war to stop Japan creating an empire across Asia and the Pacific. The surprise attack brought America into the World War 2

The whole area is an indoor and outdoor museum depicting the events before, during and after the Japanese invasion. A 98 year old survivor of the attack was happy to talk to us. Although he has a wheel chair it doesn't stop him making regular visits to the site. The museums are interesting and so was the film show but you need a few days to be able to take it all in. A short boat trip took us to the Arizona Warship which lays as a tomb in shallow waters. A walkway above it allows you to get up close to look at the wreck and pay your respects to the 900 sea men entombed in the vessel which was hit on the morning of 7/12/1941. The scene was heart rending. At the end of the walkway there's a shrine with a stainless steel wall containing all the names of those who lost their lives. A display board shows photographs of scuba divers delivering the ashes of survivors of the attack, who have since died. These ashes are interred inside the wreck.

Next was a tour of some scenic parts of the island with photo stops, especially Nu'uanu Pali Lookout which was well worth seeing. A panorama of spectacular mountains, gorgeous green landscapes and the coast.

Next a tour of the Punchbowl. This is a vast cemetery set in an extinct volcano for Americas' fallen heroes from WW1, WW2, Korean and Vietnam wars. A serene place to visit, with extensive beautifully kept lawns containing flat headstones all laid out symmetrically. At the far end stands the Honolulu Memorial which comprises wide steps leading up to the court of honour with a statue of Lady Columbia who represents all grieving mothers.

We felt a visit to Honolulu would not be complete without sampling Waikiki Beach, courtesy of the local bus. I took a long dip in the warm crystal clear water. It's a good looking beach fringed with palm trees tall apartments and mountains at both ends. A great experience, and all very impressive but it was pretty cool when I left the water.

Val and I certainly know how to maximise our time whenever we go ashore and often boast that "we take things by the throat."

Back on the ship and what better than a cool pint on the Pennant Deck with a good view of the Aloha Tower.

We had a dramatic sun set with the skies ablaze which gave me some brilliant pictures.

The saxophone duo were as polished as ever and I acknowledged Jenny afterwards.

Table for eight in the Medina but we were victims of the "tongue" again. The only way you can silence him is by interrupting him.

The sail away party was in full swing on the Pool Deck with Caravan belting it out from their lofty perch. We were given leis to drape round our necks to add to the party spirit. Everywhere people were dancing.

We knew what to expect when we went to see Philip Brown. He was just as boring as ever singing songs that have been done to death. But we were happy to listen to what the band were doing and didn't mind them drowning him out occasionally. In fairness he sang "Unforgettable" quite well but overall, he's not for me.

Still no word from Ann Widdecombe. Can't understand it, especially since she's friendly with Val's family.

And so after an educational and fun filled day we set sail for Pago Pago (pronounced Pango Pango.)

MONDAY FEB 1 Pacific Ocean. Sunny.

Here's a story to end them all. I was talking with a guy at breakfast called Larry who took the world cruise on Aurora last year. Two weeks from Southampton he met a woman on the dance floor. A couple of weeks later he bought her an engagement ring from the jewellers in the arcade. When they arrived at Honolulu they bought a wedding dress. Three months after they disembarked at Southampton they got married. He's 83, she's 81. His son was best man. She sold her house in Glasgow and her car and they now live at his house in Chesterfield. Love is unaffected by age and for them there's no time like the present. Well done.

Saw Rod and June. I had them laughing when I told them I was bound for the medical centre for some tranquillisers after listening to the singer last night.

Port talk with Emma about Pago Pago in Samoa. Spectacular scenery, paradise beaches. She advised us to keep our expectations realistic. Now I wonder what that could possibly have meant!

Took to the promenade deck and wrote a full day's journal. James stopped by for his customary chat. We engaged in three rants: obesity, irritating people and unawareness.

Good news, Ann Widdecombe has agreed to pre - dinner drinks with us in the Crow's Nest.

Lynn Frederick welcomed me when I approached her for a chat. She was good to talk to. Yes she did work on the Oceana four years ago in a duo called Serendipity. She also confirmed that the sax and the flute have the same fingering but as for sound production she said you just blow into the flute. Nonsense Lynn, you know there's more to it than that, although I didn't tell her. She told me about a passenger once who approached her during one of her performances and told her quite assertively she was a s***. He and his wife said they didn't want to listen to her. Later on, after she sang 'Dream a Little Dream of Me' his wife approached her and told her she was a c***. Lynn was heart-broken and left the stage to report the incident to the entertainment manager who banned the couple from any venue where Lynn would be performing. I would have gone further and made them walk the plank.

Another Ann Widdecombe presentation. Her ratings seemed to have dropped a little but she still had a full house. She talked about her writing and said the plots "just come." Someone asked, "Ann, have you ever thought about becoming a comedienne?"
She said "Sir, I am a comedienne" An intelligent and very entertaining woman.

How beautiful to have the sun flooding into the cabin at 5:45 pm as I began playing my flute.

Kept our date with Ann Widdecombe. She insisted on buying drinks for us but I wouldn't hear of it. We whistle stopped many subjects which included the U3A band, Jay and Monica - the two ladies I jam with each week and my creative writing group. She laughed when I read out my list of lookalikes. Val talked about travel, photography and of course Helen and Greg with whom Ann is familiar. She's a very interesting person and we felt quite honoured to be in her company.

During dinner two women told us that before they flew from New York to San Francisco there was snow over two feet deep in parts of Manhattan.

The moment I'd been waiting for had arrived in the Curzon. Clare Langan, flautist. She gave an electrifying performance of jazz, rock and classics with flute tones from heaven. The band overpowered her in parts but she was brilliant as well as confident, funny, animated and with a gorgeous speaking voice. I loved every minute and so did Val. Well done Clare. We'll be there at your next performance.

Cruising to Pago Pago, Samoa.

TUESDAY FEB 2 Pacific Ocean. Sunny.

The wake is awesome to gaze at. Thunderous, with varied shades of blue and foam being churned up by the ships propellers leaving a trail a mile long.

Port talk, Apia, Samoa. Although we have previously visited we listened and learned. Emma said there is usually a charge for using the beaches. The cheek! I don't remember a charge.

Once again James joined me on the promenade deck. This time we discussed the loud band, singing (he said he was hopeless) and health. We agreed that if you can walk a few laps of the deck you know you are at least reasonably fit. He guessed my age to be sixty!! "Well James, you're a friend for life!"

I was just thinking about wheelchair users and why most people ignore them yet most people wouldn't ignore Stephen Hawking.

I stared in disbelief when I saw Val and Clare Langan walking towards me. Val disappeared leaving Clare and I to talk. It was great get together. I told her I'd brought my Miyazawa flute on board to play each evening. She said they're good quality instruments. We talked about the Aurora orchestra and my jam sessions with Jay and Monica. Clare is interesting and very friendly. She said she'd got a book I may find useful and asked me to wait until she went to her cabin for it. She very kindly returned with a Christmas flute music book with cd of backing tracks. She'd written a note inside saying she'd enjoyed meeting us and to push the boundaries 'cos you're never too old. Love Clare. She told me to go for the high notes, "just push your chin out, it's easy"- WHAT!! Meeting her was the highlight of the day.

The lovely Swedish lady is called Eva and she told me the temperature where she lives was -20 degrees which is common. The iced up lakes can support motor cars.

I was sat near a woman on the deck whose arms looked as though they were a foot wide. When she was ready to leave it took her husband and two other men to haul her out of her seat. Poor soul. I bet she was well over 20 stone and I imagined her heart to be working flat out.

Carmen's featured a singer called Lucy Williamson who has sung for royalty. Well I bet they needed painkillers. I diverted my attention to the band who had a good flute player and I was able to avoid having to listen to her loud piercing voice. Sorry Lucy you did not impress me. I think most straight singers should perform as far out to sea as possible to enable us to retain our sanity. I saw

Ken in his black shorts. The only one in the audience who was inappropriately dressed. I was surprised he didn't get chucked out.

Nice crowd at the dinner table. All gelled. One couple were happy with the advice we gave them about Hong Kong and everyone was impressed when I read out my list of lookalikes.

We attended the Headliners song and dance show called "Destination Dance" A spectacular event indeed but I think the female singers should be consigned to a sound proof room.

Finally some sanity in the Crow's nest with the genius piano of David Taylor who also sings well within his range. It's a shame he has no personality whatsoever. But he certainly helped us to recover from the previous show.

Cruising to Pago Pago, Samoa.

WEDNESDAY FEB 3 Pacific Ocean. Occasional sun, warm and humid.

Today we cross the equator. There'll be fun and games on one of the pool decks but I doubt if they'll match those we had on the Queen Victoria in 2013.

Thunder was forecast but it didn't happen.

People fascinate me. Each morning at 7:15 am two men and a woman occupy exactly the same seats at exactly the same table. It's the power of habit and I refer to them as the "breakfast club"

The weather was hot, humid and clear with a choppy sea as I was taking my 25 minute walk. Ann Widdecombe was relaxing as I passed by when I said "Good morning Ann, you look rather pensive." She said, "I'm just watching everyone walking off their calories while I'm putting them on." Ha ha! I thanked her again for last night.

When Emma gave her talk about Auckland, the theatre resembled a chest clinic. Interminable coughing and spluttering. We've previously visited Auckland but this time we'll be free spirits.

Tom told me he's 80 years old and has written 38,000 words since leaving Southampton. He seems a very dedicated writer.

We were told that a full crossing of the line ceremony would not take place because of health and safety reasons. WHAT!! At the crossing, 'Neptune' was presiding over a tug of war between the photographers and the medics with the crowd raging. After twenty minutes I wandered off because it was a let-down. However, the weather for the equator was cloudy, grey and sunless but very warm and humid.

To secure seats, I arrived at the theatre 45 minutes before AW gave her talk which was actually an interview with a member of the entertainment staff. She was quite humorous and certainly informative but I wondered if the questions were pre-arranged. Afterwards it was the audience's turn to ask questions via the roving microphone. She's one of the most entertaining people I've ever seen. She enjoys tranquillity, and carpe diem but hates muzak. Thanks Ann, you can join our club!

James joined me for my deck walk. He was gung ho about his meeting with a newly retired lady doctor. I was to observe over the following few days that he'd be accompanying her to various venues as well as sharing the same dinner table with her. Could romance be incubating?

Some of the choir made a surprise appearance in Carmen's and my instruction was to capture Val on video. They gave an impressive performance.

Two very pleasant couples joined us for dinner. An Australian mother and son and a couple called David and Jane.

Next on my to do list was the Playhouse to see the saxophone and piano concert. Jenny played one of her own works, an unusual composition called Chasing Angels. A three movement piece inspired by her sleep problems. The first was based on "trying to get to sleep" the second was to do with nightmares and the third was about actually falling to sleep. It was a brilliant concept about changing a negative to a positive.

Ken continues to defy the dress code by wearing shorts in the playhouse after 6:00pm. Why wasn't he thrown out like I was in the Crows' Nest. Some one of his standing should know better.

Val and I peeked in at the Curzon to check on Philip Brown's audience size. Not even half full and there he was mingling with the audience and sucking up to certain folk presumably to effect a big applause at the end.

He is an extremely nice guy but he's a straight singer and definitely not for me. Better not tell Rod and June because they love him.

Cruising to Pago Pago, Samoa.

THURSDAY FEB 4. South Pacific Ocean. Cloudy and humid with some rain.

Watched a torrential downpour on the Pool Deck. It was quite a spectacle watching the rain bouncing off the deck but it was short lived.

I suspected we'd be arriving late in Pago Pago because of our delayed departure from Honolulu and sure enough the captain announced that we could expect to arrive about 12 noon. We would therefore need to be organised to be able to maximise our time ashore.

The port talk gave us the Bay of Islands, New Zealand. I advised the couple sitting next to us to forget the ship's excursion and to visit Russel independently. They were grateful and said they would. Val approached Emma afterwards to complain about the PA system. Emma seemed rather startled but Val enjoys wielding her assertiveness.

The couple who parade round the deck in anoraks fascinate me. For goodness sake were not that far from the equator! - More proof that the ship is a microcosm.

The sax and piano duo were sitting on the pennant deck and were happy to welcome me for some conversation. I told them I loved Chasing Angels. Jenny said she also composed the accompaniment for it on her keyboard. I asked her more questions about playing the saxophone. She confirmed it is the easiest wind instrument to play. She gave me a shopping list of bits and pieces, reeds, mouthpiece and cushion, in case I wanted to take it up. She also gave me their e-mail address. They are really lovely people.

Possible fact - I bet I meet more interesting people on a 127 night cruise than most people back home do in 5 years.

I decided to remove my hearing aid to check the tone on my flute. What a difference. A more mellow sound. What am I to do now, play the flute without them? I think not. I shall have them checked when I get home. I suspect they may need tuning.

While David Taylor was entertaining me in the Crow's Nest with 'Witchcraft' and 'Begin the Beguine', Larry, the fast wedding man plonked himself next to me and introduced me to Marion, his wife. She sports long artificial eye lashes. Still wants to be attractive in her 80's. God bless her.

For the epilogue it was the virtuoso flute playing of Clare Langan. Another electrifying climax to the day. Here are some of the pieces she performed; 'Symphony of the Seas', 'Traumerei', 'Ashokan Farewell', 'Hungarian Rhapsody No 5', 'Scottish Medley', a

Straus Polka and 'Theme from Titanic'. It was odd that the theatre was only half full. Anyhow she connects well with her audience who loved her. Later I bought one of her cd's.

Pago Pago, American Samoa tomorrow.

FRIDAY FEB 5. Pago Pago, (pronounced Pango Pango) Harbour, American Samoa, Tutuila Island, South Pacific. Sunny

Another paradise island in the South Pacific with dramatic landscapes, beautiful beaches and friendly people who live mainly in coastal villages. Sadly the island was hit by the 2009 tsunami.

Buildings are known as fales (pronounced farlays) and are characterised by openness. Many consist of round or oval thatched roofs supported by poles around the edge. During the day the larger fales are used for relaxing, chatting and meetings. Chiefs look after a village's communal way of life and also maintain law and order.

Rod and June told me they paid 10k for their cruise from Southampton to Auckland. Proportionately that's a lot more than we paid. In September they will be taking another cruise to include New York and Quebec. They said they'd look to us for some hints and tips.

Kevin and Denise are a total let down, not an ounce of gossip for me. I suggested they try harder!

During the sail in to Pago Pago the decks were full of people photographing the beautiful scenery especially of the mountains.

 Once we were through the cruise terminal and into the street we suddenly felt like victims of a stampede. They were coming at us from all directions. Taxi drivers and coach drivers all excitedly trying to get you to do one of their tours. We'd previously arranged to share a taxi with Carol and Vic but we all opted to go for a local tour bus instead. It looked antique with its wooden frame interior, bench seats and vertically sliding windows. Actually it was only 8 years old.

The coastal scenery is gorgeous. We made a photo stop to admire a huge rock aptly named "Flowerpot Rock" about 150 meters out to sea. The rock resembles a huge plant pot because of the masses of vegetation growing from the top. It's home to exotic birds and is quite unique.

We motored past many villages with their open sided fales, these are houses where the villagers live. You wave to folk and they wave back especially the school children who seem happy to have you on their island. Everywhere is green and fertile. We made another stop to watch the sea gushing over the rocks. We then paid our respects at a memorial to some victims of the 2009 Tsunami. There were about 20 photos of young and old etched onto the wall. Next we entered a village and witnessed some devastation to a large communal building.

It was fun making contact and getting a response from the children and they were willing to pose for our cameras. I was shaking hands with a man thinking he was the father of three of the children I had just photographed but it turned out he was our driver! I didn't realise because I'd previously only seen him from behind! Back on the coach we saw more villages and schools and the hand waving continued. Next it was a comfort stop at a supermarket which was antique by our standards. Outside was a sign "Breastfeeding Helpline."

One of the highlights was a dip in the sea. It was like a hot tub, refreshing and very comfortable. The hills almost formed a circle around us and it felt like paradise. Afterwards Vic somehow hurt his foot when he descended from a step and the poor guy had to limp back to the village.

It was then time for a well-earned beer but we couldn't find a bar! Eventually we found a shop to satisfy our needs. I sat on some steps with a large bottle of beer to be close to the locals. The others went off for somewhere more comfortable. But I was happy enough thank you very much. I bought another beer when Ken rolled up and joined me. He told me he'd lost his wife to cancer. We found lots to talk about before shaking hands with a few of the locals. I felt really good as I walked back to the ship because of the enjoyable afternoon we'd had. Disaster struck though, as I neared the terminal - I couldn't hold it any longer, and you can guess what happened. Enough said ha ha!

Later Val told me that Carol and Vic thought I was rude because I remained on the steps while they went off. Nonsense, nothing wrong with wanting to keep company with the locals in a foreign land.

Lucy Williamson didn't entertain us, she actually tortured us and did the same to her songs. The blurb said she has sung for royalty. Well I hope they were wearing ear muffs. I think a lot of singers suffer from delusions of grandeur. On the way out of the theatre I told Ryan of my disappointment but members of the entertainment team don't like to mock the stars of the show.

We cross the International Dateline before arriving at Apia tomorrow. We lose a day. Instead of Saturday it'll be Sunday. Work that one out!

Upolu Island, Samoa tomorrow

SUNDAY FEB 7. Apia Harbour, Apia, Upolu Island Samoa. South Pacific. Sunny.

Upolu Island, like its neighbour, American Samoa has stunningly lush interiors, beautiful beaches and friendly welcoming people.

Apia is Samoa's capital and is situated on the north coast. The island was another victim of the 2009 tsunami.

Traditional culture in Samoa is built on faith, family and music. Nearly 100% of the population are Christians and the literacy rate is also close to 100%.

We lost Saturday because we traversed the dateline.

Often our destinations provide us with a welcoming party such as dancers or musicians. It's always a pleasure to look down from the Promenade deck to be entertained. This morning we were greeted by a large choir of men and women all dressed in white who sang on the quayside from a marquee because of the showers. Events like these are quite moving, and certainly add to the holiday spirit, a great start to the day. Afterwards the rain cleared to give us lovely hot sunshine.

As we were negotiating a taxi tour of the island, a couple, David and Jane, approached us and asked if they could join us. No problem as we hit it off with them when they shared our dinner table. $120 between the four of us seemed like a reasonable deal so off we went for one of the most enlightening and interesting days since Southampton. Our driver introduced himself as Sonny; he was knowledgeable, funny and spoke reasonable English.

The country roads are a joy with very little traffic. Everywhere is an undulating landscape of vivid green vegetation.

First, was Robert Louis Stevenson's House. He spent his last years here because he felt the climate would benefit his tuberculosis. He was very well respected by the locals and was only 44 years old when he died. It's an impressive house with balconies and verandahs and a setting of extensive open lawns, flowers and trees. We peeked in at some of the rooms and marvelled at the olde worlde furniture. We also helped ourselves to fresh papaya. Very tasty.

We motored on along the peaceful roads and then stopped to view a high, narrow waterfall with lots of blue butterflies fluttering about. I called them elusive because they wouldn't keep still for our cameras.

We began to bond with Sonny as we continued our journey passed villages and churches. It was Sunday and very busy for the locals who were attending Mass.

Val saw some washing on a line and asked Sonny to stop. The family invited us in. A little boy of about ten promptly gave Val a big kiss on the lips! There's a certain shyness among these lovely people yet they were willing to be photographed, especially the children. One boy had a guitar and he was quite happy for me to play it. Val and I sang "Aint She Sweet" which was well received with a good applause. Who would have thought we'd be entertaining the locals at a village on a South Pacific Island. Definitely one of life's golden moments. One of the boys appeared with plates of food. Not sure what it was but it resembled dry dumplings and tasted alright. Somehow I felt very special after our visit and kept on saying "what lovely people." We also felt happy that David and Jane were enjoying themselves.

More dream roads with seldom another car in sight. It was heart breaking though to witness the aftermath of the tsunami. The devastation to parts of the coastline and to some villages was not pleasant to see. One could only imagine the plight of those people on that dreadful day.

During our tour Sonny liked educating us and we enjoyed firing questions at him. We even gave him a song!

We arrived at a paradise beach called Lalomanu with white sand, palms and distant hills. Sonny told us we could stay as long as we wanted. There were about fifty small wooden beach fales lined up. They were on stilts, painted turquoise and yellow with mosquito nets and curtains. The fales are used for holiday accommodation and are run by the locals.

The crystal clear sea gave us a refreshing dip with good views of the chalets and palm trees. After about 30 minutes of bliss we found a bar and had a beer each. We bought a coke for Sonny.

As we travelled on there was not a boring moment as we took in the beautiful surroundings of this fertile island.

It felt rather odd to see a Catholic Church almost the size of a small cathedral across the road from another village. We went inside the church and admired the magnificent white interior and colourful stained glass windows.

We then entered the village rather cautiously not knowing exactly what to expect. A group of youngsters greeted us and soon we were chatting away and laughing as they posed for photographs.

The village chief is 84 and we were shown his house.

The shallow oblong concrete well was also interesting, it's actually the communal bath.

Compared to what we have, the living standards here are quite primitive, with open sided communal rooms, with either thatched or tin roofs. A young woman caught my eye and I wandered over to take her picture. As I approached her I didn't realise I was actually in her bedroom! Her three week old baby was asleep on the bed and she offered to wake her up for a photo. I suggested she let her sleep. The girl's sister was sat close by. More photos. I shook their hands and asked them their names. They were really friendly. I said "I am John" and I thanked them as I said goodbye.

While we were taking more photos of these lovely people and their children, a boy appeared and kindly gave us bananas. The warmth we were shown was quite moving. Another village with more golden moments that will live with us forever.

During our drive back to Apia we enjoyed looking at yet more villages while waving to the locals who never failed to wave in return.

Back in Apia we found a small bar where Sonny was happy to join us. We thanked him for being a brilliant driver and guide. The agreement was a four hour tour but we actually got six and a half hours for which we paid him extra. Of course he was delighted. It was then handshakes and hugs. David and Jane thanked us enormously and said without us they might not have had such a good experience. We enjoyed their company tremendously.

Dinner for six with fairly good company. We talked about how cruise companies can rip you off especially with trips and on board shops and how we wise up to it.

It was cacophony with a capital C in the Curzon. We endured three women called the Supremes who were painfully dreadful and the cheek to have their own conductor. As we were leaving the theatre someone who'd seen us singing for the Samoan family said Val and I were a much better act! Fame at last!

Cruising to Auckland, New Zealand.

MONDAY 8 FEB. South Pacific. Sunny.

I missed my walk because I got delayed through talking to various folk. Let's get my priorities right. If I have a choice between walking and gossip then gossip takes precedence!

Ken told me he writes over one thousand words a day in his journal. That tops my output, but is it about quantity or quality? Brevity is a skill and can help reduce quantity. He also talked about the difficulties of coping after his wife died but found solace through bereavement counselling.

One can always rely on Iris for a good story. She told me she knows a couple on the ship who are "professional complainers" They kicked off about their kettle and curtains and asked for the carpet to be replaced claiming it was dirty. Hey presto! They were given an upgrade. Iris saw them on a previous world cruise when a similar complaint had the same effect. She went on to say she knows of two other people, one of whom has a wheelie frame the other a wheel chair. She said they are fake invalids but it gets them priority mobility. Again she said she had a similar experience with them on a previous cruise. And yet there is a lady on the ship who is genuinely severely disabled who is quite happy to do trips on her own.

I suddenly felt disillusioned with Emma when she gave her talk about Wellington NZ. I have christened her the "queen of superlatives."

Many folk agreed that last night's performance of the Supremes was an insult and they should not have been allowed to inflict so much pain onto an innocent audience. But worst of all at the end we were asked to applaud about ten times for various people connected with the show. We nearly ended up with RSI!

We heard that a guy called Simon from the entertainment team has been sent home on a flight from Apia for being drunk after having previous warnings. It's one thing when passengers get drunk but when the staff do it, shame on them.

There's a definite problem on the ship - obesity. It's time the diet police were brought on board. I've heard of "stop smoking cruises" Why not have "stop over-eating cruises."

Kool Blue played some good numbers in the Crow's nest, but I suspect the bass player is blasé about his talents.

I sent my pint back because it didn't taste right but I think they tried the placebo effect on me!

The show featured a singer called Rietta Austin. What a sweetie. A plump New Zealander in killer heels who made us laugh with her self-deprecating humour. She had a good voice although she screamed a few high notes when she was quite capable of doing otherwise. I liked her Burt Bacharach songs. A good act, totally unpretentious.

Chanced on Jane and David. He said I look like Hank Marvin! Jane said yesterday's experience was epic and once again thanked us.

Cruising to Auckland. NZ.

TUESDAY 9 FEB. South Pacific. Sunny. Dark blue ocean.

Vic told Val he'd been to reception three times to pick up the Ibuprofen she'd left there for him to collect. Each time they claimed they hadn't got it. When Val went to investigate "Lovely" said they'd actually got it and then handed it to Val who promptly gave her a hand bagging for withholding the gel and for opening its sealed envelope.

The port talk was about Akaroa. NZ. Interesting scenery with nice beaches but there's a 25 minute tender. I'll need to put in another priority disembarkation request otherwise we could miss our private tour.

Took up my customary position on the Promenade Deck when I chanced on James and Anne. I suspected romance was in the air and I wasn't wrong. I was talking mainly with Anne. I mentioned my job before I retired, stress, and the evils of PPI insurance. I also told her about the helpline and my interest in the flute and piano. She's a retired GP and very interesting. Her son suffers with bi-polar. He has a music degree, teaches music, plays classical guitar and strums 1930's songs. A shame he isn't on board, we could arrange a jam.

Tom, the writer said he never works out a plot beforehand. He simply allows it to unfold as he puts pen to paper. I'm so lucky being surrounded by interesting people.

As I was walking across the pool deck I could have been in a morgue. A row of women on sunbeds were fast asleep and God bless them they all looked as though they'd pop it any minute!

Fortunately my first experience in the laundrette didn't resemble a scene from Eastenders. Far from it. The occupants were quite friendly. One guy told me he was thinking of doing a world cruise on the Queen Victoria but he's arranged to attend an open day first on the said ship with a meal included. A sort of recky, but it's costing him.

I do most of my journaling on the promenade deck and many people have noticed I'm a writer. I tell them it's not a secretive thing, I simply enjoy writing a detailed record of my experiences on the cruise ship, and by the time I reach Southampton on 10 May I will have written the equivalent of a book.

A woman with three companions said "Look, there's John from Poulton le Fylde." I couldn't remember where I'd met her, probably on the dinner table some time ago. She was on the committee at Chorley U3A. She told me she took a cruise on the Black Watch where a guy took 50 ukuleles on board and gave lessons. She joined the group and enjoyed it. I forgot to ask if they entered the passenger talent show. If they did, I shudder to think how they must have sounded!

It was late afternoon as I gazed out over deck 7, the sun created a million tightly packed diamonds on the calm swell - a sight to behold.

David Taylor played two requests for me in the crow's Nest: 'Solitude' and 'Mood Indigo'. I would have loved to have jammed along with him. I often wonder if the musicians enjoy playing or do they see it mainly as a job?

The Curzon Theatre was almost full for Stephen Garcia's performance. He's an excellent magician, and very funny.

I was captivated but Val was quite indifferent. She thinks magicians are a man's thing. Anyhow acts like his certainly beat most straight singers.

Chanced on June and Rod and we all decided to romp round the atrium taking photos of each other. They'll make good souvenirs because after all they've been good company.

Cruising to Auckland. NZ

WEDNESDAY 10 FEB. South Pacific. Sunny, cooler. Razor sharp horizon.

Larry joined me for breakfast. Poor soul, no personality and very little conversation but he appears to enjoy my company.

It was Dunedin NZ for the port talk. We've already booked a private train journey followed by a tour of the city. It's big on Scottish ancestry so perhaps we'll get bagpipes.

I'm speculating about James and Anne. Looks like they've found love on the high seas. Will they be exchanging e-mail addresses when they disembark or will they have other plans? I wonder if he's told her that even on the voyage he's in touch with his lawyers about his divorce. I do though, wish them well.

The choir performed to a packed house in the Curzon Theatre. They sang beautifully with songs from Westside Story, South Pacific and others. I particularly liked their harmony and occasional counterpoint and Val certainly looked the part singing her head off. "Gareth Malone, you need look no further"

A guy in the elevator was holding a guitar book. I asked if he'd brought his guitar on board and when he said he had, I suggested a jam and it wasn't long before we were in his cabin. Well, I thought I was a bit forward for bringing my flute on board until I saw his equipment. There was his guitar, amplifier and wires all over his bed. I asked if there'd been any knocking on the walls. He said no because he plays very quietly. He's been playing a year but already owns a number guitars. We've agreed to get together sometime before Sydney. His name is Mike. So, flute and guitar on the high seas! That's something to look forward to.

David has retracted on Hank Marvin and thinks I look more like Michael Palin! So many folk know my name. Either they have good memories or I'm easy to remember because of my bohemian appearance.

It was late afternoon and as I gazed out of the cabin window I wished my flute was as beautifully sounding as the ocean was as beautiful looking. I vow I'll never give up trying to achieve a rich and sweet singing tone, and even on the ship I'm working to that end every evening while Val is getting ready.

Stephen Garcia performed more magic and comedy to another packed house this time in Carmens. The audience love him. I was howling at one of his jokes. Later, June said my laughter was so infectious that it was me she was mainly laughing at and not the performer.

Our grievance about not being able to have world cruise status paid off. Customer services told us it was because we were doing it on two separate ships but to keep us sweet, they booked us into the Sindhu Indian Restaurant - very plush indeed - a creatively luxurious restaurant with yummy food that puts the medina in the back yard! A polite couple from Leicester were seated at the next table and seemed quite happy to fire questions at us about cruising.

Rietta Austin again in the Curzon with more self-deprecating humour but I preferred her previous show. Some of her high pitched notes sounded a little screechy but she's still a sweetie.

Tomorrow we arrive at Auckland. NZ

THURSDAY 11 FEB Waitemata Harbour. Auckland NZ. Sunny.

Auckland is New Zealand's largest city. Located in the north of North Island it boasts a wealth of attractions. The Sky Tower is its guardian angel.

Saw Stephen Garcia in the Lido and complemented him on his excellent performances. Told him we need more acts like his because straight singers are usually very boring. Very friendly guy. He's forty three, has two children and works one cruise ship per month.

We spent the day scratching the surface of this great city.

Took the hop on hop off to Bastion Point which is on high ground. The area is significant for the protests that took place there in the 1970's by the Maoris who were having their land taken from them by non-Maori New Zealanders. The ornamental gardens, a large oblong pond and an obelisk as a memorial to New Zealand's first labour prime minister were interesting as were the grassland and trees. The views of the city and surrounding waters are excellent.

We were then taken to the museum to pick up another bus. It's the driver' responsibility to synchronise the recorded commentaries with the bus's position. Our journey took us past many landmarks but it was the timber houses that gained our attention. These come in all shapes and sizes covering every price range. We actually drove on the motorway for a few minutes before stopping at Parnell Village.

This is an upmarket suburb and one of the most affluent in New Zealand. Particularly interesting were the timber shops, boutiques and restaurants - all individualistic and tastefully painted. The backs of the buildings are equally attractive and worth exploring.

They have walkways with quaint restaurants and a profusion of plants and flowers - a photographer's haven. We decided not to eat there as we felt it would take up too much time. Instead we took the hop on back to the ship for a swift lunch.

We followed our plan and took the ferry to Davenport. I don't know why, but I thought Davenport was an island when in fact it's part of a peninsular. We spent the whole afternoon there. The coastal path was interesting and lined with timber mansions with corrugated iron roof tops. All the while we had impressive views over the harbour to the city.

Our map was quite basic but with the help of some friendly locals we managed to find our way up to North Head. This is an extensive hill top and at one time was used for coastal defences. The Head is a warren of military tunnels and chambers which we entered. We could see a little but a torch would have been useful. Outside the views were remarkable in all directions including a huge beach below us.

We walked back the same way and witnessed an amazing sight. A guy was standing on a sort of surf board paddling his way across the harbour to the city. A bold undertaking indeed requiring a tremendous sense of balance.

Eventually we were able to satisfy our cravings when we found a nice bar. It was early evening as we sat under a parasol with a couple of cool beers. All was very pleasant as we reflected on the day. But the bar prices - Oh dear! But as Val rightly said, "Stuff it, we may never get the chance again."

Easy ferry back to the city before boarding the ship for a half hour crash out in the cabin.

It was dark as we were cruising out of Auckland, the cabin window provided some great night scenery of the city lights flooding the water with masses of colourful reflections for my camera.

We decided to escape people by having a table for two. Be assured were not being anti-social!

No straight singer to endure, instead it was a guy called Julian Smith who played the soprano sax. He came second in Britain's got talent. He's far from being pretentiously manic like most performers, instead he's laid back and speaks very calmly. A skilful instrumentalist but some jazz would have been welcome. But nevertheless a great finale to a great day.

Bay of Islands tomorrow.

FRIDAY 12 FEB. At anchor, Bay of Islands. NZ. South Pacific. Sunny.

The Bay of Islands is one of New Zealand's prize possessions. A superb marine park with 144 islands in crystal clear water and many secluded bays.

Arrived early for the first tender tickets but the staff turned up late without an apology.

Aurora anchored later than planned because the Auckland authorities advised us to reduce our speed because it was the whales mating season. Add to this an engine failure on one of the tenders and of course we also arrived late at the tender port.

The tender port is close to Waitangi where in 1840 the treaty was signed between the Maoris and the British Crown.

To save time and energy we took the shuttle bus to Paiha and then the easy ferry to Russell which afforded good views of some uninhabited islands, hills and the distant view of Russell.

Russell is a charming village with single and double storey white timber buildings which include a church, museum a colonial police station, boutiques, galleries, bars and restaurants all separated from the gracefully sloping beach by a narrow tree lined lane called the Strand. The area is an absolute gem.

It was hot as we made our way up to Flagstaff Hill and rather challenging especially since I was constantly having to adjust the sheath on my little toe. We looked at many expensive timber properties en-route and enjoyed the lovely views down to the village. All the while the crickets were in full voice but you never see them.

Flagstaff Hill gives a 360 degree panorama of hills, mountains and bays. In 1844 the Hill was the scene of protests by the Maoris who objected to the Union Jack Flag and cut the flagstaff down four times.

We met a friendly NZ couple who told us the second baby girl born in NZ to European Immigrants was in fact the couple's ancestor.

A ship's tour arrived and we wondered how much they'd paid for the privilege! It's a shame the staff on the tour desk don't tell you how easy and inexpensive it is to do the trip on your own.

Flora and fauna was next in the form of woodland path that looped down to Russell. We were in a kiwi area where dogs are banned. Unfortunately we didn't see a kiwi, but we were captivated by the sight of Russell below. The tall trees on either side of our track provided good sun shade and we were favoured with much bird song. We were two very contented tourists indeed. We strolled for a while on the Strand before indulging a cool beer and lunch al fresco under a big sunshade. A perfect setting.

Back on the ship we sipped another cool beer on the Pennant Deck while gazing out over the bay.

The Crow's Nest beckoned us for pre-dinner drinks with Lynn Frederick playing some tasty numbers on her flute and sax. If I could have her in my band back home there would be no question about doing gigs. Val thinks Lynn dresses too young. I don't think so, she just enjoys being trendy.

Good table for six including David, Jane and a Belfast couple. David is a Keith Richard lookalike - one more for my list! He tells me I have a slight Liverpool accent!

I am not a cinema goer but "The Irrational Man" at the playhouse appealed to me. A down in the dumps philosophy professor gets involved with a female student and then finds a zest for living when he decides to kill a corrupt judge. Good plot, good ending.

Cruising to Wellington.

SATURDAY 13 FEB. South Pacific. Sunny

Sat with Eva, the Swedish lady. She loved Russel and thanked me for recommending it. Her mobile showed that it was -30 degrees in her home town. We talked music and cruising. She's writing a cruise journal. How sensible!

Sydney was Emma's subject for the port talk. She could have suggested going independently to Manley on the ferry but she didn't. Shame, would have made an inexpensive and exciting morning out for first timers. But the cruise desk don't like telling you that because they lose money if people do their own thing.

As I've already mentioned one of my passions is talking to people. Here's another story from Iris: She was once on a cruise and got insulted by a waiter who threw a menu at her. After a number of complaints about him, P&O offered her £200.00 compensation. She refused. They raised the amount to £300.00. She refused again and threatened court action. She was then offered £1000.00. She kept holding out but eventually accepted their final offer of £1200.00!

Poor Val, she told me while she was in Horizons the handle fell off her cup and she got saturated with hot coffee. Her blouse, shorts and bra took a drenching. Reception eventually agreed to pay the laundry bill. I wonder if the costing for a cruise allows for compensations to guests who are not happy with this or that.

I was having a nosy and saw a notice on the inside of a staff door which read: "Smile, there are passengers on the other side!"

Bravo, Val has fixed it. A priority disembarkation card has been sent to our cabin. We'll be on the first tender at Akoroa to enable us to be on time for our private mail run trip.

I can sense some discontentment from the self-service and dining room staff, probably to do with conditions and pay. Freedom dining does not give them tips.

Spent many happy hours on the Promenade Deck bringing my journal up to date and people watching. Am I having too much of a good time?

Saw Piano a Deux in the Playhouse. A man and wife team. He's English, she's from Singapore. They played four hands classical piano, which was clever and amazingly entertaining. They took it in turns with their announcements and were really quite funny.

It was Champions bar for a pint and music from Caravan. They're a polished Asian band with a staggering repertoire. They sang a long Beatles medley which was quite good but not as good as my pint. The lead singer is a little odd, he stares out at the audience in one direction.

Julian Smith again at the Curzon with his soprano sax but it was hopelessly lacking some jazz. Next was a New Zealand singing sensation called Will Martin. He looks 18 but he's actually 47. Strange. He's a good pianist but his singing didn't grab me. The last number though was good when Julian Smith joined him in a duet.

Wellington tomorrow.

SUNDAY 14 FEB. Aotea Quay, Wellington Harbour. NZ. Sunny.

Wellington is New Zealand's capital and is situated on the southern Tip of North Island. The city is a haven for walkers and sightseers.

We berthed close to a huge logging depot with The West Parc Stadium nearby. The views of the harbour and beyond had the promise of a great day ashore, which would be our last day in North Island.

The shuttle bus took us into Wellington where we enjoyed looking at the shiny high rise buildings, but the funicular was our first priority.

It was opened in 1902 and ascends to a dream vista. Probably the place to get a taste of the sheer beauty of the area. We looked down over the central city, the harbours and the distant mountains layered in shades of grey. Scenic delights. Cameras at the ready, not forgetting Aurora resting sedately at the quayside. The terminus building contained a small transport museum with restored carriages on display. Naturally we sat in these and took each other's photos.

After we explored the top we opted to walk down back to town. Our route took us past many places of interest. The first being the botanical gardens with curly whirly pathways, huge trees, flowers, shrubs, cacti plants and rockeries. The crickets were singing non-stop which added to the atmosphere but a volunteer worker corrected us by telling us they're not actually crickets but cicadas.

The delightful pathway continued to curl down and brought us to a huge grass area with a brass band playing who were really quite good. Another path led down through a historic cemetery with lovely undulating ground. We then passed over a motorway bridge through some more cemetery before reaching street level.

Fancy being half way round the world and having lunch in a Burger King. But as I was aching for the loo I felt it was the best option.

The Te Papa museum near the waterfront is worth a visit. We learned about the Maoris, and immigration from Europe. We also sampled "the earthquake experience." We were sitting in a mock up living room of a house that literally shook and vibrated. The commentary was quite graphic and heart rending. After looking round some other galleries I sat down to adjust the sheath on my little toe when a rather eccentric woman approached me and said she sympathised with me. Later we saw her again with her husband and we started talking. They live in NZ and told us the current hot weather was their summer.

The harbour is a vibrant place with buskers and has a number of diving boards for daredevils who enjoy showing off their skills. It was fun capturing some of their feats on camera. We were just thinking about a beer when we chanced on the NZ couple yet again. Another conversation. Conclusion, a lovely couple.

Presently we found a bar and joined two women from the Aurora. They were drinking beer out of what looked like square jam jars with handles. We followed suit. We laughed and talked excitedly and all agreed that Wellington was a hit. They told us they're Jehovah's Witnesses but made no attempt to covert us!

During our walk back to the ship we came alongside a slow moving goods train laden to capacity with thousands of logs which was on its way to the depot for export. The workman on the rear truck beamed into my camera as I took his photo.

The paparazzi who had previously taken a valentine picture of me had it on display in the photo gallery at £17.50. The cheek! What an audacious rip off! How do they sleep at night? I wonder how many they actually sell.

I chanced on Brenda from Carleton and had her laughing when I told her I'd been traumatised by the price of the valentine photo.

Val went to bed while I went to the theatre. I saw GP Anne who told me she'd just spoken to her friend back home who was having her ninetieth birthday. She was one of the Bletchley Girls.

What I expected to be a good end to a brilliant day was actually the opposite. It was Lloyd Davis, an award winning comedian. I'd like to know if his awards were presented out of sympathy for telling corny jokes! Heard them all before.

Akaroa tomorrow am.

MONDAY FEB 15. Akaroa. Akaroa Harbour. South Island. Sunny.

Akaroa is Maori for "Long Harbour."- Stunningly beautiful.

As we cruised into the harbour the mountain we could see from the cabin window resembled a huge forested wall which was quite spectacular.

We were still having anxieties about meeting our man on time but fortunately our priority disembarkation card allowed us on to the first tender without having to queue. What a relief!

Akaroa made an instant impression - a paradise coastal village surrounded by a horseshoe of mountains with ready-made compositions for our cameras!

We were about to embark on something out of the ordinary - a tour in an area of New Zealand with the crème de la crème of picture postcard landscapes.

Our mail man arrived on time who introduced himself as Robin. He showed us into his shiny red mail van which was actually a small minibus and welcomed us to the Eastern Bays Scenic Mail Run. He explained that over a 5 hour period we would be delivering 147 items of mail mainly to remote farms, settlements and a village.

Without delay we were firing questions at Robin who was happy to oblige with his vast knowledge of the countryside having once been a conservationist.

We commented on how quiet the roads were with an amazing lack of vehicles. We understood why when he told us that the UK and NZ are roughly the same size but the UK has a population of 65 million while NZ has 5.5 million. He drives 120 kms. a day, 5 days a week with no traffic lights, no roundabouts, no one way systems and no hold ups whatsoever. I call that happy motoring.

He told us there'd been a small earthquake the previous evening. Houses shuddered and pots got broken. How sad.

His deliveries frequently took us off the beaten track into isolated areas where the mail was placed in drop off boxes which came in all shapes and sizes: round, square, cylindrical and decorative. A few of them even looked like miniature doll's houses, and they were all supported on pedestals of various shapes and sizes ranging from short poles, dead tree trunks, and stones. Many of the boxes were painted in bright colours. He could often drop the mail without having to leave his vehicle because the boxes were at window height. Sometimes he would also collect mail from the boxes if the pointer was in an upward position.

We had the lot. Unspoiled landscapes, beaches, rock scenery, a crater rim, an old isolated church, a village, sign posts with unusual names like Starvation Gulley and Decanter Bay Road, and of course we could stop at any time for photos.

Often the best parts of the landscape were the bays, Decanter Bay, Pigeon Bay and Le Bons Bay. All the more scenic because we were able to view them from elevated positions. "Artists, photographers and poets you need look no further."

Half way round we stopped at the side of a road that had a battered old picnic table with two benches. Quite unexpectedly Robin produced a table cloth and spread it out for flasks of tea, coffee, cheese, biscuits, chutney and fudge cake, all home-made. What a surprise, what an occasion, and what hospitality. By then we had well and truly bonded with him and took photos of him as host!

His advice to folk who rush round is to "stop and smell the roses."

We stopped at Okains Bay village store. Opposite is an earthquake damaged school with only 13 pupils. At the store Robin barters fruit for fresh milk straight from the cow, and as there was no refrigeration in his vehicle for the one and a half litres of milk he'd been given he decided to drop it off at his homestead. We drove on and soon came to a remote track with acres of trees and then descended into a small dell where his house nestles in 18 acres of land. He went inside while we had a brief look round. The bird song was beautiful. His wife spends a lot of time tending their plot making them self-sufficient in fruit, veg, walnuts and eggs.

Our final sightseeing experience was Le Bons Beach. Robin assured us it was the best beach in New Zealand - a long wide stretch of sand with the sea gently rolling in with high crags like book ends at either end. We walked the whole length and only saw five other people. Robin met us at the other end where we all took photos of each other. Then, after a few more deliveries, it was the final leg back to the village, while still marvelling at the scenery including Aurora in the distance.

The whole trip lasted five and a half hours and we made him feel good for taking us to paradise and back! He'd almost become a friend and I had to coax him into accepting ten dollars extra.

We walked along some of the main street, peeked inside a charming timber church and then had a late lunch and a beer al fresco. Finally we ambled along the waterfront to capture more gorgeous pictures before boarding the tender. Could anyone from the Aurora possibly match what we experienced?

After we crashed out in the cabin Val decided to stay in while I went to Carmen's to see the mentalist perform. It was a good show even though his tricks were a little weak except the last one where he asked a member of the audience to pick any number from a telephone directory and of course that number was written down in a sealed envelope. How do they do it?

Table for seven. A1 company, all complaining about the price of things.

Val chose to have an early night while I went to the Curzon on my own. James and Dr Anne joined me. She'd had a few drinks and I could smell it on her breath as she was getting quite affectionate towards me - God bless her! Heaven knows what James must have been thinking.

I made an exception to being entertained by a straight singer. Laura Broad from Birmingham. Lovely voice, classically trained, down to earth and unpretentious. I loved the way she moved her hands and arms in time to her songs.

Port Chalmers tomorrow am.

TUESDAY 16 FEB. Port Chalmers (For Dunedin). Otago Harbour New Zealand.

Dunedin is the South Island's second largest city and is situated on the south east coast. After the Maoris, the Scots were the first people to settle there. Dunedin is the old Gaelic name for Edinburgh.

Port Chalmers is a container port and we were able to watch a commercial ship at close quarters being loaded up with a huge cargo of logs from the logging depot. Robin had previously explained that NZ is a big exporter of timber to China, with the timber often coming back as furniture. Interesting.

Our private tour bus took us to Dunedin which is 10 kilometres away with pleasant coastal scenery en- route.

Dunedin railway Station, is a palatial building in the Flemish Renaissance style which is fronted by ornamental gardens. Equally impressive is the interior with its tiled walls, floor and balconies.

It was a pleasant change to be sitting in an eighty year old wood panelled railway carriage with netted luggage racks.

When we set off I had to use my assertiveness skills to silence a couple of guys who were talking above the commentary. They were very reasonable and said "sorry mate."

The railway follows the Taieri River Gorge and climbs a total of 250 meters to Pukerangi, our destination.

Soon we were soaking up the drama as we snaked our way through tunnels, across viaducts, rocky terrain and bridges. The sight of the deep gorge was awesome. Other features included lakes, wooded areas and grassland.

We were standing behind the safety bars at the end of the rear carriage watching the tracks paling into the distance while the terrain was being reeled off either side to the rhythmic clickety clack, clickety clack! We also took up positions in between the carriages, again within the safety bars and because we were in the open air we felt an intimacy with the ever changing topography. Our positions gave us good views and whenever we approached a wide bend, the graceful curves of the train was quite something to look at and especially when we were crossing a viaduct.

Some of the stations are little more that big painted sheds with windows and station names. We got off to stretch our legs at Hindon which was once famous for gold bearing quartz mines during the gold rush.

Our turn around point was Pukerangi which means "hill of heaven," Again we were allowed off to have a brief look at the scenery. On the way back I was standing between carriages, wind in my hair, drinking a large bottle of beer and hopefully making a good subject for Val's camera!

Back at Dunedin station as we were photographing the lovely old interior I heard the sound of bag pipes coming from outside. I rushed out but sadly I only caught the last few bars and the piper had gone.

Our adventure continued with a coach tour. The 29 year old driver was good company as he drove us round his beautiful hilly city, which is up market and affluent. The poor area did not look poor to me!

We got off to marvel at Baldwin Street. At nearly 350 meters long with a maximum gradient of 35%, it's the world's steepest street. I imagine the residents all having healthy hearts. We were told the views from the top are magnificent. Two heavenly beaches were next with stop offs for photos as we beamed in on the surfers.

The whole day was one big adventure and gave us another huge stock of photos to add to our prolific collection.

Back in Port Chalmers we boarded the ship and I felt like hitting the sheets for half an hour when the cherry descended upon the cake. I suddenly came alive when I heard the sound of bag pipes! I dashed up to deck seven and there they were. Two young women in tartan kilts on the quayside, one playing the pipes and the other playing a drum who occasionally gave us some dancing. Who would have thought that half way round the world I would be listening to bag pipes? I recognised some of the pieces as 'Mari's

Wedding', 'Atholl Highlanders', 'Mason's Apron' and 'Am
Grace'. I was hooked on the whole show. A visit to Dunedin sure
would not have been complete without some Scotland. A big finale
to a big day.

I wandered on the Pennant Deck and chanced on Kate in her
wheelchair and her mother. We discussed the price of my valentine
photo and Kate agreed that at £17.50 it was a rip off and confirmed
what Val had said that materials for the photo cost a mere 20p.
Shame on the photographic department.

Table for six. We've previously dined with one of the couples, the
other couple met on the internet and were later married. She gave
us the most banal and detailed account of their wedding day, two
years previously, without leaving a stone unturned. It was torture,
the most boring drone of all time. She was non-stop and held the
conch without giving anyone a chance to speak. I tried in vain to
change the subject and felt that it must have been my punishment
for my day's self-indulgence! At one point I said to myself, "Come
back Melbourne Muppets all is forgiven" Val and I pressed our
feet together signalling that enough was enough. We excused
ourselves and promptly left. I vowed if I ever saw that dreadful
self-centred woman around the ship again I'd make her walk the
plank!

Had a beer in the Crow's Nest and watched poor Lynn Frederick
performing in semi darkness. On the way to the cabin we went
onto deck seven, and what splendour to see the ocean draped in
moonlight.

The NZ Fjords Tomorrow.

WEDNESDAY FEB 17. New Zealand Fjords. Occasional sun with
mist gradually clearing.

*Fiordland National Park which comprise Dusky Sound, Doubtful
Sound and Milford Sound is a world heritage site and the most*

dramatic and scenic part of New Zealand. Rudyard Kipling
described Milford Sound as the eighth wonder of the world.

The Dusky and Doubtful Sounds were misty, with some drizzle, but there was "magic in the mist" which added to the atmosphere. The low cloud clinging to the cliff tops and mountains gave an awesome spectacle. No colour, just black and white with shades of grey. Eerie. We were restlessly hopping from port to starboard and back again to make sure we were not missing anything of interest. Our cameras had gone into a frenzy.

A member of the paparazzi asked me if I'd like my photo taken against a torrent. I said "No because I've fallen out with your department"
"Why sir"
"Because I had to be treated for shock at the medical centre when I saw the valentine photo of me on display for £17.50
She replied by saying "Have a nice day sir"

Managed a jam with Mike, the guitarist in his cabin. He uses a small Yamaha amp and backing tracks. He has an Epiphone guitar and enjoys heavy rock. I wrote out the chords for a 12 bar which he struggled with at first but eventually got there. Then it was Blues for guitar and flute. My tone was superb. He has a damaged left hand finger and struggles with certain chords but tries not to let it hamper his progress. I thought, well at last I'm having a jam. He's a nice guy, ex Royal Navy.

It was late afternoon when the captain announced that due to technical problems there would be a delay in entering the Milford Sound. A disappointment as Milford is the climax. Then bravo! 15 minutes later we were able to go ahead.

An Indian summer. Everything changed. We were gazing at thousands of waterfalls. Many were gushing and thundering into the sound while the majority resembled silver ribbons, sometimes in parallel draping down hundreds of meters. The scene was almost mystical. Again we rushed from port to starboard and back again frightened of missing a trick. Again our cameras went into overdrive. We were witnessing nature's formidable wonders at her best.

It was comical to see the waitresses arrive on deck. Everyone was busy gasping at the scenery and the last thing they wished for was a drink. The poor souls were wandering around with empty trays trying to make good for the loss of takings at the bars inside.

Conclusion; the New Zealand Fiords can rival those in Norway.

Dined with David and Jane while rejoicing about the fiords. The couple are good sporty folk and David certainly likes to laugh.

It was time to investigate the Dolly Parton lookalike show in Carmen's. Oh dear! She got two members of the audience each to wear a pink hat and bang a tambourine while she sang. Of course it was our cue to make a hasty departure.

Jim (principal) and Brenda from Salwick joined us for a drink in the Crow's Nest. I used to think Jim was a bit haughty taughty but I've warmed to him. Later they showed us their cabin which was an inside allocation on arrival. They had been given a disabled cabin which dwarfed ours. But not for us. We like our outside picture window.

So, it's goodbye kiwis and soon it'll be hello possums!

Cruising to Sydney.

THURSDAY 18 FEB. Tasman Sea. Sunny

The past week has been a whirlwind of exciting destinations with the fiords as an epilogue. We now have two days at sea to ground ourselves.

Huge graceful swell with a deep pitch. I'm fortunate that sea sickness does not affect me.

Piano a Deux were sitting on the table next to me at breakfast. I made the first move and then we connected immediately. Lovely couple. I told them I'd be at their evening concert. They disembark at Singapore to perform one concert and to look after her mother for a few weeks before returning to the UK where they have plenty of work. They were keen to hear about my band, my flute and piano. He said he understands the problems people face with the bass clef. We talked about retirement and she agreed that sadly many folk retire without hobbies. She asked my name and then gave me a card. He's called Robert and she's called Linda Ang. She asked me to e-mail them. What a delightful couple.

Saw Larry, he's been quarantined for the past four days with gastro enteritis. God bless him. Marion has recovered.

We kept our slot with the Australian Immigration Inspection. The smarmy guy from Headliners who felt obliged to entertain us recently on one of the tenders was directing people to their interviews. He was at it again sucking up to people and telling them to smile. He didn't get the chance to direct us because we looked the other way. He has an ego the size of an air ship.

Chanced on Mike. He's requested a jam for tomorrow. I'm definitely game.

As I walked the Promenade Deck I began to feel sad about leaving the Aurora on Saturday. So much has happened. So many nice people.

Back in the cabin I played some very reasonable flute while looking out over the swell and the spindrift.

More Piano a Deux in the playhouse. First it was Schubert and then amazingly 'Colonel Bogey' played in different classical styles like Mozart etc. Very clever. Then at great speed he recited composers' names with Linda at the piano. Again very talented and quite funny. Afterwards I shook his hand and gave her a hug, she said "Don't forget to keep in touch John." Nice.

Dinner with John and Chrissy with a gorgeous sun set flooding in through the windows. They told us they met on the internet five years ago.

Laura Broad again in the Curzon. As expected, excellent voice but rubbish songs except when she duetted with a two of the Headliners and then we were treated to some surprisingly good harmony.

Night cap in the Crow's Nest, and while I was listening to Lynn Frederick for the last time I felt that it would have been something to have jammed with her.

Val and I asked each other what is special about the Aurora. For Val it was being able to eat al fresco on the Pennant and pool decks. For me it was journaling and people watching on the promenade deck.

Cruising to Sydney.

FRIDAY 19 FEB. Tasman Sea. Sunny. Choppy.

As we disembark tomorrow we spent much of the day saying our farewells to all those who had become our friends.

Saw Ken and wondered if he ever wears a top other than a short sleeved white shirt!

Australian John and his wife disembark at Sydney for a two week break before cruising back to Southampton on another ship. John told us by the time we arrive there on 10 may all three Queens will be in port.

Talked with Ian and Jonquil, my theatre friends. He's retired after 35 years in the police force. We discussed discipline. Lovely couple.

Next it was James and Dr Anne. A big hug from her.

I went looking for Iris and Tom and found them in the Crow's Nest.
More hugs and handshakes. Tom has written 44,000 words since Southampton.

Saw David and Jane. He showed me a draught of part of a book his homosexual uncle had written in the days when you kept your sexuality to yourself.

James and Dr Anne again. She advised me that everything should be taken in moderation.

Another jam with Mike. I've now got him playing in three blues keys having written the chords for him. We had a good blues session on the high seas. Very enjoyable, especially when his wife came in and said we sounded brilliant. She recorded us on her mobile and when she played it back I was rather impressed. They said they'd sent me a copy. Another souvenir!

Peeked in at the art exhibition. You get the odd painting that grabs you like a yacht under a cliff but most were pretty ordinary. It must have been a good experience though for many and a good way to socialise. Some will have a new hobby to take home with them.

Sat with Carol and Vic for a drink in Champions while we reminisced before hugs and handshakes.

The Medina with Kevin and Denise and Aussie John and his wife. John is a very experienced cruiser and is familiar with most locations.

Well, James and Dr Anne have finally done it. They're holding hands! Romance on the Aurora! Good luck to them. Is it too late for a ship's wedding? Anyhow I've enjoyed their company and wish them well.

Sat in the theatre enduring Donna somebody screeching her head off. I bet my companions were getting fed up with me forever complaining about naff singers.

A lady approached me to say she'd enjoyed Russel and Long Beach and thanked me for recommending them.

More hugs and goodbyes in the Curzon exit. Oh dear, how emotional.

CONCLUSION. Part one of our world cruise has been an exciting whirlwind, with 17,020 nautical miles under our belts.

Sydney tomorrow am.

PART 2

SATURDAY 20 FEB. Circular Quay. Sydney Harbour. New South Wales, Australia. Sunny.

Sydney is the Capital of New South Wales and one of the largest cities in Australia and is best known for its beautiful harbour which boasts the distinctive Opera House and the Harbour Bridge. Sydney is a haven for walkers and there are lovely beaches within an easy ferry ride and for those who just want to explore it's the perfect city.

5:30 am. I could make out the outline of Sydney Harbour Bridge and the Opera House. I thought about those who'd bought a £200.00 ticket for the evening's performance and hoped they would enjoy it.

Last minute photos of the interior of Aurora rather for memories than for works of art. The views from the Pennant Deck were exceptional which included the Harbour Bridge, the Opera house and "there she was", the Queen Elizabeth out at anchor. On another deck just a short distance away I could see the Four Seasons Hotel which we'd be staying in for one night. All rather exciting, even more so when I saw the lovely Asian lady from Piano a Deux who gave me a hug and said "Thanks John for sharing your thoughts and please keep in touch". How kind!

So it was goodbye Aurora and hello Sydney, which was our second visit. It's one of the most picturesque harbours in the world and convenient for passengers as you're off the ship and straight into the city.

A guy in baggage reclaim was loading a guitar onto his trolley. I said it was a pity we didn't meet on the cruise, we could have had a jam but he said he was only a beginner. It wouldn't surprise me if quite a number of folk had taken instruments on board. We were early for our taxi so I wandered off to the Fortunes of War pub and asked if there would be any jazz booked for the evening but I was told that the pub could no longer afford to pay groups of musicians. A singer guitarist would be performing in the evening. Not for us.

Our taxi failed to arrive at 10:00 am and by 10:45 am we decided to use the trolley and push our luggage to the Four Seasons Hotel but we were up against terminal security who became quite confrontational when they said they wouldn't allow it. We eventually paid 40 Australian dollars for a taxi with journey time of less than four minutes. We checked in at 11:15 am. The concierge told us that we'd been ripped off and phoned the original taxi company who told her they'd picked up another Reginald at 10:00 am. Obviously they hadn't checked the full name. Anyhow I shall claim the money from the travel agents when I get home. The delay was disappointing because we had plans but fortunately everything worked out satisfactorily. Our luxury room was situated near the top and afforded excellent views of the streets below and of the skyscrapers.

We put Sheena's itinerary to the test. (Sheena lives in Sydney and is the daughter of our next door neighbour back home.) So it was a ferry from Circular Quay to Watsons Bay with lots of harbour scenery which included the Opera House, the Bridge, racing yachts and of course Cunard's Queen Elizabeth out at anchor - all quite spectacular.

From Watson's bay we followed our instructions and walked to South Head. The interesting route took us past Lady's Bay, a nudist beach nestling far below our path. I felt some of the men there were exhibitionists because they knew they could be seen from the path. They seemed to delight in letting it all hang out.

We were greeted at the end of the walk by Hornby Lighthouse - very sedate in red and white circular stripes. From there the views were superb including the cityscapes.

As we were walking back we hit on a dream beach called Camp Cove and very soon we were in the water taking a long refreshing dip which was very pleasant indeed. At one point I suddenly became quite anxious when I saw a shoal of small green fish leaping out of the water that took me unawares but I soon realised they were harmless. Later, I asked a couple of locals if they knew what the fish we called and I was surprised that they didn't know.

Back at the lovely Watsons bay, folk were eating fish and chips at the famous Doyles on the ferry pier so we decided to follow suit. Nothing like a good nosh while relaxing in the shade and enjoying something that's alien to my diet and washing it down with a delicious cool beer. All was well with the world.

A woman who I was talking to earlier approached me saying she agreed with me that the men on the nudist beach were exhibitionists. Thank you madam.

Another enjoyable ferry ride back to Circular Quay, and then a short walk to the Mercantile Pub which we visited three years ago. Then it was beer and Irish music from practically the same band as last time. Wonderfully atmospheric.

Back to the Four seasons for a rest and a preen then out again for dinner. It was Saturday night and what a scene. I have never seen as many log legged luverlies out enjoying themselves as state of the art fashionistas! The music from the pubs were flooding out onto the street. A little overpowering perhaps but certainly vibrant.

We found a nice Italian and ate al fresco. Val had pizza, I had a huge spaghetti Bolognese.

The walk back to the Hotel was more like a limp and before we crashed out into bed we took some good night shots of the street below and the tower blocks. After a disastrous start to the day it was a happy ever after story.

Sydney day two tomorrow.

SUNDAY 21 FEB. Sydney. A little drizzle at first.

As we were walking through the magnificent lobby of the hotel we were able to start our day on a high note, no pun intended! It was culture in the form of a gentleman impeccably dressed in a suit and bow tie playing a grand piano. And at 8:30 am it was unusual to be greeted with live music in a grand hotel. We sidled up to him to get close to his excellent playing and then we engaged. He asked where we hailed from and then he told us he'd recently visited Garstang - a
Town near to where we live. Small world! I requested "Witchcraft" which he played beautifully and I visualised myself playing along with him on my flute.

We agreed to walk across Sydney Harbour Bridge and back. A good decision, and at 1149 metres long we were able to combine exercise and the crème de la crème of sightseeing, which included the occasional jogger! The harbour is nature's masterpiece with some science thrown in. The two liners had changed places. Aurora was at anchor while Elizabeth was alongside - it's always interesting to see the sights from different viewpoints. The tasty area to the left of the bridge is called Kirribilli which is very affluent and contains the residences of the Governor General and the Prime Minister.

Val was quizzing one of the security guards who told her they were not allowed to discuss their work except to say it involved structure security which means they stop people from climbing the iron work. She also thought that they were also on suicide watch. There is some speculation as to their exact role but I heard later that they carry out twenty four hour patrols and are on the lookout for terrorist attacks. Anyone visiting Sydney for the first time would be well advised to walk the bridge for some top class photographs.

Morning coffee next. It was al fresco at a little place at the Rocks - the historic part of the city. A busker was paying the guitar some distance away and sounded very pleasant.
The Museum of Contemporary Art was worth a visit. One of the galleries held a Grayson Perry exhibition which we waived because there wouldn't be enough time to do it justice.

On the 4th floor terrace we enjoyed more views of Sydney before getting into conversation with a woman Val had met in the choir on the Aurora. The woman introduced herself as Joyce and showed us her "art journal" which comprised cuttings from the Horizon Program, watercolour sketches of the places she'd visited with descriptions. I told her it was a credit to her... She's a mental health nurse who will shortly be travelling to Asia to work as a volunteer with ex sex slaves. An extremely interesting woman.

Back to the Four Seasons Hotel for our luggage and 12:15 pm taxi to the cruise terminal. Queen Elizabeth was awaiting our arrival to give us express check in. A string quartet welcomed us into the atrium and soon we were in our room - an outside cabin on deck one on the port side. The bottle of sparkling wine in the ice bucket looked tempting but we decided to save it for the sail away party. Our picture window gave us intimate views of the Opera house and some of the harbour.

So, there we were on The Queen Elizabeth, which was to be our home for 79 nights. We looked forward to many journeys into the unknown, many adventures and lots of interesting people to meet.

After a quick bite in the Lido we left the ship to go walking. It was most pleasant while strolling round Circular Quay with our cameras that had not had chance to cool down after our morning's escapades! We passed the Opera House and entered the botanical gardens park. The undulating stretches of lush grass, the back lit trees and the city tower blocks provided us with some great photography.

We chanced on Andy and Julie and let them know in no uncertain terms what we thought of their friend who babbled on the other night about her wedding. Andy and Julie just smiled neither agreeing nor disagreeing. Perhaps they're more tolerant of self-centred people than we are.

Val was feeling the strain of a hectic day and wasn't keen on going to the Mercantile. But my persuasion paid off - it was amazing how she bounced back to life when we got there. We experienced the best pub atmosphere of all time.

We perched ourselves on tall stools with beers and cameras while allowing the music and the atmosphere to suck us in. As the fiddle, guitar and whistle belted it out we soon engaged with the whole scene. An intimate gathering of folk were all there for the fun, for a knees up and certainly to let their hair down. The jigs, reels and songs were almost non-stop, making us feel part of a big bubbly personality. A guy appeared and played the bodhran, another the spoons and a guy got up to sing. There was dancing, foot tapping, laughter and masses of fun. Val couldn't resist a dance and when she hit the floor the locals made her very welcome. What an atmosphere.

A man was sitting at the bar with a rather long sort of lizard draping round his neck and a young woman was happy to let us photograph her with a lizard draped round her neck. All rather odd.

Later, I was talking to two of the musicians who are aptly called Shindig and told them we were from the Queen Elizabeth and that we'd really enjoyed being at the Mercantile.

So we drank the last of our beer feeling our second day in Sydney had been a great climax - a big cherry on a big cake. We were in high spirits as we strolled back to the ship while thinking of the bewitching effect of Irish music.

Didn't feel like dressing up for dinner so we chose the Lido instead.

Finally the Royal Court Theatre where Amanda Reid, the entertainment manager introduced the entertainment team, one of whom was Jane Edwards, the choir mistress who had the same job on the Oceana. The Cunard singers and dancers performed one number before the main act which was an Australian called Chris Cable, a maestro of the clarinet and sax - an absolute feel good occasion.

Val went to the deck party and saw the firework display to see us off. She also took some colourful night shots of the harbour during sail away.

Newcastle tomorrow 8:00 am

MONDAY FEB 22. Maiden call. Channel Berth No1, Newcastle Harbour Newcastle, New south Wales, Australia. Sunny.

Newcastle is the largest coal exporting harbour in the world and was a penal settlement until 1822.

At 3:30 am the ocean was bathed in moonlight which partially lit the cabin. It was almost spiritual.

It was light at 6:00 am and I could see hundreds of sightseers stretched along the shoreline of the Hunter River to watch Elizabeth making her maiden call to Newcastle.

At breakfast I shared a table with an interesting Australian couple. His hobbies include pottery, dancing and teaching yoga while she enjoys painting. They would make good table companions. While we were on the shuttle bus to town I had to endure what the Buddhists would call unhealthy speech. A woman delighted in babbling on and on with verbal trash, completely sabotaging the volunteer guide who was doing her best to give us information about Newcastle.

At Queens Wharf we caught the tail end of a ceremony comprising ships officers, bell boys and local dignitaries to mark Elizabeth's maiden call. Val took my photo posing with one of the officers.

As we made our way along the waterfront in the direction of what looked like an attractive beach we found ourselves talking to a guy whose catamaran was berthed nearby. He introduced himself as Glen and told us about his exploits as a sailor. He started walking with us and asked if he could board Elizabeth, we told him it wasn't possible without a security card. We eventually went our own way because we were not sure of his motives.

Nobbys Beach is supreme. A long curve of sand, turquoise sea with a raised headland at one end and a couple of cafes at the other. Val decided against a dip because the sea was too rough but I couldn't resist. I was in paradise dancing with and negotiating the waves. Occasionally one would hit me unawares and send me reeling. But what fun. It's best to ride the waves but you need to get your timing right. It's an exhilarating experience. I also enjoyed some body surfing but I wished Val would have joined me.

We were talking with a pleasant couple who are passengers on Elizabeth. The subject must have been music because he produced his mobile phone and said "Look I'm not going to show you a picture of my grandkids" instead it was a picture of his Fender Strat.

We were deafened when we heard thee cannon fire shots and found out later it was another acknowledgment of our ship's maiden call.
A hill nearby looked inviting so we found our way to the top and discovered Scratchley Fort which was built in 1882 to defend the city against a possible Russian attack. It's now a museum. The views to Nobbys Beach and headland are spectacular.

We walked back through a lovely area called Foreshore Park and after looking at a few shops felt there was nothing more to detain us so we took the shuttle bus back to the ship.

I made my first visit to the library which resembles a modern Waterstones. The library occupies two floors which are connected by a teak spiral staircase. There is also a section with desks and computers. I took out a book of witty poems by Liz Cowley for some easy reading, nothing heavy thank you.

There was no one in the yacht club so I helped myself to some grand piano but not for long as I felt someone may come in and disapprove.

During my flute practice no one banged on the walls which is good. Either my flute was being appreciated or the people were out on the first sitting. My routine will be the same as it was on the Aurora. Flute practice each evening while Val gets ready for dinner. Hopefully by the end of the voyage my technique will have risen to a new level.

The Tiffany String Quartet sounded quite sublime after the Irish Music in Sydney. They're female with a glum looking viola player. We also looked in the Golden Lion Pub and listened to a guy called Herbie Denton playing the piano. He seems quite good and has a sense of humour.

There was a mix up with our table arrangements in the Britannia Restaurant which resulted in a table for two but we've been promised a table for eight tomorrow.
The Royal Court Theatre was a packed house for "Beatlemania" with an Australian band called the Beatle Boys. They're quite good but not as good as the British equivalents.

Cruising to Brisbane.

TUESDAY 23 FEB. At Sea, South Pacific.

More magic moonlight in the night.

I'm continuing where I left off the Aurora by walking at least 15 minutes a day on the Promenade Deck. It's the best way of getting intimate with the sea and affords excellent people watching. The other exercise you get is through walking to various venues inside the ship which equates to some mileage over a week.

A young guy from the entertainment team was telling me he earns £2900.00 a month with no board to pay. I doubt it very much - he was trying to make himself look important.

Attended our first port talk with Matthew who we know from previous sailings. He's grown a beard but I'm not sure if it suits him. Anyhow his talk was about Puerto Princesca in the Philippines where we're scheduled to call instead of Cebu.

Val has joined the watercolour class. Not for me, but let's hope she can soon start exhibiting!

As I was writing my journal in the Garden Lounge I noticed a lady with a most unsightly disfigured face. Poor soul. Maybe the result of a horrific accident.

I'm thinking about writing to Amanda Reid to ask if she could arrange a get together for fellow musicians by putting an ad in the daily programme. Nothing like a jam on the high seas which could lead to an appearance on the passenger talent show.
The afternoon matinee in the Queens Room featured the Duo Diez. Guitar and violin. A man and woman playing Spanish music. Very talented but I prefer the classical guitar to be played sitting down. They didn't quite connect for me in fact I fell asleep.

I took to a recliner on deck 3 as a way of getting off the merry go round. I did some writing while occasionally looking up at the beautiful ocean and watching the many shapes and sizes walking by.

The shopping arcade has many outlets for books, designer jewellery, wines and spirits, clothing, toiletries and general. But because everything is overpriced, my purchases will be from necessity rather than choice.

Quiz time in the Golden Lion. A knowledgeable lady, called Margaret from Australia joined us and helped rack up our score. The young woman asking the questions comes from Fleetwood and has a voice like Caroline Ahern.

We joined our table for eight in the Britannia Restaurant. A motley gathering, including David and Muriel who are both retired vicars, Gordon and his Swedish wife Annette, and Brook, who was a physiotherapist and his Asian wife Vicky who was a nurse. They're all retired. I hoped it wouldn't take long to bond. Gordon showed me how to tie a bow tie which is really quite complicated.

The theatre had no appeal so we looked in at the Commodore Club and was treated to an excellent rendition of 'Embraceable You' from the pianist. You can't get a pint in there, only wines and spirits which are grossly over-priced.

Each evening we have Ovaltine and Horlicks before retiring.

Brisbane tomorrow am.

WEDNESDAY FEB 24. Multi user terminal, Fisherman's Island Brisbane, Queensland, Australia. Sunny and hot.

Brisbane is the capital of Queensland; it has a wealth of parks, monuments and historic buildings. The Brisbane River runs through the heart of the city - perfect for a cruise on a City Cat to enjoy some sightseeing.

The shuttle bus took 40 minutes to take us into the city. We began our itinerary on Queen Street - a vibrant and modern thoroughfare full of trees and silver skyscrapers. Next it was a long walk over Victoria Bridge in the hot sunshine while occasionally looking back at the dramatic city skyline.

We found the Southbank and no sooner did we start our riverside walk when we saw the Segways. That was it. I decided to fulfil my dream and have a go. First, I was given some tuition. You stand up straight and bend slightly forward to propel. You gently turn the handlebars to the left or right to turn, and to stop you stand up straight. Not easy at first but I soon got the knack. The guy said I was a natural! Then we were off. I felt quite confident wheeling my way with the instructor along the Southbank to the far bridge and back. What fun. There was I ringing my bell and telling folk I'm having my second childhood. Afterwards I felt quite pleased with myself and Val certainly seemed to enjoy being a spectator. Fortunately she'd filmed me. The instructor is Venezuelan and emigrated to Brisbane 5 years ago for a better life.

The Southbank Walk has lots to offer including great views across the river to the city and the attractive Southbank Parkland. The whole area is one big beautiful scene. The short "rainforest walk" which included a Nepalese pagoda, was pleasant and shady. We chanced on what looked like an outdoor swimming pool but was actually a spectacular man-made beach complete with sand. I'd had my fun, it was then Val's turn. I found some shade while she went in for a dip. She loved it and thought it was an unusual experience to have skyscrapers for company.

We hopped back over Victoria Bridge to a Farmers Market for some lunch. It's a vibrant and colourful scene with many stalls selling local and exotic food including takeaways. We bought two large vegetarians meals - Brisbane style and then sat on special cardboard boxes while tucking into the delicious food. The atmosphere was buzzing - another great experience.

Over the bridge again because The Queensland Art gallery was beckoning. It's a large space age building on the banks of the river and contains paintings and installations to marvel at or even to make you feel bemused.

We walked back along Queen Street in search of a wine outlet for Val to replenish her stocks. No luck until we asked a guy where we could buy wine. He told us where we could get it and personally escorted us there, along the street down an escalator into a shopping mall to a "Bottle Shop" How very kind of him. After Val had bought her supplies I asked the sales assistant if trade was good he said it had rocketed due to the number of cruise passengers taking stocks back to the ship!

Finally we found a nice bar to relax with a beer. We got talking to an English couple who live and work in Brisbane. They were very interested in our cruise and offered to buy us a drink. We had to decline because of the clock and when we were leaving it was hugs all round. People can be so nice.

I saw a woman in the Atrium having her photo taken with her cruise card hanging round her neck. Maybe she wanted to look important and looked upon it as a fashion accessory. Strange!

Table for six as the two vicars were absent. Brook, the physiotherapist believes that all obesity is self-inflicted. After my main meal I asked for cheese and biscuits minus the cheese and biscuits! And was given a plate full of prunes, peanuts and chutney. How wasteful.

We watched a ventriloquist called Dean Atkinson who was funny in parts especially when he operated mouth masks on two members of the audience.

Cruising to Yorkeys Knob.

THURSDAY 25 FEB. Coral Sea. Sunny.

At breakfast I sat with an Australian couple who told me they were once on a cruise ship when a passenger appeared with bag pipes and played them while the ship was leaving port. Everyone cheered. Well, after that I don't think anyone should fear taking an instrument on board including the kitchen sink!

I wrote a note to Amanda Reid to ask if she'll put an ad in the daily programme to enable me to meet other musicians. I also found out you can book hour long piano slots so naturally I made my bookings.

Port talk about Manila. We've already decided to visit the old town of Intramuros independently. Tragically it seems that of the 2.5 million people who are poor, 30% are living below the poverty line with the huge shanty towns causing problems for many children who don't have childhoods because they are sent out to help make ends meet.

We used our invitations to the wine tasting event which was free because we are previous cruisers. I was surprised that it wasn't a ploy to get us to buy expensive wine. You were given wine to taste at four separate tables followed by a brief lecture about the grape. We had a total of two red and two white and at the end there was questions and answers. Someone asked "How much a bottle?" Brook's question was "How do you get away with it?" Mine was "What time is happy hour?" Everyone laughed.

Captain's reception in the ball room. Managed two free glasses of sparkling wine while circulating in our formal evening wear. The floor was awash with folk holding their drinks, looking like royalty and trying to draw attention to themselves. The captain told us that Elizabeth has 1200 Australians on board, 400 Brits and 500 other various nationalities including a lot of Japanese. Surprisingly there were very few Americans. Maybe the Australian numbers will drop when we reach Hong Kong making way for Americans to board. We latched onto a lovely Australian couple called Diane and Andrew and we've arranged to meet them in the Golden Lion after Cairns.

During dinner Muriel was telling us about the prejudices she has had to endure because she was a female vicar. We think the other two couples have inside cabins, nothing wrong with that but it's the same on every ship, people are always eager to defend their choice by saying they only use the cabin for sleeping so what's the point of an outside. Nonsense. Imagine a house without a window.

The Royal Court Theatre gave us an acrobatic duo called Deja vu. Fairly entertaining but it was little more than twenty six variations on a theme of doing the splits. The killer came when he sang two songs. Either he should go on the voice transplant list or go back to Russia to consult the career advisory service!

Cruising to Yorkeys Knob

FRIDAY 26 FEB Coral Sea. Sunny and hot.

The lady I saw a couple of days ago with the disfigured face sat at my breakfast table with her husband. She was kindly and quick to get into conversation. But oh my God, whatever happened to her?

The weather was hot and calm for cruising through the Whit Sunday Islands in the Great Barrier Reef. On the whole it's magnificent scenery but rather lacking as individual subjects for our cameras.

I cannot get a signal on my mobile which means I cannot receive a code to give me internet access. I need a connection to carry out my banking transactions to avoid loss of interest.

I peeked in at Val's art class. She was sharing a table with four other women who were applying a wash with their brushes. She told me later she thought she'd made a mistake by joining, partly because she was the least experienced of all the women. So what will happen to the artist's materials she bought?

At last I received a signal and code on my mobile and then Val helped me to get connected to the internet. It was running very slow but I managed to complete my banking transactions and it took 15 minutes to send a short e-mail to Jay. Fortunately we've qualified for a lot of free access.

Took to a recliner in the shade alternating between writing, sleeping and watching the shapes or rather misshapes walking by. That's entertainment!

Good news. Received a letter from the asst. entertainment manager who has given me four forty five minute piano slots over the next week or so. It's now official, I can keep up my practice in the Yacht Club on the beautiful grand piano.

Later Amanda phoned; she has kindly agreed to put a notice in the daily programme inviting passenger musicians to get together.

David and Lynn from Australia met us in the Golden Lion. We'll be sharing a minibus with them in Rabaul, Papua New Guinea. Lovely couple, looking forward to their company.

Surprise, surprise, chanced on Gerald, the Scottish Australian we met on the Queen Victoria. He was holding hands with an Asian woman who probably thought his purse was more attractive than his personality. He's a reasonable sort but on the Queen Victoria he never learned my name.

An Australian harpist /vocalist called Alena Conway was our treat in the Royal Court. An excellent talent. Played the harp beautifully and accompanied her own voice as well. She was wearing a long white dress and looked charmingly angelic under the white spotlights.

Yorkeys Knob tomorrow am.

SATURDAY 27 FEB. Ship at anchor, Yorkeys Knob. Coral Sea. Queensland Australia. Sunny and hot.

Yorkeys Knob, Cairns is the gateway to Queensland with the Great Barrier Reef being one of the world's greatest wonders.

Boarded the tender to shore then took the shuttle bus for the eight mile journey to Cairns - the gateway to the Great Barrier Reef. When we arrived, the first thing to impress us were the parks and palm trees. And it was interesting seeing a shop selling Didgeridoos - hundreds of them, mostly painted in bright colours. If I'd have bought one to play on the ship I wondered how the passengers would have reacted!

We missed our opportunity to do a snorkelling trip to Green Island so instead we stayed local. The temperature was unbearably hot but we enjoyed walking along part of Chinaman Creek with palms and a backdrop of mountains and some strange birds. We saw

Tony and Sandy waiting to take a helicopter ride over the Barrier Reef. They said they'd paid £500.00 but felt it would be worth it.

We were told that we could swim in the lagoon but it was difficult to locate until we realised that the area we were looking at was actually the lagoon. It's man made and complete with sand, a lovely setting on the edge of a park. Val went in for a dip and looked as though she was really enjoying it but I decided to refrain because of a cough and a mild headache. So I sat down and relaxed while watching the leggy luverlies sauntering about.
The opposite end of the waterfront was decked out with palms and grassy areas. A good place for a stroll but lunch was beckoning.

Exotic food, that's what we like. We found a good al fresco, overlooking the sea with our table almost on the pavement. A friendly waiter brought Crab in batter followed by spaghetti on Thai salad which was like eating fire but we were given plenty of water. The slow service was acceptable because it enabled us to remain there for an hour and twenty minutes to relax. The beer had a slight aniseed taste - something different, but we enjoyed it. Overall it was a good dining experience

As we were walking back to the shuttle bus we saw something quite unexpected. Fruit bats, also known as flying foxes, hundreds of them hanging from some tall trees squeaking and squawking right there in the centre of town.

After we returned to Yorkeys Knob we discovered a beach, which was heaven in miniature. A short curve of sand with trees at each end and a glorious sea. Couldn't wait to sample it if only to cool off, but a local couple approached us and warned us not to venture in because of the crocodiles, sharks but mainly the box jelly fish. How disappointing. But the stingers can make you ill and have been known to be fatal. Nearby was a pole with a large bottle of vinegar attached which you apply to the sting if you're an unfortunate victim. If the couple hadn't been there we could have ended up in hospital!

As we made our way to the tender it was goodbye to the East Coast of Australia, and thank you possums!

Back on the ship we somehow missed the sunset but there was a magnificent afterglow providing us with some stunning photographs. I had my camera set on creative mode for the definitive picture.

What better way of concluding our time in Australia than Val filming me playing Waltzing Matilda on my flute with the map of Queensland on the television screen for the background. I practiced the piece and was ready to be filmed but Val wanted to do it her way. I was furious because it could have been an original idea. Although my flute sounded good and was synchronised with the map she'd lost it and I ended up playing the last few bars to a map of the world. She threw my camera on the bed and wouldn't give it another try.

Sat in the ball room because no other venue appealed to us. Enjoyed watching the dancers and listening to the band. They often play numbers from the American song book. When I tried to get Val up for a jive she said she was tired and decided to have an early night. Saw Vicky who asked me to join her. She was on her own and probably wanted some company. She loves being whisked round the floor by the host dancers. She's very accomplished and moves very gracefully. Her husband, Brook, is a non-dancer despite his parents being dance instructors. So she relies on host dancers on cruise ships and dance partners at home as dancing is a big part of her life. She said that over the years some men wanted relationships with her but she has always remained faithful to Brook. I was surprised when she said she was an old lady at 72. WHAT! I would have placed her at late 50's. And thanks Vicky for telling me I don't look anywhere near 69. I explained that my contribution to dancing was limited to very basic rock and roll. She wanted to jive with me but alas we didn't get the opportunity.

Cruising to Rabaul.

SUNDAY 28 FEB. Coral Sea. Hot and sunny.

Saw an invalid lady in the Lido coughing her heart out into a napkin. Fortunately the dining assistants were wearing hygienic gloves!
I sipped my early morning tea while watching the army of deck stewards setting out the recliners and wondered what sort of a future those guys could expect.

The weather was hot with a lovely warm breeze and the sea was calm as I walked for fifteen minutes round the Promenade Deck. Afterwards I noticed an elderly man on the pool deck who at first sight looked like a woman because of his large breasts. Odd.

The art gallery which is really a shop, displays some amazing works as diverse as the artists who paint them. Landscapes, cityscapes, seascapes, still lifes and figures adorn the walls, all there to help us while away some pleasant time. I asked the curator why the last limited edition number was always 195. He said it was the maximum number of pictures that could be made from a single printing plate before any loss of quality.

Tony and Sandy were gung ho about their helicopter flight over the Barrier Reef. They paid £500.00 for forty minutes of bliss. I wonder how much of it they saw through the camera lens. They're interesting people who'd make good friends.

A doctor gave a lecture about travelling and health. In a nutshell, sanitise the hands, keep hydrated and be active and don't forget the sun cream. Didn't tell us anything new but I enjoyed his style of presenting rather than the content.

Some culture in the Queens Ballroom with the Tiffany String Quartet. As expected it was listening and visual magic. One of their pieces had the singular name of PLINK PLANK PLUNK – a brilliant demonstration of pizzicato. But some Gershwin would have been welcome.

One hour piano practice in the Yacht Club with the beautiful grand to myself. A little unnerving at first because of some dance tuition that was taking place but I bit the bullet because it was officially my time. Boy did I struggle. I didn't realise that nearly two months absence from the piano could have such a disastrous effect. I ploughed through "Georgia" and "Embraceable You" relentlessly and it all came good especially when the dancers left and I could then relax. I managed some other pieces, but I couldn't remember "Yesterday." But it was a good feeling sitting at a grand piano at sea. The woman who'd booked the next slot was interesting to talk to. She had lessons when she was seven but gave it up and then resumed playing fifty five, or sixty years later. She played some lovely Bach. My next slot is on the 6th march, the day we cross the equator.

What in heavens name is going on with my flute? Sometimes I can produce beautiful tones but today I struggled. Clare Langan where are you? Have a heart, and come aboard and give me some one to one"!

Another Captains reception in the ballroom. We targeted a couple who were happy to talk with us. They live in Kendal. He was a little self-assured. Later I realised why -Val told me they are ex teachers. I quite enjoy meeting people at these events and certainly for the free booze.

Vicky always departs the dinner table after her main course to keep her dates with the host dancers and leaves Brook on his own. We also left early along with the two vicars to catch the Jazz in the Garden Lounge. A great show even if some of the numbers were a bit off the wall. The bass player was superb on his five string. Afterwards we looked in the theatre to see if we were missing anything. Nothing. Just an unimpressive female howling her head off. After ten minutes the four of us left.

Cruising to Rabaul.

MONDAY 29 FEB (leap year.) Coral Sea. Hot calm and clear. Cruising through the China Straight gave us superb views of the surrounding tropical islands which are mainly green and sparsely populated. The straight connects the Coral and Solomon Seas.

The port presentation was about Hong Kong. Another wonderful destination to explore with endless possibilities on the cards.

When I took to a recliner on the Promenade Deck with a couple of books I asked myself what I wanted most from my cruise. I tried to be philosophic about it and thought about "Inspiration" But I'd read somewhere that inspiration is for amateurs. After thinking about it I said to myself "Yes that's quite true"

A lady gave a talk in the Admirals lounge about visual journaling. She uses art books for her journals and showed us three of them. The pages were full of watercolour scenes, drawings and collages as a record of her travels. The text however, was very minimal, but overall her journals were interesting and arty.

Our evening was dominated by Dixieland jazz in the Garden Lounge. The vicars joined us for the first show. Big, feel good music. Afterwards it was dinner and when we'd eaten our main course the four of us went back to the second show for a completely different play list. It was forty five minutes of super jazz, courtesy of brilliant improvisations and a bass guitarist who'd had lessons from God.

David and I went to see John Nations, the phenomenal juggler I saw on the Aurora. As previously he was springing round the stage projecting his astonishing abilities accompanied by his unique brand of humour. David was transfixed especially with the climax.

Rabaul tomorrow am.

TUESDAY 1 MARCH. Bay Road Wharf, Simpson Harbour, Rabaul. Papua New Guinea. Sunny and hot.

Rabaul is situated on the east coast of the island of New Britain in Papua New Guinea, a poor, mainly agricultural town that has seen many problems. The area sits on the 'ring of fire' in the Pacific where volcanos and earthquakes erupt. In 1942 the Japanese invaded and turned it into a supply base for their Pacific fleet.

It was pointless getting up at 6:00 am to see Mount Tavurvur as it was in sight for most of the morning.

Our mini bus tour was arranged by Lynn from Brisbane. We drove along pot holed roads with black ash piled up on either side, from the 1994 eruption. Our first stop was the hot springs with Mount Tavurvur smoking in the background. We had to pay an admission charge to a woman occupying a dilapidated shelter of wooden poles and palm leaves. We were told she owned the land. It was a scenic region even though it was desolate and covered with volcanic ash. The hot springs were interesting, with steam pouring off them. The water was very hot to the touch.

The other attraction was seeing the women and children who provided masses of colour. Their clothes were as colourful as their wares, which were spread out in a long row on the ground. Sarongs, tops and hats were hanging from cross posts and a profusion of handbags, ornaments, clothing and cheap jewellery. We were well received, especially when we handed out chocolates, and the women and children didn't mind being photographed. I was slightly alarmed when I noticed quite a few of them had red teeth as though their gums were bleeding. Val explained it was caused by the betel nuts they use as a stimulant.

When we arrived at the war museum we were greeted by a group of women singing "She'll be coming round the mountain," which was very entertaining but by the tenth verse I'd photographed them to the max.

The people in Rabaul all seem to have a passion for wearing brightly coloured garments which help to make one's photographs that bit more appealing.

The museum contains artefacts from the Japanese occupation including texts, photographs and bits of aircraft. We also entered a Japanese bunker which was really quite eerie. Took more photos of children having first given them chocolates.

Our next stop was a hill top which I think is known as "Tunnel Hill". The Japanese dug many tunnels there, which were used as air raid and military shelters. Some of the entrances are still visible. On the summit is an observatory where volcanic activities are monitored mainly of Mount Tavurvur. The views down to the harbour are superb with Queen Elizabeth taking centre stage.

The highlight of our tour was a visit to a local school. We were allowed in the classroom where Val handed out lots of pens. Then the children, who were aged about nine or ten screamed out a couple of verses of a song, all fifty three of them were crammed into one room - very touching. It was then classroom number two where a maths lesson was in progress. The children all seemed to look the same in their yellow shirts and of course we took more photos and as before, the event was quite moving.

The Japanese used slave labour to dig tunnels to house their barges.
We visited a barge tunnel which was more like a large cave. It houses the remains of barges which are full of rust but nevertheless very interesting. The vessels were used to supply ships in the harbour with munitions and supplies.

More mums, more children, and as we were handing out the last of the chocolates a toddler with no clothes on came running up to me for his prize. It was quite amusing.

We were dropped off at the market which sells mainly food and after a quick look round we walked back to Elizabeth for lunch. On

121

the way we saw the New Rabaul Guest House. It had a curved tin roof, corrugated tin canopy and was fronted by a tall wire fence!

It was hot and humid when we returned to explore the open market. Everywhere was decked out with colourfully dressed people - many had red teeth. Large displays of fruit and vegetables were all attractively arranged on trestles. We were on a photographic walkabout. Sometimes you feel a little intrusive, but out of respect it's best to ask first before trying for the perfect portrait. Usually they don't mind. I would say the market is not just a haven for photographers but a haven for people watchers.

The temperature was white hot and we would have loved a beer but sadly we could not find a bar and wondered if any even existed.

It was then time to leave Rabauls' treasures and head back to the ship having bagged many great experiences. But it was the people who stole the show, and if sand is to Blackpool then volcanic ash is to Rabaul!

It was a pint in the Golden Lion and then a deck recliner while reflecting on a brilliant day ashore.

Back to the Golden Lion for forty five minutes with Herbie Denton. He's a good pianist and singer but I didn't like his songs. He's good at sharing his personality with the audience though.

At dinner I noticed that the women can babble a bit. What is it about the human tongue! I've also found out that Brook is an ex-army major.

I'd looked forward to seeing the comedian, one Jeff Stevenson, but he just wasn't funny. The proof of a good comedian is when one keeps awake. I actually fell asleep.
Bravo. My request to meet other musicians has hit tomorrow's daily programme. I'm looking forward to seeing what happens.

Will anyone turn up? And if so how will I work it? Perhaps I should play it by ear - no pun intended!

Cruising to Puerto Princesca.

WEDNESDAY 2 MARCH. Bismarck Sea. Equator Day. Sunny, hot.

As I was relaxing in the Garden Lounge, coffee in one hand, pen in the other, which I sometimes liken to a magic wand, I started cursing it because creativity was just not happening. Folk drifted by delighting and also repelling my eye. Gerald said good morning minus my name, but oh dear! his lady friend does not have the legs for semi stilettos.

Matthew presented Shanghai with a big choice of excursions. We may opt to do the ten hour Garden City tour which will give us the opportunity to see some of Chinas' interior. We may also be able to take the shuttle bus to the Bund during the evening.

It was mayhem on the main pool deck for the crossing of the equator ceremony. Neptune and his entourage were overseeing the initiation ceremony in which the polliwogs (those crossing the equator for the first time) get covered in dyes and all sorts of yuk before being thrown into the pool. The crowds were really enjoying the show especially when the captain leapt in, fully clothed. Everywhere was a mess and I wondered if the pool water would be filtered before being emptied into the sea.

When I arrived at the Admiral's Lounge with my flute I felt apprehensive because I didn't know what to expect or who to expect. Would some talented musicians turn up? Would we soon be having a jam session? But I waited, and waited. Alas no takers. No one turned up. It was a case of "all dressed up with nowhere to go." What a disappointment. Perhaps I should try another ad, say after Hong Kong.

The sea was like a mill pond as I laid on a recliner with my book of Liz Cowley poems which sadly failed to impress. But the themes were quite good.

At 5:00 pm I kept my date with the grand piano. The Kendal couple turned up and said they liked my playing. Afterwards I continued to work on' Embraceable You', 'Georgia' and 'Solitude'. I played a good 'Gypsy Tango' but I struggled to remember some of 'Yesterday'. "If you don't use it you'll lose it". Anyhow, by the time I get home I won't be out of practice. I was able to play for a full hour. When the "Bach" lady arrived she let me watch her play some amazingly fast scales with both hands before she gave me some brilliant Bach. My tastes are not restricted to classical music I enjoy playing other music as well.

More music in the Garden lounge with a recital by Caroline Holden, the resident harpist. I was early so I was able to get into conversation with her. She's Scottish. When I mentioned my flute she asked me to bring it along. I politely declined because I have not practiced with her. However, we've tentatively arranged a jam possibly in the Admirals Lounge. She's an accomplished musician and gave us a mix of classical, folk and the 30's and I also enjoyed listening to her accompany her voice. I harmonised to some of them but Val accused me of being disrespectful. But later Caroline said she liked my singing. At last, looks like I'm going to get my jam after all.

We stood at the back of the theatre while a male singer got four people to join him on the stage for some comedy. The audience were hysterical, and that was our cue to leave. A lady walked out with us and introduced herself as Helen Fischer an Australian author and soprano singer. She was dressed like royalty and enjoyed being extravert and funny. She doesn't have a cabin she has a suite. Val has persuaded her to join the choir tomorrow. Oh the joys of people!

The ballroom is always a good standby if the theatre fails to impress.

The band played quality music and it was fun watching the dancers.

Addendum: I assumed we'd be crossing the line around early afternoon but I discovered at a later date we crossed it at 5:36 pm which meant I was actually playing the grand piano as we were crossing the equator.

Cruising To Puerto Princesca.

THURSDAY 3 MARCH. Pacific Ocean. Cloudy, warm.

Some drama while sitting in the Garden Lounge - a sudden torrential down pour. It was exploding off the glass roof and bouncing off the pool deck. People were fleeing but some remained in the pool and probably enjoyed the excitement and knew the rain would soon clear.

Another wander round the art gallery. I was gazing intently at the paintings and imagined how they'd look on my walls. When I let the images seep into my head they become mine and then there's no need to make a purchase!

I thought the lecture "Sleep perchance to Dream" was a flop. Why do some speakers tell us things we already know although we did learn about the dangers of OSA? (obstructive sleep apnoea). Perhaps it would have been useful if we'd been given some techniques to help us get back to sleep having been awake for long periods.

Matinee concert with the Duo Diaz. Diaz is Spanish for ten, which is the combined total number of strings on their instruments. Their playlist included Bach/Gounod's 'Ave Maria' and a classical guitar piece called 'Asturius'. The violinist was the best, another musician who was taught by God. At the end the audience were on a high.

There was a poor turn out for the Tiffany String Quartet in the Garden lounge but it didn't stop them playing music from heaven. I latched onto the cello and by isolating it from the other instruments I became quite intimate with it which helped because I was seated only two and a half meters from it. The music from a string quartet, just like an old master painting has never been bettered.

At dinner I sat next to Muriel, the retired vicar. We discussed counselling and the mental health helpline and I discovered she's not the conversationalist I expected her to be, given the type of work she did.

Commodore Club for jazz on the piano and harp. Disappointing because Caroline didn't play her harp, she just sang a couple of numbers which were fairly enjoyable but the genius pianist sang and played two Cole Porter numbers brilliantly. Don't buy drinks in the Commodore, you'll be broke by the time you leave the ship. I'm not sure if Val's happy about the jam I've arranged with Caroline in the midships bar tomorrow night.

Lastly, it was Julian Smith, Soprano sax, performing in the Royal Court. He performed on the Aurora but this time round I thought he was pretty boring.

Cruising to Puerto Princesca.

FRIDAY 4 MARCH. Pacific Ocean. Sunny and hot.

Port talk on Busan South Korea

I was enjoying my daily dose of caffeine in the Garden Lounge when the famous Helen Fischer approached me to say hello and to dramatise. She's slim, and was wearing expensive casual gear. What a card. I guess she'll be in her eighties but what confidence and what a Venus she must have been her younger days. She'd be the life and soul on our dinner table.

I carried on with my writing hoping some genius words would leap onto the page but alas it didn't happen. I have to be content with basics or more positively "Just stop and think a little harder." I've always found that mental exercise is harder that physical exercise.

When I turned up for my piano slot, an elderly woman in white framed glasses was playing very loud classical music. An obvious accomplished player. She had no intentions of stopping until I told her I'd booked the piano….When you press down the sustain pedal the keyboard moves one centimetre to the right but it doesn't affect the sound. I'm now concentrating on quality and not quantity and seeing definite progress.

Gerald and his Asian totty joined us for the quiz and we clocked up11/20. A good result. But heavens! why are some of the questions so monotonously trivial?

The vicar's absence from the dinner table allowed us all to descend into notoriety!... Vicky told us she takes statins and blood pressure tablets.

The midships bar was quiet so Caroline agreed to a duet. I improvised on a couple of numbers but felt capable of a lot better. The applause though was welcome. She suggested we put in some practice and meet tomorrow evening in the room on the corner near my cabin but I'm apprehensive about the "crew only sign" on the door.

Just before each bed time it's the Lido for Horlicks and Ovaltine and some people watching extraordinaire - the late night eaters. They're usually obese, often females with enormous bottoms helping themselves to pizzas and cakes - comfort eating, or just plain gluttony. Perhaps the NHS should send them on a will power course!

Cruising to Puerto Princesca.

SATURDAY 5 MARCH. Celebes Sea.

Port talk Jeju-do, an island off the coast of South Korea.

Garden Lounge for my usual mornings writing fix. This is made up of my previous day's news. You have to keep on top of it while it's still fresh or you're in trouble. Fortunately, I always make notes as I go along.

Among the shapes and sizes who come and go there's one woman who intrigues me. She's fortyish. Massive. Always wears a black top and black three quarter length slacks and carries a big blue rucksack, which seems to be a permanent accessory. What on earth does she put in it? Why is she constantly hauling it around the ship? What drives the poor soul? ... But then I suspect folk might find me intriguing and say; "There's that weirdo again, he's always writing".

Elizabeth is cruising through a group of islands, some of which are inhabited and I imagine the officers on the bridge will be identifying them while charting the ships course.

Chanced on Muriel in the library. First I was telling her about Tom Singleton and the problems he seems to be having with me, and then about how Val got involved with the controversial paintings in the hospice chapel. Muriel thinks I'm interesting and a good conversationalist, she said she loves talking to me. "Thank you Muriel. Praise makes good men better and bad men worse" so they say.

I sometimes enjoy relaxing under the canopy on the Lido pool deck and don't know which is more interesting, reading my book or people watching. I chuckle when I see older women bulging out of their bikinis. God bless them. All the while I was preoccupied with meeting Caroline for a jam. Alas it didn't happen.

I entered the door marked crew only and there was no sign of Caroline. I knocked on a couple of doors to no avail. Nothing.

Naturally I was disappointed. However, when I saw her at her concert she apologised and said she'd given me the wrong meeting place. We've agreed to meet at the correct venue during the next few days.

Jay has e-mailed me to say she's happy with the band and that the Burn Naze venue still exists. She said I am being missed. She also said that tracking Queen Elizabeth is very exciting.

I still cannot get connected to my bank. Terribly frustrating.

Puerto Princesca tomorrow.

SUNDAY 6 MARCH. Maiden Call. Puerto Princesca. Sulu Sea. The Philippines.

Puerto Princesca is the capital of Palawan, a long and narrow island and one of 7,100 islands that make up the Philippines.

To celebrate our arrival we were treated to a spectacular demonstration of dancing and drumming. The quayside was transformed into a kaleidoscope of youngsters in beautifully coloured costumes performing a variety of formations to powerful drum rhythms. There was even a tribal dance. This show was a welcoming party on a huge scale. Unforgettable.

When we walked off the gangway and through the canopy some local women gave us beads to place around our necks. We wore the beads with pride.

To make up the numbers and to secure a good deal, some Aussies invited us to join them for a trip to the Subterranean River which was actually on our list. Twelve of us piled into a mini bus which apart from Val and I, comprised Gordon and Annette and four Australian couples.

Our first stop was the money changers where we were given Philippine pesos for Australian dollars to enable us to pay for the trip. You could tell you were in a developing country by the humble shops, cafes, masses of overhead power cables and tuk tuks.

It was a fast one hour and twenty minutes drive to the UNESCO site, sometimes bumpy but with plenty of scenery to take in. Lush vegetation, hills, wooded areas, wayside vegetable stalls and shacks with toddlers sometimes roaming around lines of washing.

We made a comfort stop where the 'ladies' was indicated by a three quarter length caricature wood carving of a female holding herself as if she was dying to wee! Hardly dignified and especially since the toilet tissue dispenser was actually hanging on the outside of the loo!

The Australians were a boisterous lot who enjoyed airing their sense of humour but they were good fun.

We boarded six seater boats with stabilisers made from bamboo. Then we were put to sea for an exhilarating fifteen minute passage to the shore near the subterranean entrance. A short walk along duck boards with trees either side took us to our starting point where we were given life jackets a hard hat and an audio set before being rowed across the small estuary in a sophisticated canoe.

The entrance resembled a grotto in sea green waters like something out of a fairy tale book. Our oarsman switched on his powerful hands free flashlight advising us to keep our mouths closed as protection against the bat droppings. We were then taken through some of the most awesome sights we have ever seen. A revelation, an epiphany. Forty five minutes of snaking along a river within what I can only describe as a long continuous twisting and winding chamber of ochres, gold, whites, greys, blacks and silver. Nature's sculptures greet you at every turn. These are known as speleothems…mainly biblical lookalikes. Christ, the Virgin Mary, The Holy Family, a cathedral, and an eagle. We even saw a naked lady with a perfectly rounded bottom and of course many other shapes that you could personally put a name to. It was an eerie experience with a feeling of mystique with devils lying in waiting! Imagine spending a night in there with bats, spiders and snakes!... Our cameras were still clicking as we re-entered the estuary. You then realise just why it is a world heritage UNESCO site. It had also recently been given the status as one of the new seven wonders of nature.

The buffet lunch was a delicious feast of local recipes, with a bottle of lemonade thrown in. Afterwards we wandered round the colourful shacks where you could buy casual cloths, gifts and cooked food. Many hawkers were selling pearls.

During our return journey the Australian men wanted to see a cockfight, so we drove off the main road and followed a rural track. But the anti-blood lobby amongst us voted against it. The spin off was that we were able to stop at a village to get some close ups of shacks. We also photographed children sitting on a trailer with a bullock harnessed to it. It's always interesting to see how people live.

It was 5:00 pm when we arrived back and felt that for £25.00 each it was indeed value for money. There was still plenty of time to explore because the ship wouldn't be leaving until late. We decided to waive a cool beer in favour of a little local sightseeing and a photo shoot.

The Cathedral of The Immaculate Conception dominates the area. An imposing building in blue and white with twin steeples. It was full inside, probably for mass as it was Sunday. Near by a game of basketball was in full swing.

The Plaza Cuartel was worth seeing. A picturesque garden area with trees, plants and various interesting features, chief of which were various monuments and placards telling the stories of atrocities committed by the Japanese after they invaded during the

Second World War. Near to where we were standing 150 American
Prisoners were herded into bunkers and burned alive by Japanese soldiers. 11 men managed to escape with the help of some locals.

We photographed a shanty settlement a distance away which was close to the sea and suspected the shacks were built to rehouse the homeless after the devastating 2013 typhoon. One feature I couldn't understand was why the pedicab rickshaws were decorated with flowers.

We wandered round some narrow back streets which we soon realised were actually front streets. No need to feel intrusive as the people were quite friendly. A man was tending his fighting cocks, all six of them in wooden cages. Two tiny shops were interesting because of the twelve inch square serving hatches on the outside wall.

Two women were eating in a small garden behind a tall wire netting fence. We said hello and they invited us in to a tiny garden. One asked if I'd like some of her food but I politely declined. She asked if we'd like a drink. I handed over some money which she gave to someone who returned with a huge bottle of beer for Val and I to share. The woman is a widow aged 38 her friend is also a widow, she's 34. The elder one couldn't believe my age, she thought I was much younger. Her children appeared and were all smiling. Then of a sudden she sang "Love Story" for us, well on key with a nice voice. Youngsters appeared who actually took our photographs from behind the netting! It was an exciting experience being welcomed in by this woman and her family, even more so when we danced together with Val in video mode. There was a cheerful, friendly and heart-warming atmosphere on both sides of the fence. After we hugged these lovely people we walked away feeling elated.

To end our day we drank some cans of beer in a timber built shop. The young man who served us told us the shop belongs to his mother and he looks after it on Sundays. During the week he teaches computer studies at the local collage. Two police women arrived who were happy to talk with us. I think they said they were tourist police. The Bach piano lady was walking by and then joined us. Her name is Nancy.

After dinner Val retired while I went here and there seeking some final pleasure. I wasn't up to jiving with Vicky, besides she might have embarrassed me! She was on the dance floor but I managed to avoid her

Julian Smith, saxophonist, was playing his last number after which a singer hit the stage with 'It's Not Unusual', 'Delilah' and 'It's Now or Never. I think these musical clichés should be chucked into room 101! My Ovaltine gave me relief.

A Great day. The epitome of what cruising is all about.

Cruising to Manila.

MONDAY MARCH 7 Sulu Sea. Small swell, hot and sunny.

Sat with the vicars in the Garden Lounge. I was explaining how the mental health helpline works. Muriel thinks I apologise too much. Well, I can always take advice from a woman of the cloth!

Matthew gave us Nagasaki. It all seems to centre on the atomic bomb explosion and we were told that we may find some of the exhibits in the museum quite disturbing.

Could not understand our on board statement so it was to the pursers desk for an explanation. Easy! We have a windfall…$250.00 each on board spend which we were not told about when we booked the cruise. The money will more than compensate for the loss of interest I have incurred on my current account.

We had arranged to do Shanghai independently but our windfall prompted us to book the ten hour Garden City Tour.

Over to the ballroom for the passenger talent show. Sometimes I like being entertained by the sheer lack of talent, and wonder how folk can have the cheek to perform. The Fleetwood girl was compere and Val accuses her of talking to us as though we are gaga. First to appear was a young brother and sister wearing daft white framed sun glasses. All they could offer was a sing along to a CD while activating their arms. The only attribute was their confidence. Mother was frantically taking their photos. They should have been at school not on a cruise ship. Two excellent dancers next doing the Paso doble. A guy then sang 'Can't Help Falling in Love,' but had he known about me he would have enlisted me to sing the harmony and I might have boosted his ratings! A woman sang 'When Irish Eyes Are Smiling', but the poor soul went off key a little. Finally another couple danced a good waltz. The show however, was another experience and something to write about.

I enjoyed lazing under the canopy on the Lido pool deck while reading my book and listening to jazz, but as always my eyes become diverted with human being watching.

We're certainly getting our fair share of captain's receptions. "We're only here for the beer." Loved the two glasses of sparkling wine and the piano trio who were playing the American Song book. We latched onto a couple from Yorkshire who are experienced cruisers. Often when a couple stand on their own they welcome the company of others for some sociability and then everyone talks excitedly. I value these events because they don't exist at home.

I was surprised to see David at dinner in his vicar's suit and white collar. He asked if he could say grace. Val wasn't in favour, but I encouraged him to proceed.

Goody! Val finally got me logged on to my bank accounts. Relief at last.

Caroline was just finishing off to an empty space and it was too late to arrange a jam with her.

Manila tomorrow.

TUESDAY 8 MARCH. Pier 15 South Harbour, Manila Bay. Manila, Philippines. Hot and sunny.

Manila is the capital of the Philippines and is situated on Luzon, the country's largest island. The city is a mix of old and new.

I was a passenger on the Queen Victoria when she berthed here in 2013 but sadly I was sick and in quarantine and was unable to leave my cabin; but this time was different, I was going to make up for it.

When it comes to entertaining, no one does it better than the Filipinos. The quayside was teeming with youngsters in dazzling costumes. We were given a massed drum recital, followed by another group playing large, wooden xylophones and enormous pan pipes. We even had clowns on stilts. I was told the ceremony was not just for us but equally to welcome those Filipinos who made up part of the crew.

After we left the gangway and walked through the canopy two young local women were handing out gifts of beads and fans to the passengers. Just like at Puerto Princesca we felt that we were on the red carpet.

Once we were through the gates it was mayhem with taxis and minibuses clamouring for fares. A few of us squeezed into a taxi to take us to Intramuros which is the old, walled part of Manila.

The Cathedral was our first call and was packed. The friendly congregation were singing enthusiastically, some standing, while clapping and throwing their arms about. It was almost a party atmosphere. We just followed suit. I then began to hand out chocolates to the children but some nuns suggested I did it outside as Mass was about to begin. The children followed and once outside I got mobbed. Hands were coming from all directions in desperation to grab the chocolates. I had a frenzy on my hands until they exhausted my supply.

A young local called Darryl talked us in to seeing some of the sites on his tricycle with a side car attached. It was fun but quite hairy being peddled round the streets, often weaving our way in and out of the traffic; sometimes we felt like sitting ducks, but he seemed skilled enough, and would stop occasionally to let us take photos.

We saw a church, some nuns in a garden and a monument with a sculpture depicting rape and death committed by the Japanese during WW11. Some of the streets in Intramuros have a third world feel making it an interesting and photogenic place to visit. We looked in the gorgeous courtyard of an old Spanish house before climbing up onto the city walls. The ramparts gave us some good views of a golf course far below and tower blocks in the background. Below the walls we saw a WW11 'execution' wall with many bullet holes.

Darryl dropped us off at Fort Santiago. He had given us good value, so we paid him accordingly. He took the money to his lips and promptly kissed it as though it was gold. We said we'd look out for him later at the cathedral if he was around, to take us back to the ship.

Fort Santiago was built in 1571 and has a chequered history. The imposing stone walls and a large portico entrance sits by its moat. The fort area is now an historic park which provides a very pleasant stroll. The fountains, trees and flowers make pleasing photographs. There are also many ruins: a theatre, an imposing residence now littered with bullet holes, dungeons, a cannon with a collection of shells, plaques and monuments. The Japanese were here and committed atrocities; they found the dungeons quite useful for the torture and killing of 600 Filipinos and Americans. In the distance I noticed a shanty town and thanks to my zoom lens I bagged a great picture.

We walked back to the Spanish House for lunch and decided on an upstairs restaurant called Barbara's specialising in Spanish and Filipino recipes. An excellent choice. Soup, buffet and a beer for £10.00 each. It looked like a period setting with big oval mirrors, chandeliers and old furniture. Two guitarists and a double bass player were singing at every table and when they came to ours I got up and joined them with harmonies for 'Yesterday', 'And I Love Her' and 'Can't Help Falling in Love'. It was a happy event. Those guys would be a good attraction in the Golden Lion on the ship. Three young waitresses in long traditional dresses didn't mind us taking their photos.

Back in the court yard there was a small shop selling bicycles with bamboo frames which appeared to be extremely well made.

Daryll was at the cathedral with his humble contraption waiting to take us back to Elizabeth. We passed a couple of streets where the shops and apartments were all huddled together in a clutter with junk on the pavements. Some of the shops were little more than shacks. Again overhead power cables were everywhere. Eventually we came to a park and Daryll waited while we went in to take some pictures. We talked to a group of secondary school students who told us they were having an outdoor drama lesson.

We felt sympathy for Daryll as he peddled us back in the hot sunshine. His thin legs were like machines and we wondered how much strength he'd need be able to pedal the sheer weight of his trike let alone two adults. Once again we were holding our breath a few times as he weaved his way through the traffic but he did a superb job. A lovely guy, and I couldn't help feeling sorry for him. He was happy though when we paid him over the odds.

Delectable cool larger on the Pool Deck with Lynn and David from Australia while engaging in some small talk.

The heat began taking its toll and forced us to crash out in the cabin but upon waking we felt even more exhausted but it gradually passed.

A pint in the Golden Lion with Herbie Denton on the piano. You'd think his piano keyboard was an anvil from the way his hands crash down, and please Herbie sing some better songs.

From The Royal Court Theatre a guy called Paul Gauntlet performed a mixed bag of singing, tricks, juggling and escapology. Failed to impress at first but he eventually made his mark.

A brilliant day ended with good theatre and that was it, or so we thought it was. As we were walking past the ballroom we noticed about 500 balloons in a net suspended from the ceiling. We guessed that the balloons would be released and descend upon everyone and create mayhem. We were right. But instead of watching we decided to join in. Soon the balloons rained down on us and the object was to keep as many airborne as possible. It was aerobics with a difference. We were frantically leaping about with our hands and arms in all directions to keep the balloons in the air for as long as possible. The last one touched down after 27 minutes. The next challenge was to burst them and that took 10 minutes and by the end we were quite out of breath, but what an uninhibited way for adults to engage in some great childish fun.

Cruising to Hong Kong.

WEDNESDAY 9 MARCH. South China Sea. Calm, cooler, partly sunny, very comfortable.

Lecture entitled "Affairs of the Heart" given by Dr. McMinchin. He outlined all the things you can do to maintain a healthy heart, the majority of which I know already.

Some peaceful relaxation on the Lido Pool Deck with my book ended when "Changez" plugged in. They produce a good beat but little else. I stayed for two numbers before seeking solace elsewhere.

Some of the paintings at the passenger art exhibition were passable, but the general standard seemed a little poor. Vicky's "goldfish" failed the test, but her other pictures compensated. The tutor was eager to tell me that the Queen owns two of his paintings. It was interesting to talk to him about art but I had to dash off to the Royal Court Theatre to film Val singing in the choir.

It was a reasonable performance but they sang off key for a few moments causing me and the woman next to me to go oooh! Oh dear! Compared to the Aurora's standards under Natalie, it was second rate, and I don't think Gareth Malone would have been impressed. Perhaps Jane Edwards should put a little more effort into helping the choir perform better. Afterwards they all paraded to the grand lobby and posed on the stairs for photographs.

During my piano practice I was forced to endure three Australian women who were laughing raucously. But they didn't put me off and they left after 15 minutes. Then there were two dancers who seemed to want the place to themselves. They left not long after the others and then it was bliss and I was able to make good progress.

When we arrived at the dinner table David told us he'd brought his own bottle of wine to share but had to pay $20.00 corkage charge. Well that was a red rag, so I walked up to the sommelier and told him the charge was immoral and tantamount to theft. I also complained to the maître d' who told me they had no sway over charges. Anyway, back at the table everyone supported me.

They all disembark tomorrow, and after I briefly filmed everyone it was e-mail exchanges, handshakes, hugs and good wishes. The worry now was whether our replacements would be as good company

Relief - my banking transactions are now complete for March.

I sat through the whole of Caroline's late performance at the midships bar and although she's a good musician and singer, I've become disillusioned with her. It's the same music over and over. But she did take my request..."Wild Mountain Thyme." Sadly at the end of her recital I was the sole member of the audience. She said she'd be free on 21 March and I agreed to her request to let her see some of my music first.

Hong Kong tomorrow.

THURSDAY 10 MARCH. Ocean Terminal. Victoria Harbour Hong Kong. China. Misty. Cool.

Hong Kong is one of the world's greatest cities. Colourful, vibrant and no dull moments.

The morning mist hanging over Victoria Peak and the skyscrapers was quite eerie but the greyness and slight rain cleared later.

The ship's berth couldn't be more convenient. You're off the ship and straight into Harbour City, a mega shopping mall with 700 up market retail outlets, 50 restaurants and 2 cinemas. You need lots of time and plenty of money to do it justice. The design is very shrewd because cruise ship passengers have no choice but to walk through part of it for the exit to the city. The shiny marble floors are immaculate and give off arty reflections.

We hit the streets of Kowloon with a walking tour Val had produced some months previously, but first we had to negotiate a short journey on the underground. Not easy, but we got help from some courteous locals. After we boarded the train we discovered we were travelling in the wrong direction and when the train stopped, we got off with a very kind young man who escorted us to the correct platform.

First on our itinerary was the street of florists. Shop after shop, all open fronted, beautifully clean with tiled floors, selling every flower imaginable including bonsai, cacti, pot plants and made up bouquets etc. The colours adorned the pavements making the scene almost psychedelic, and as we wandered up and down the walkway our cameras were going mad. It was floristry on a big scale and well worth seeing. We were told that most of the flowers are imported from Holland. We saw another florist shop nearby called The Hing Fa Flower Market with a reception area that resembled a 5 star hotel with prolific flower stocks adorning the walls away from the floor area. Conclusion… They like their flowers in Hong Kong!

Birds and bird cages were next, again on a grand scale. Song birds of every feather twittering and chirping. What an eye opener, or rather an ear opener. The pavement was like a corridor with birds seemingly content in their designer cages on either side. A few sparrows had found their way to the sacks of bird seed and were busy pecking away.

Well, apart from birds and flowers it seems that gold fish are as popular. There are many shops selling these and other exotic species. Sadly, many of the fish were contained in polythene water bags with barely enough room to manoeuvre.

I didn't fancy the food market but I succumbed because it was on the itinerary. The first floor was decked out with masses of vegetables, some unidentifiable. Up another flight and it was the same picture only this time it was meat. Butchers galore, again we struggled to name everything. One guy in his white apron and red crocks kindly put his knife down and was happy to pose for a picture.

We thought about eating when we arrived at the top floor but changed our minds because the diners were all locals with many sitting on blue plastic stools and besides I wondered about the hygiene standards. Naturally we took photos for the record but felt rather intrusive. No one seemed to mind but I bet they were thinking "Go away, I don't want to be photographed when I'm eating."

Val had a haircut Hong Kong style in an upstairs salon. It looked a bit seedy probably because the floors needed sweeping, and there was a cat at large. The huge mirrors though, in big black frames were overpowering yet oddly fascinating. The young local guy took his time and only charged her £10.00. She was quite happy. Cunard would have wanted about £45.00

It's easy to fall in love with Kowloon, it's a vibrant and colourful part of the city with dazzling street scenes of vivid signs and hoardings suspended above the pavements, street markets, street food from open stalls, an abundance of shops, bars, restaurants, high rise tower blocks and huge tenements and parks. There's a picture at every turn of the eye.

You'll marvel at Ladies Market. It's a vast street market selling mainly women's goods which seemed to be dominated by bras! The place was almost like a warehouse. The sheer quantity and choice of female wares was staggering.

We found a nice upstairs restaurant for lunch and a rest. It was noodles on a hot plate for me while Val had chicken and rice - very tasty and so was the lemon tea, and all reasonably priced. One of the waitresses was wearing a face mask.

After we walked round a bit longer and took more photographs we decided to head back along the Nathan Road. On the way we looked in Kowloon Park. Three separate groups of men were poring over a board game which could have been mah-jong. There was a tense expectancy on their faces as though the stakes were high. It's a pity we didn't have time to see more of the park as we've heard it's very beautiful.

We walked the final leg back along Canton Road and continued to be fascinated by all we saw, and at the end of the walk we found a shop for Val's wine. My energy levels were ok but Val was flagging. Not bad after seven and a half hours on our feet, excluding lunch of course. I suggested we lick the plate and see what was happening by the harbour. It was a good move and as it was nearing evening we bagged some great pictures of a junk with illuminated red sails.

Hong Kong is undoubtedly one of our favourite cities. A photographic gem.

So once more we trod the marble floor of the palatial shopping mall before boarding Elizabeth.
Paperwork was waiting for us in the cabin notifying us that we have reached Cunard's highest status. We are now "Diamond," and that means extra perks which include a luncheon in the exclusive Verandah Restaurant, wine tasting and double internet time.

People were gathering on deck 3 for the laser show, but I enjoyed looking at the skyscrapers which were casting vivid reflections in the harbour with the night junks drifting by.

Three new couples joined our dinner table. Hanna and Eric from America, Susie and David from America, and Linda and Jeff from England. Seems like we've got good replacements but I'm reserving judgment. And then it was the inevitable "how many cruises have you done?"

We were entertained by a Chinese troupe in the theatre. The girl with the spinning hoops amazed me. The rest were pretty ordinary.

No alcohol, we had Ovaltine instead and then it was bed with our heads still spinning after an amazingly enjoyable day.

Cruising to Shanghai.

FRIDAY 11 MARCH. East China Sea. Cold and windy. Sea choppy. Cloudy.

The Café Carinthia is a luxurious place with fresh flowers and ocean view windows, perfect for journaling. But they like you to buy a coffee. I never do because I can get one free in the Lido.

Listened to Matthew give his port presentation about Kagoshima Japan.

Our internet accounts now confirm we have been promoted to diamond - the top passenger status. This gives us 8 hours free internet on the current leg and various other perks.

The sea has developed into a huge swell which is always dramatic to watch especially from eye level in our cabin.

Spent the day wandering round - the library, art gallery, the shops and the Garden lounge.

In the Golden Lion, the young quiz master asked "What is the national flower of Austria, not Australia, you know, the Austria in Germany." Of course he then left himself open to much ridicule.

Dinner. Hanna told us she is a music teacher and so we've arranged a jam at my piano slot tomorrow evening. The rest of the table said they would want to attend. Later she suggested we all go to the theatre together. Totally against my independence. I succumbed just to be sociable, but only the once.

I was half hearted about the show but it was actually good entertainment. A guy called Pingxin Zu played virtuoso dulcimer with a video screen showing us what his hands were doing. We got the 'Entertainer', Pachelbel's 'Canon', 'Turkish Rondo', the 'Sabre Dance' and others. A delightful player, very energetic.

Cruising to Shanghai.

SATURDAY 12 MARCH. East China Sea. Cool and sunny. Calm sea.

A petite Asian woman was doing tai chi on the deck. She looked good, and I liked her handsome flowing movements. I learned it many years ago but perhaps I should take it up again.

While it was coffee and creative writing in the Garden lounge I managed to talk with the young Filipino woman who was watering and spraying the plants. She told me it takes a whole morning to water the ship's plants - a job she really enjoys.

The port talk was about Yokohama. Matthew is a good presenter but I feel he should stop and take stock. My advice to him would be to slow down and cut back on the staccato a little.

The matinee concert was quite good. A duo called Ben Godfrey and Matthew McCombie played classical music on the trumpet and piano, an unusual combination, but the music hit the mark. I particularly liked the pianist playing Debussy's 'Reverie'.

I saw Tony, the guy we met at Nobby's Beach. He was lamenting about Hong Kong, and said the view from Victoria Peak was obscured by mist. I sympathised because on a clear day it's one of the best harbour views in the world.

I had a warm up my flute for a while in the cabin and then went to the yacht club to meet Hanna. I felt nervous and wished Jay could have been with me. We launched straight into the music, 'Georgia', 'Charade', 'Angel Eyes' and others. She's a cool player and we sounded well together. Our table mates turned up to give us plenty of applause; Nancy was also present and she enjoyed it. Well I've done it, I've finally managed a jam, and also have a jam to look forward to with Caroline!

Another poor turnout in the Garden Lounge for the Tiffany String Quartet and I wondered if the music lovers had gone into hiding. But it was our pre dinner treat - music made in heaven. I asked for

Schubert's 'Ave Maria' and when they played it I felt myself choking up. I often wonder if music has helped me to become enlightened.

There were lots of compliments at the dinner table for Hanna and I but heavens! she's one heck of a chatterbox!

Shanghai tomorrow.

SUNDAY 13 MARCH. Wusongkou International Cruise Terminal Huangpu River. Shanghai, China. Cool.

Shanghai is China's largest and by far the world's most populated city and is located on the country's central coast.

We completed a tour of the ancient city of Suzhou, which has a 2500 year of history. The itinerary lasted 10 hours and covered 4 venues: three for the eyes and one for the taste buds.

During the journey our guide told us the population of Shanghai is 24m which is the same as for the whole of Australia! (I have verified these figures) yet it seems inconceivable. Mile after mile of landscapes contains hundreds of tenement blocks which are grim, soulless and not pleasant to look at.

 After an hour and a half drive we arrived at Suzhou for venue No1 which was the Silk Embroidery Research Institute. It's where clever women work their magic with silk embroidery to create exquisite works of art. These include landscapes, seascapes, flowers, birds, animals, architecture and portraits of our Queen Elizabeth, Princess Diana, the Mona Lisa and many more. If you stand a few feet away they look like photographs and it's interesting to look at the different shades of silk that make these masterpieces look so lifelike. Some of the pictures are even more remarkable because they are "double faced or double sided" which means that while a picture is being 'sewn,' a completely different one is being produced on the reverse side of the canvass with the same needle but sometimes two. They are feats of genius with some art work taking months to create. You can watch some of the women at work and they don't mind being photographed but they never smile or give eye contact. Finally we looked round the gallery and marvelled at everything on display.

During our short journey to our next venue we came by a run-down part of the city with masses of overhead cables partly blocking out some of the buildings. There were rickshaws and we saw a man on a scooter with his three small children on board, one on the front, two at the back and not a crash helmet between them!

Another feast for the eyes was venue No 2. Suzhou is known as the Venice of China, I wouldn't put it quite like that but the long stretch of canal our boat traversed held our attention while our cameras were clicking frantically. A ramshackle jumble of dwellings, bars and eateries line each side of the narrow waterway. The buildings are of brick and timber and only a few meters high and come in all sorts of shapes and sizes. They are ancient, all huddled together and highly individualistic. Some are partially built on wide stilts and others have tiny balconies and verandahs. A few of them looked as though they were about to topple into the canal. Some of the concrete steps were leaning sideways through subsidence. Red lanterns are a symbol of national pride and adorn many establishments. We saw balustrades, children, adults, plant pots and the occasional washing hanging out. And the bridges were interesting, they're ancient and made of stone and come in different designs. It's fascinating to see how the other half live and fires the imagination. I guess the residents enjoy a community spirit and I'm wondering what occupations they have. There is no symmetry here, hence its charm. We were completely absorbed.

Venue No 3 was lunch in a posh hotel. Ten of us shared a table with a "lazy Susan," this is a glass turn table from which food is served. The attentive waiting staff gave us various dishes of vegetables, meats, rice and a bottle of beer. At one point the lazy Susan had a projecting spoon from one of the dishes which caught Val's glass of beer which spilled all over the table.

Venue No 4 was top of the bill. The Humble Administrators Garden. A classical garden built in the 16th century by a retired magistrate who referred to himself as humble. It's a UNESCO site and an idyllic place to visit. Some of the features include ponds, small lakes capturing reflections, pavilions on elevated rocks, terraces, bridges, one of which is zigzag. There are walkways, rockeries, pagodas and an abundance of trees and shrubs. There is no need to compose a picture you just point and shoot. Here is a small sample of the names of some of the garden's attractions: Orange Pavilion, Green Ripple Pavilion, The Mountain in View tower, The Pagoda Reflection Pavilion, The Tower of Reflection, The Moon Gate, The Fragrant Isle, The Small Flying Rainbow Bridge, Little Surging Wave Hall, Celestial Spring Tower and Fragrant Sorghum Hall. All lyrical descriptions and a perfectly inspiring place to take one's morning walk.

There was congestion on the expressway as we headed back to port and because we were late we felt it would be pointless to try and get to the Bund.

The dinner table was buzzing with tales of Shanghai especially from Hanna, and her interminable tongue. I think she should have self- awareness lessons or consider her table companions and have her tongue super glued! Again the extra veg arrived only to be wasted. Eric, her husband is so passive and a man of few words. Heaven forbid two super tongues.

The Queens 7 piece band were fabulous but we felt compelled to see what was happening in the theatre. We didn't stay long because some award winning woman was screeching out "Don't Cry for Me Argentina."

Cruising to Pusan

MONDAY 14 MARCH. East China Sea. Sunny, cold, windy, choppy sea.

I was forced to wear my coat for my morning promenade walk, but I enjoyed the invigorating exercise and the salty taste of the sea.

Port presentation on Osaka Japan.

Another taste of paradise in the Garden Lounge with my coffee and pen until Changez invaded and killed off the peacefulness. What makes people think that we need noise when we're perfectly happy to relax without it? The band would have been much more appealing in a sound proof room.

I said to Val that I believe the American song book is the equivalent of the old master paintings, never been bettered. But she disagreed.

Another wine tasting event with four very brief lectures plus wine and nibbles. It's all pretentious. But there was no attempt to make us buy. I think the exercise is to keep the "diamond" guests happy. When it came to the questions, rather than risk a handbagging from Val for asking something humorous I asked " Which is the correct way to hold a glass of wine?" the answer, by the stem! Well, you learn something every day. A guy called Allen echoed my feelings about Cunard ripping people off. He's cruising "right round" and he showed a lot of interest when I told him about the mail run in Akaroa.

If you don't keep a check on your on board account you'll be charged gratuities which is another rip off. Val still had a charge of $230.00 which the purser's desk kindly removed.

A couple joined us for the quiz in the Golden Lion and we scored eight out of twenty which is quite good considering the super trivial questions they sometimes ask.

At dinner I avoided eye contact with the babbler for as long as possible until she caught me in her woeful waffling web and then it was an endurance test. She continues to get her extra veg with most of it going to the seagulls!

I do wish Linda would show less cleavage - might stop them popping out and dropping into her gravy! Seems that she and Val have become buddies because they are both not fans of Princess Diana.

Looked in the Queens Room and then had a peek in at the theatre. A big guy in a big penguin suit was just standing there like a pudding, howling his head off which meant it was our cue to make a hasty departure.

Pusan tomorrow.

TUESDAY 15 MARCH. Pusan International cruise terminal, Korea Strait. Pusan, South Korea. Cool, Sunny with blue skies.

Pusan is South Korea's second largest city after Seoul. Mountains, Markets, temples and beaches await those fortunate enough to be able to visit the country.

Alas there was no welcoming party on the quayside to charm us off the ship!

A very pretty local young woman welcomed us onto the shuttle bus while handing out maps. She then became our guide for the 15 minute transfer to the Nampadong district where Val and I did our own thing.

Our hit list started with the Lotte Department Store. It's the largest of its kind in the country with upmarket shops and marble floors. The Aqua Mall hosts the world's biggest musical fountain show; (according to the Guinness book of records). Water jets from high up in the atrium and from below create dramatic cascades which are set to classical music. We had Flight of the Bumblebee, Swan Lake, The Marseillaise, and the Flower Song to name a few. The climax was the 1812 Overture which was spectacular. The South Koreans had certainly made a first good impression on us, but there was more to come.

The roof of the building or the observation deck is known as the Sky Park, an extensive area of walkways, patios, flowers and plants. A pleasant area to wander round while taking in the panoramas which include mountains, the harbour, high rise tower blocks, Pusan Tower, a Buddhist Temple and of course the busy streets, all under a clear blue sky.

The Jagalchi fish market is a vibrant and busy scene. A huge rough and ready roof only building, of wet floors and an enormous variety of fresh fish and sea creatures often displayed on gigantic plates and bowls placed on the floors. There was enough stock to feed a multitude. But it was the women who captured our attention. They wear wellies, and layers topped with big plastic aprons with head scarves and enormous visors. They really look quite comical. Most of them were seated on small crates as they carried out their work. The site is a magnet for cameras and we felt the women made better pictures than the fish did.

Equally exciting are the side streets with goods cluttering the outsides of the shops and hoardings which look as though they're dripping down at 90 degrees towards the pavements.

The shuttle bus took us back to the ship for lunch and then we were out again to grab the rest of our itinerary.

We weaved our way up the streets and found the entrance to our final gem, Yongdusan Park at the top of numerous wooden steps. The park is set on a hill 49 meters high and overlooks the harbour. Some of the attractions include the Pusan Tower, octagonal pavilion, statues, bronze dragon tower, flower clock, a Buddhist temple and the Pusan citizen's bell and pavilion.

We came by three young guys from Seoul who were very friendly and although their English was poor they were eager to make an attempt at communicating with us. They're drama students and when I mentioned Shakespeare they knew what I meant. Val and I sat on a bench with a huge pink plastic heart behind us while they took our picture and made a gift to us of a Polaroid photo. How kind. Later we asked a group of young people if we could have their photo, then it was six smiles beaming into our cameras. Part of the way down to street level is by way of a green escalator that was out of order, much to Val's dismay because she was flagging a bit.

Finally it was time for Val to replenish her wine stocks. After forty minutes of scouring the streets we managed to find an outlet and bought six bottles.

Nancy sat with me in the Lido self-service while we sang Pusan's praises and then we talked about music. She said she no longer listens to the Tiffany string Quartet because she thinks the lead violinist sometimes plays off key. I said I hadn't noticed. Nancy then said the violinist from Duo Diaz had also noticed. Perhaps her hearing is at fault!!

On the quayside there was adequate compensation for the lack of a morning welcoming party- a trio of dashing young women in red hot pants and short red and white jackets were playing the drums to say farewell to us. It was good entertainment as we watched them from the promenade deck.

We had the usual Herbie Denton banging the piano keys and I had to send our beers back because they were flat.

The Royal Court gave a great show to end a great day. A guy called Kenny Martin entertained us with sax and clarinet, an accomplished jazz man. "Night Train" was brilliant and he brought the house down with numbers Jay and I adore. It's music to die for. The guy is a quality musician. Why can't we have more like him?

Jeju-do tomorrow.

WEDNESDAY 16 MARCH. Maiden Call. Jeju-do International Passenger Terminal. Jeju-do Island, Korean Straight, South Korea. Sunny, very warm.

Jeju-do is South Korea's largest island and is situated about 49 miles south of the mainland. It's known as the Island of the Gods and has similarities to Hawaii in terms of geography and climate.

We were greeted by a troupe of about fifteen youngsters who were each playing a drum while dancing on the quayside. They wore colourful traditional dress that was so bulky you couldn't tell whether they were male female of some of both! It was good entertainment though.

A short journey on the shuttle bus took us to the Gwandeokjeong Pavilion in the town centre. This is one of the oldest buildings on the island. A large decorative open sided structure with many simple red columns supporting the roof. The pavilion fronts the army training grounds which was built in 1448. Close by are comical statues known as Stone Grand Fathers. These were considered to be gods offering protection and fertility. And were placed outside gates to ward off demons.

After consulting our map we decided to walk to the coast to see the Dragon Rock. The route wasn't easy to follow so we were forced to ask for directions a few times. We came by a narrow river in a minor gorge with a small hexagonal pavilion perched above it on a rock and the wooden steps alongside gave me a superb picture. As we were crossing a bouncy bridge we got into a sketchy conversation with a friendly couple from Seoul, who's English was poor. (How is it we expect everyone to speak our language?) It seemed odd that they should ask us to take their photos on our cameras. Anyhow, it's always heartening when folk are willing to engage.

The sea shore was covered with black lava rock and the sizeable dragon rock actually resembles a dragon.

Unfortunately there wasn't much else to see until we walked round the waterfront and chanced on the Haenyeo. It's the name for the Lady Divers. These super fit women are aged between 50 and 90 and catch fish with their bare hands. They wear wet suits, face masks and flippers but no oxygen and can hold their breath under water for up to two minutes. They have iron will and used to be known as matriarchs. Orange containers are buoyed nearby for their catch. A couple of the divers surfaced wet and dripping and we grabbed some photos but they refused to let us have a close up.

We decided to head back to Elizabeth because there was nothing else of any interest to detain us.

After lunch Val crashed out in the cabin and just by chance I found myself on a photo binge from deck 10. The surrounding port area is really quite attractive with a white lighthouse perched on a hill. During the sail away I took photos of unsuspecting people as they danced and of some as they relaxed with a beer. I felt rather pleased with myself as I gave full rein to my pokey nosed zoom lens.

Later the sea became a mill pond.

Golden Lion with Herbie Denton at the piano. Hanna and Eric joined us. But what a tongue she has - a compulsive talker. Eric just accepts her.

The show consisted of the two bands, the string quartet and the Cunard singers and dancers. We didn't stay long because one of the singers murdered "Cry Me a River"

While I was trying to log on the internet I caught Caroline again performing without an audience and felt it must have been soul destroying for her.
Nagasaki tomorrow.

THURSDAY 17 MARCH. Matsugae Pier, Nagasaki Harbour. Nagasaki, Kyushu, Japan. Sunny and warm.

Nagasaki is the capital of the island of Kyushu in Japan. It was the second city after Hiroshima to be hit with an atomic bomb during WW11. Today, Nagasaki is a major port and ship building centre.

We underwent an intense immigration check in the ballroom after which we were called to two immigration desks before we were allowed into Japan.

Elizabeth was conveniently berthed very close to the city centre.

The Oura Catholic Church and the nearby Glover Gardens stand on a hillside overlooking the harbour. It took us 15 minutes to reach them by walking up a narrow street, which is lined with shops. The church, which was built in 1865 stands in its own grounds, and is painted grey and white with a steeple. There was a £4.00 admission charge but no photos allowed. The cheek!

Two pedestrian escalators took us up to the gardens and residence of Thomas Glover. He was a Scottish merchant who came to Nagasaki in 1859. He established a trading company and contributed to the modernisation of Japan with ship building and coalmining. He was a generous man, who died in Nagasaki in 1911. You can look round his residence and stroll through the beautiful gardens resplendent with flowers and water features while enjoying the views of the harbour. There are many references and a statue to Madame Butterfly. This setting supposedly inspired Puccini to write the opera.

In the distance we saw a cruise ship under construction.

Scottish Traditional Music was being relayed into the gardens. But we couldn't understand why the Japanese would want to play Irish music as well. Surely they wouldn't want to celebrate St. Patricks' Day!

While we were waiting for the tram, a kindly Japanese lady gave us some change as a gift to make up the correct fare to take us to the peace park.

In August 1945 Nagasaki was the second city after Hiroshima to be hit with an atomic bomb which killed 74,000 people and injured a further 75,000. There were 156 double survivors; this means that 156 people survived both the Nagasaki and Hiroshima atomic bomb blasts.

Firstly we visited Hypocentre Park where a tall black square column set within two wide stone circles marks the exact position where the bomb exploded 500 meters above the ground. A black casket contains the names of some the bomb's victims.

The Peace Park is equally moving and contains The Fountain of Peace which was built in remembrance of victims of the bombing. The changing patterns of the cascades represents the beating wings of a dove.

We met an elderly man who miraculously survived the blast because his boss told him to go to another factory. The moment he entered the building the bomb exploded and he was thrown behind a big pillar which blocked the heat ray. He asked us to water his flowers using a ladle which symbolises the intense thirst the survivors felt.

The highlight of the park is a 10 meter high bronze statue for world peace. The right hand points upwards to the threat of nuclear weapons while the outstretched left arm symbolises world peace.

There are sculptures and many other peace monuments to see, which have been donated by various nations in their quest for peace. Our experience of the park was heart-rending.

The atomic bomb museum gives you an idea of the horrors of the nuclear explosion. Some exhibits include twisted girders and articles that were found after the blast, numerous photographs and descriptions, medical photographs of victim's bodies, photographs of human organs damaged by radiation. Survivors testimonies, personal belongings many of which belonged to children There is a description of the atomic bombing and many other exhibits. The bomb was called "Fat Man" and there is a cutaway model on display. The museum is not for the squeamish.

I thought of T.S. Elliot when I saw the 3D virtual film of the wasteland, a grim landscape of complete destruction.

Outside is the peace monument which consists of a circular expanse of water running slowly over the sides with 74,000 diodes which light up at night to represent the number of dead. I think the day will remain with us for the rest of our lives.

Took two more trams back to base and during the journey I watched as a number of school girls crashed out probably through exhaustion. Thanks to Val for all the research she carried out to find out how to use the trams.

The Queens Ballroom was full of Dixieland jazz lovers with Kenny Martin the star of the show. He played clarinet along with three other wind players from the band and of course there was piano, bass and drums. For me the ultimate pleasure is playing jazz on my flute and I would love to have joined those guys.

Hanna still babbling on at the dinner table. More extra veg for the waste bin.

Three women from London called the Spinnets entertained us with1940's songs. I stayed for the whole performance and enjoyed their harmonies.

Kagoshima tomorrow.

FRIDAY 18 MARCH. Kagoshima, Marine Port Kagoshima Bay.
(also known as Kinko Bay) Kyushu, Japan. Rainy.

*Kagoshima lies on the Southern tip of Kyushu which is the most
southerly of the four main islands of Japan and is mainly popular
because of its close proximity to the volcanic island of Sakurajima.*

The day was a washout but we were determined to get something
out of it. We took the shuttle bus to town and made our way to the
ferry terminal to take us to see Sakurajima which is one of Japan's
most active volcanoes. Sadly it was mainly shrouded in mist so we
decided to change our plans. We noticed an aquarium nearby and
felt it was the last place we would want to visit, but the rain made
it a "needs must."

We had no regrets. An aquarium a la Japanese. I think we must
have seen every species of fish on the planet: big fish, little fish,
speckled, coloured, sharks, sting rays, sea spiders, sea horses, jelly
fish and lots of sea creatures we couldn't identify. I don't know if
the displays contained genuine coral or not but it was all very
beautiful. We forgot about the weather by immersing ourselves in
this amazing place.

Eventually we were shown to a small theatre with a large pool to
watch the antics of five dolphins. What was amazing was how the
young trainer communicated with them. She got them to perform
spectacular acrobatics like leaping out of the water in three's,
swimming blindfold through hoops, and leaping through hoops in
mid-air. She even got them to glide along the tiled edge of the
pool. We felt conspicuous because we were the only westerners
present, but no one seemed to care. The fun continued and these
lovely animals seemed to be enjoying it especially since they were
constantly being rewarded with morsels. We were given a
demonstration of a dolphin's ability to see by exposing one to a
white board. No response. But the black board caused a splutter
and a splash. One dolphin leapt many times to touch a fluffy ball
which was suspended high above the pool. It was interesting to
watch the trainer's hand movements to get the dolphins to respond

and I wondered whether they'd only perform once they'd bonded with their trainer.

We resumed the last of our tour and then sat down for a coffee where a Japanese couple allowed Val to take a photo of their baby.

We left the aquarium in high spirits because we felt that Kagoshima had been kind to us.

The rain had eased a little so we took the ferry to Sakurajima Island. After we docked we walked a short distance along the road hoping to find something of interest and sure enough we spotted a big torii on a small hillside, (toriis are gates at Japanese shrines). We walked the short distance to the top and discovered a beautiful red timbered shrine enclosed by tall trees. The shrine is known as Tsukiyomi Jinja. It was built about 1300 years ago and was moved there from its original site after it got covered by lava during a volcanic eruption in 1914. There is an observation deck but no views because it was misty. Numerous pieces of paper containing prayers were hanging from branches and shrubs.

At the ferry terminal we approached a lovely Japanese woman on the information desk with a few questions. "Why do many Japanese use chopsticks"?
"Because of the Chinese influence".
"Why do lots of Japanese wear face masks"?
"Because of asthma and hay fever and also for preventative reasons". We told her that the Vietnamese use the masks for very different reasons, mainly to keep their faces pale as it's considered to be attractive, but she wasn't aware of this. She told us she was 26 years old and was brought up in Canada where her father was a scientist. She now lives in Kagashima. She told us the shrine we'd visited was dedicated to one of the Shinto gods.

Back on the mainland we decided to return to port because of the rain. While we were waiting for the shuttle bus Val approached Trevor Newby, the ballroom band leader to say how fantastic the jazz was last night. But we were surprised to learn that him and his

159

wife Jane, the choir mistress, dislike jazz and prefer melodious music.

As I sat in the Garden Lounge torrential rain was beating down on the glass roof with the pool deck awash and deserted. Very dramatic.

I was thinking of writing the rest of my journal in free verse, but I can't seem to get started. I guess it's laziness. If I could though, I'm sure it would boost my communication skills.

I still practice my flute each evening but I'm critical of every note I play. Including staccato, legato and quality of tone. Who knows by the end of the voyage my flute might have grown wings!

Linda has mainly covered up presumably because of her cold, so we were spared from her flashing tits while trying to eat. I imagine they are a bit droopy when she undresses! And then there's Hanna, god bless her, simply cannot hush her tongue. She not only wasted her own food but the extra veg as well.

Val and I went to the theatre on our own but the gang of six followed afterwards and we all sat together. Not happy with it because we value our independence.

We endured the Cunard Singers and Dancers before Kenny Martin came on to bewitch us with his jazz magic. A great talent.

Once again Caroline was playing the same repertoire and had an audience of only two. Perhaps if I could get a jam going with her we'd fill the place!

Cruising to Yokohama.

SATURDAY19 MARCH. Pacific Ocean. Clear, cloudy, mild, choppy.

I broke the mould by taking my 15 minute walk on deck 10. One must walk outside the box occasionally.

As is my custom I grabbed a strong coffee then sat in the Garden Lounge to hone my writing skills. Occasionally I would look up to see who was coming and going. I take great delight in observing people whether it's approving, condemning or just merely laughing at them.
I think I'm becoming the ship's cynic but then others may feel the same towards me. The Japanese passengers are quite comical. They're all petite and wander round in groups with one of them always carrying an expensive camera.

Matthew is slipping into complacency. He's slightly rushing his port presentations. My advice to him would be to prune the history, talk more about the destinations and certainly use more pauses. His subject was Hiroshima.

We seldom eat in the restaurant at lunchtime because it can be such a lengthy affair that stops you from attending some of the ship's programmes on time. The Lido self-service however is more convenient and offers good choices.

Another matinee concert with the classical piano and trumpet duo. They're excellent and I imagine if you're learning to play the trumpet you would need to be an uninhibited type.

Jam session with Hanna. We played some of Jay's pieces but Hanna is so heavy on the ivories that I had to ask her to play a little quieter, and when she sang in her high pitched voice I asked if she could play the songs as instrumentals which she did, and of course she made a better sound. She's a really good accomplished player and I enjoyed improvising with her and although it's a nice change to duet with a pianist I feel more comfortable with Jay.

Val and I like to think we're very knowledgeable but far from it. Our quiz score was so embarrassingly poor that we refrained from passing the sheet to the next table for marking. And as for the young quiz master, what an inflated ego he has! I also think he should be sent for further training.

Won't have to endure Hanna's babbling and her food wastages after tonight, her and Eric disembark tomorrow. As for Linda, she was modestly attired with her tits fully contained. She and Jeff also disembark tomorrow. After I video'd them it was hugs and handshakes all round, and after my embrace with Linda she said to me "You're a bit different". Good, she's noticed. I don't want to be like others, I value my individuality. But overall and apart from a few irritations I've enjoyed their company.

Royal Court Theatre for Palladium Night. My saviour was the band because the singers were in desperate need of voice therapy.

Yokohama tomorrow.

SUNDAY 20 MARCH. Yokohama. Daikoku Pier. Tokyo Bay Honshu. Japan. Sunny.

Yokohama is Japan's largest seaport and has a huge China Town. Yokohama is also the gateway to Tokyo.
Yokohama and Tokyo are situated on Honshu which is Japan's largest island. From here we were taken to Tokyo. From the coach we could see vast numbers of new vehicles parked up in grids awaiting export. There were thousands of them which included cars, trucks and diggers and it was then that you realised why Japan is the world's third biggest economy. We also saw mile after mile of industrial units, testimony to the country's economic strength.

Tokyo is the capital of Japan and is the most populous metropolitan area in the world.

The coach dropped us off at the Kabuki Za Theatre in Ginza which is Tokyo's moat famous upmarket shopping, dining and entertainment district. One square meter of land here costs over 10 million yen which equates to £7147.00. Gleaming skyscrapers tower over posh thoroughfares and the lamp posts on both sides of a particular road each bore the national flag and the trees in between gave me a photograph with a very attractive perspective.

Mathew had previously told us that Tokyo contains few if any signs in English. Val proved him wrong by taking photos of signs in the railway station where English is well represented.

As we walked through the park towards the Emperor's Palace three young girls were happy to pose for us while we took their photo. It's always a good feeling in a foreign land when the local people are willing to engage with you. A look back towards Ginza presented some pleasing scenes of modern tower blocks fronted by groups of small trees.

The Emperor's Palace is a sedate black and white structure in the traditional Japanese style. It's set on elevated ground overlooking a moat and double arched bridge. We felt the palace wasn't the only photogenic subject - equally it was the people. A lone sentry in his impeccable uniform was standing guard in his sentry box. Also a lone policeman impeccably dressed and wearing a face mask was standing nearby looking quite bored.

We sat and had a coffee outside the park snack bar and watched a couple of Japanese flags swaying beyond the distant trees. We then undertook some more intrusive photography. You know the shots you want and take a few calculated risks to get them lest you get caught. Folk wearing face masks seem as common as folk taking selfies.

We came by a building with an entrance like an atrium comprising a huge open drum like canopy with a glass dome and trees either side which seemed to beckon us. A sign said Marunouchi Square. We found ourselves inside a little garden area with small trees, shrubs flowers, cherry blossom a small lawn, a rockery, a shiny skyscraper and a raised rotunda with plants and benches. The place was truly idyllic with lots of al fresco diners giving it an intimate feel. We thought the Mitsubishi Museum was out of place here believing it contained machinery but we discovered it's an art gallery with 200 paintings by Toulouse Lautrec. We felt a visit would take too long.

Our next call, again by chance was an open flea market. Tables were teeming with mainly small antiques and for those without a table they used the ground instead. We both like portraits, so we were happy to wander round secretly taking photos of the stallholders. Again we saw some people in masks.

If we'd had more time we would have travelled on a bullet train but at least we saw a couple of them gliding into Tokyo station on the overhead track. These trains can attain speeds of up to 200 mph.

One never knows what awaits. After hearing chanting and drums we crossed the road to investigate and there was Allen and Annette. Without any preamble, Allen and I were invited onto a red platform and given green and white jackets to wear, and two small cymbals each with red tassels. It was then time to perform. A drum, flute and chanting provided the sound while we and a few others kept time with our instruments. It was a real feel good occasion, and the small crowd that had gathered, some in masks, created a pleasant atmosphere. Afterwards I was given a small bell as a gift. Well, I made my debut in Tokyo with Val's video to prove it! We couldn't tell if it was a religious, political or maybe a charity event? but we wished we'd have asked.

We expected Tokyo's restaurants to be well outside our price range, so we opted for something a little more modest. We found an eatery where you choose your meal from a numbered photograph. You put your money into a slot and tap in the reference number. A ticket drops out with your change. You take the ticket to the counter and your meal is served. All very efficient, cheapish and tasty. I had curry and rice, Val had noodles with something she couldn't recognise.

Tokyo's streets are spotless and full of posh shops and tower blocks. Three more young women kindly posed for Val's camera. We followed a sign to the Tsukiji Hongangi Buddhist temple. It dates back to 1657. It was destroyed by fire and rebuilt only to be destroyed by an earthquake. The present building was completed in 1934 and combines many architectural styles. The interior is equally impressive. It's peaceful, and you can watch the incense burning while enjoying the aroma.

There was an open market outside and we saw a woman spinning cotton from wool. A duo, one with a Paul McCartney bass and the other with a long wooden wind instrument kept us entertained.

Tokyo was well worth the visit and we felt a great sense of achievement for having packed so many memories into five hours.

We sat on the coach and waited 25 minutes for a couple and after the
guide made a phone call we eventually left without them.

Back at the port we waived the ship and got straight on the shuttle bus to Yokohama. Our drop off and pick up point was at the Minato Mirai central business district near the Landmark Tower. This is a huge structure containing a five star hotel with 603 rooms, many restaurants, offices, clinics and has a sky garden on the top story.

The amusement park is interesting and has many state of the art rides including a ferris wheel that looked taller than the London Eye and because it was dusk we were able to capture some amazing photos, the best being of the deep coloured reflections in the lagoon.
Annette approached me in the Lido, "Hi John." We raved about Tokyo and then turned to health and why so many obese people give into temptation with poor diets. She told me her cholesterol

level is high and she takes statins. She said her parents died prematurely of heart disease. I mentioned my medication but told her most of my problems were psychological! hah hah! She's a really nice woman.

I got Herbie Denton to sing a Buddy holly number, but like most of his songs he murdered it. We need some jazz in the Golden Lion.

We now have two Iranian couples on our dinner table. They seem amicable and are non-Muslim. I don't think the wine waiter was happy when we had to remind him to bring the wine that had been left for us by our disembarking table mates. I think he has a grudge against me for kicking off about the corkage charge.

Two lovely Japanese women in kimonos played violin and shamisen. This has a long neck with three strings and a small square sound box. They played a mixture of Japanese and Western music. The Beatles "In My Life" was particularly notable. Their act was a brilliant finale to a brilliant day.

Cruising to Osaka.

MONDAY 21 MARCH. Pacific Ocean. Light cool wind, sunny, choppy.

Attended the port talk about Okinawa. It's Japan's southernmost island where the people like to think they're a bit different to the rest of Japan.
Val told me she'd chanced on Amanda and has requested more jazz. Let's see what happens.

I was talking to a guy called Neil, 76 from Cairns, Australia who uses a mobility scooter. He has difficulty walking because of circulation problems and has stents in his leg veins. He and his wife disembark at Southampton before touring Europe for a month. Jolly good luck to him.

Tony, (Helicopter) Cairns, told me he made a complaint to the tour office about his harbour cruise in Hong Kong which cost over $100.00. It was advertised as two hours long in a junk. It was actually one hour long and wasn't in a junk. He was furious. The tour office no longer deal with complaints, it's now down to H/O in Southampton. He said it's put him off cruising again with Cunard.

At dinner the Iranians were happy to talk to us about cruise destinations, and of course Val and I were happy to flaunt our knowledge. Susie was on her own as David was unwell. I offered to accompany her to the theatre later on but she declined.

The Spinetts put on a brilliant show. They sang 1940's songs in period outfits while moving rhythmically round the stage. Afterwards I told one of them that after Kenny Martin they were the second best act to appear on the ship and what a nice change they made compared to boring straight singers.

Osaka tomorrow.

TUESDAY 22 MARCH. Maiden call. Osaka. Tempozan Wharf, Osaka Bay. Honshu, Japan. Sunny and warm.

Osaka is a large port city in Honshu and the third largest city in Japan.

Looks like there's a health scare because the Lido is no longer self-service. Probably Norovirus. We're being served by staff wearing plastic gloves.

As Elizabeth was creeping into port I was watching a fire boat making beautiful fountains with the sun and a glass skyscraper in the background. It would have made a winning picture but regretfully I'd left my camera in the cabin.

Crowds of locals were eager to see Elizabeth for the first time, and we were welcomed by a 32 pc brass band booming out various tunes including Obla Di. Receptions like these makes one feel quite important!

We boarded our coach for our tour of "Ancient Japan," a whirlwind experience with a lovely guide and some amazing photography.

An hour's drive along modern highways took us to the city of Nara which is famous for temples and art dating back to the 8th century. First on our list was a visit to the Todaiji Temple, the world's largest wooden structure containing the world's largest bronze Buddha which is 15 meters high. The entrance is by way of a wide walkway and a torii gate. The interior is vast with many wide wooden pillars. A group of people were lighting incense which was giving off a pleasant aroma. There were also smaller Buddhas and all one could do was to marvel at the whole scene. A class of extremely well behaved 8 year olds with their teacher were happy to pose while we took their photos.

Wild deer roam the grounds and we were asked to watch where we were putting our feet. In Shinto religion the deer are revered as the messengers of the Gods.

Still in Nara our next stop was the Kasuga Taisha Shrine. Unfortunately we were not allowed to enter as a christening service was in progress but one of the main features was the long incline leading up to the shrine with 2000 stone lanterns lining the way. These lanterns are 3 ft. tall with some covered in moss. They are lit with candles twice a year. Another item of interest were the hundreds of what appeared to be naval graduates in full uniform being initiated presumably by a Japanese monk.

During the coach journey to Kyoto, our guide produced a large card containing the numerals one to ten and their corresponding pronunciations. It was a fun lesson in how to count in Japanese.

The Ana Crown Plaza Hotel in Kyoto is quite well to do and that's where we had lunch. It was a mixture of Western and Japanese cuisine comprising smoked salmon salad, soup with two breads, chicken breast with pasta and veg, sushi, ice cream and coffee. One of the courses was served in an octagonal box - joy of joys - a delicious meal served by smart, friendly and cheerful staff.

Afterwards we were allowed to photograph the marriage reception dining room which is very plush. A young woman in a kimono let us have her picture as she stood in front of a massive vase of flowers. Then the hotel director appeared and took her picture with Val and I stood either side of her. We guessed from the way she was dressed she was someone important, but she was actually a waitress!

It's little wonder that Kyoto is a world heritage site with so many treasures to visit. The Golden Pavilion or Rokuon-ji was next on our list. A three storey structure with the top two storeys covered in gold leaf. Its history dates back to 1379 and was owned by an important shogun before it became a Zen Buddhist temple. It's a scene of sheer magnificence standing on the edge of a glassy pond with ornamental trees growing from tiny islands. The gorgeous reflections added to the beauty. Four girls in flamboyant kimonos kindly let us take their photo. We ended by walking round the grounds with many steps to climb and more photographs to take.

The narrow uphill street to the Kiyomizu Dera Temple is atmospheric in its own right. Good quality souvenir shops and cafes line the colourful street and there were many young women in kimonos. At the top you are greeted by a large red pagoda, a few other buildings and of course the great temple. The views over Kyoto and the distant mountains are remarkable. Once again we had young women posing for us but our guide explained that some of them are actually Chinese. But nevertheless they looked good in their kimonos which they sometimes hire.

We took an interesting short walk along a hillside track to a beautiful small pagoda and when we looked back we had a better view of the temple. It's another huge wooden structure which stands on a hillside and has many supports like stilts. It dates back to 798.

After following the track downwards we came upon a spring flowing from the base of the hillside. If you drink the water you might be rewarded with health, wealth and wisdom. So that was our itinerary complete with more scenic gems under our belts, and while Val likes her facts and figures I tend to be more visual.

It was 7:30 pm when we arrived back at the ship. A letter was waiting telling us that the ship has a norovirus outbreak and that we are to take the following precautions: try to avoid touching the hand rails and the buttons in the lift, avoid hand shaking and hand to mouth contact. Try to use the cabin toilets and not the public ones and most importantly wash hands frequently and use the hand sanitisers. Oh dear!

We dined in the Lido instead of the restaurant to enable us to go to the jazz under the stars at 9:30 pm. The jazz sounded a little disjointed but we still enjoyed it. The bass player for me was the star. Most of the music was familiar to me through Jay.

We looked in at the Royal Court. It was "Vanity Fair." I was looking forward to some 1930's music but one of the male singers went hopelessly off key when he sang "I Get a Kick out of You." Then the two women started singing a number that was so dreadfully screechy we decided to make a hasty departure.

For a change, after we had our Ovaltine, we took a bible black walk.

Cruising to Hiroshima.

WEDNESDAY 23 MARCH. Pacific Ocean. Sunny, Slightly choppy.

I've taken to using my elbow to press the switches in the lift to lessen my chances of getting the norovirus.

Tried some creative writing in the Café Carinthia. An idyll, but the waitresses are so ingratiating. "I don't want to buy a coffee, I can get one free in the Lido"

When the captain made an announcement about the norovirus I realised how serious it was. He basically repeated the contents of the letter we received last night. Now it's up to the entire ship to pull together to beat this thing. Naturally we were concerned and trusted that our day ashore would still go ahead tomorrow.

It was almost comical watching the young Asian woman sanitising the door handles and glass doors in the Winter Garden. Most people were touching them which meant she was having to constantly repeat the process with only the odd person opening the doors hygienically. It's amazing how many people are so unaware.

I continue to find it funny watching the Japanese wandering round in groups. I think I read once they only become individuals at night!

One of the Iranian couples joined us. He told us he has no time for the media and propaganda and that all religions in Iran get on because they love one another. He told us that his wife is the boss and we learned that their winters can be minus 10 degrees and plus 40 degrees in summer.

Attended a lecture about the Atomic bombing of Hiroshima and learned that the co-pilot of the Enola Gay, Robert Lewis, wrote in his log "My God what have we done"

The Matinee featured Rouge, two young women playing classical guitar and flute with music from South America. Superb talents. "The Queen Elizabeth hath been transformed into paradise." After this my flute goes for scrap metal and my guitar ends up as firewood!

Afterwards, we were talking with Nancy about tours when she introduced us to ABC... "Another bloody cathedral" or castle!

Took a walk on deck 10 and when I came by the golf practice nets. I couldn't resist the irons and although my shots were good I became bored after about 8 balls. And yet in the early 70's I was obsessed with the game.

Yacht club for my piano practice. I played Embraceable You, Georgia and Solitude. A couple came in to practice their dance steps and I felt they wanted the room to themselves. Tough.

The ballroom orchestra gave us "Jazz under the stars" in the Garden Lounge. Dixieland at its best. A tonic. I told the bass player he had a gift. I think I have a fixation with bass players!

Everyone at the dinner table seemed happy, with the Iranian men confirming their wives are boss yet the wives do all the cooking. I still haven't connected with David yet.

Fantastic entertainment in the Royal court; String Idols. Two female violinists from Tokyo who trained at the Royal Academy of Music. They played both classical and modern with lots of harmony and counterpoint. I liked their costumes and the way they moved round the stage. Please, please let's have more music like this. Val thought they were a bit screechy and walked out.

Surprise, surprise. I chanced on a guy we met on the Queen Victoria. I remembered his name, Andrew. We exchanged room numbers to arrange lunch.
Hiroshima tomorrow.

THURSDAY 24 MARCH. Maiden call. Hiroshima, Itsukaichi Berth, Seto Inland Sea, Honshu, Japan. Sunny, cool.

Another beautiful full moon in the night illuminating the sea.

Hiroshima is a major industrial centre and a thriving city. It has a picturesque port surrounded by mountains. Hiroshima is best known as the first city in the world to be hit with an atomic bomb.

A maiden call for Elizabeth, yet no welcoming ceremony. Odd.

I have named the morning "Beauty" and the afternoon "The Beast."
You'll see why when you read on.

Again we saw vast numbers of cars and JCBs lined up on the quayside awaiting export.

We embarked on Cunard's tour to Miyajima which means Shrine Island.

First it was the coach and then the ferry. As we neared Miyajima Island, we saw the huge orange torii gate which was the centre of attraction and to confirm what we've heard, it did appear to be floating on the water.

Once ashore we were surrounded by beauty. Our lovely guide tended to impart too much information which was our cue to stray. Miyajima is a sacred sight and a world heritage national treasure dating back to the 6th century. We entered a walkway lined with little quaint shops and cafes before coming out at the waterfront which gave us an intimate view of the torii gate with a backdrop of mountains.

The shrine is located in a small inlet and is built on stilts. A wedding was taking place in the main shrine and we were amazed that we were allowed to take photographs. The bride was seated sedately in a long white silk dress and a huge white hood. The hood veils her jealousy, ego and selfishness and is a symbol of a gentle and obedient wife - a ceremony vastly different to ours. We passed through rooms, halls and corridors with the dominant colour of orange. Outside was a fabulous pagoda, stone lanterns and the odd stray deer.

A large wooden structure caught our attention and after climbing many steps to get to it we went inside to a large empty hall with many wooden pillars. The view over the bay from there was magnificent.

Back to base for the shuttle bus to Hiroshima. We had difficulty finding the correct platform for the tram to the Peace Park and when we asked a local woman, she kindly escorted us to the correct location and then I took the risk of giving her a hug - it paid off - I got one in return! The trams are very efficient and run in the central reservations of the roads. The journey took 30 minutes and was quite an experience.

The first thing to hit you are the remains of the exhibition hall which was built in 1915. It has been renamed the Atomic Bomb Dome and remains a symbol of peace and a reminder of that dreadful day on August 6th 1945 when an atomic bomb called Little Boy exploded 600 meters above the ground instantly killing 70,000 people, with total deaths of 140,000 through burns and radiation. Miraculously the bomb ripped out the inside of the exhibition hall leaving the structure intact.

The Peace Memorial Park covers a vast area with the hypocentre monument situated in a side street. Some of the sights include the cenotaph, the children's peace monument, the memorial mound, the peace bell and the Flame of Peace which will only be extinguished when all nuclear weapons have been eliminated.
 The peace memorial museum shows graphic displays of the consequences and effects of the atomic bombing of the city. There are films, artefacts, children's clothing, a child's tricycle, medical photographs, general photographs, models, maps, possessions, a mock-up of three people with dripping flesh, building materials and testimonies. It was a solemn atmosphere as people moved quietly from exhibit to exhibit. I think everyone was affected by it all.

We walked through the park again to pay our last respects and came upon the peace clock tower. Each morning the clock chimes 8:15 to mark the time the bomb exploded. As I write this I feel my eyes watering, my experiences of the two peace parks and museums will stay with me for the rest of my life. Holidays are not all fun and games they can be seriously educational as well and I must add that our excursion cost a fraction of Cunard's price.

On the way back on the coach I was talking to a guy who thought I'd got a slight Liverpool accent!

A local troupe in period costumes put on a lavish show of drama and dance in a warehouse on the quayside. Whatever was being acted it was the triumph of good over evil with demons and swords. A drummer and piccolo provided the sound track to a very colourful and entertaining affair indeed and since there was no welcome party this morning we were adequately compensated.

The Iranians are very friendly and we're beginning to bond with them. Raza showed me some photos of himself when he was working as a civil engineer.

The McDonald Brothers entertained us and gave a better performance than when they played the Aurora.

 As we were leaving the theatre Raza linked my arm, he always calls me John. We saw Jane Edwards from the entertainment team and I think I upset her when I suggested the McDonald Brothers should replace the Cunard singers because the McDonald Brothers don't sing off key. She said she wasn't aware that the Cunard Singers sing off key.

I was surprised that our Iranian friends wanted to go to the disco and because they were unsure of its location they were very grateful when I escorted them there.

Cruising to Okinawa.

FRIDAY 25 MARCH. Pacific Ocean. Cloudy and fresh but warmer. The sun was streaming into the cabin at 6:25am. Big swell.

Terry Waite filled the theatre for his lecture. A brilliant speaker. He spent 5 years in solitary confinement in a prison in the Lebanon after trying to arrange a meeting with four hostages. He left us on a cliff hanger by saying he would continue his story at his next lecture.

Lunch date with Andrew and Pam from the Queen Victoria. They used to live in Rochdale and had a newsagents. They now live on the Isle of Wight.

Rouge are among the best classical performers I have ever seen. The guitarist is a virtuoso and together with her big piled high curly hair, had me captivated as did the flautist whose tones are heavenly. When they played Schubert's Ave Maria I was choking up.

A masquerade ball took place in the evening and I think some of the passengers actually look better in masks!

We were granted express dinner to allow us to go to the jazz under the stars which as always was good.

Afterwards we saw a brilliant male and female act at the Royal Court called the Power of Two. They opened with a clown routine where she was pulled in all directions after which she revealed herself and both performed the most amazing acrobatic and balancing act. They then gave us an aerial show on drapes which included the use of a huge metal ring.

Okinawa tomorrow.

SATURDAY 26 MARCH. Maiden Call. Naha Cruise Terminal Naha, Okinawa, East China Sea, Japan. Mainly dry with sunny spells.

Naha is the capital city of Okinawa one of the Japanese islands situated in the East China Sea about 400 miles south of Japan. It retains its own language and culture, boasts some of the longest living people in the world and is home to 32 US military bases.

A small traditional band in gorgeous national costumes played for us in the cruise terminal. A great start to the day.

We took the shuttle bus to Naha centre. Terry Waite was sat opposite and I wanted to make my acquaintance with him but someone else had bagged him.

Our objective was the Shuri Castle which is classed as a must see and to get to it we took the monorail which turned out to be one of the highlights of the day. Luckily we were at the front and had a drivers view. The trains run on concrete and steel tracks many meters above the ground and our four and a half mile journey was one complete thrill even more so because the route is curly whirly rather than completely straight and there are brilliant views. The driver was impeccably dressed in his blue suit, blue hat and white gloves. A very smooth ride and a remarkable feat of engineering.

A 15 minute walk led us to a pleasant park that took us uphill to the entrance to the Shuri Castle. Before we entered we watched some Japanese dances given by young women with solemn expressions. They wore beautiful kimonos and performed slow movements, rather like tai chi.

The castle is set on a hill - a red timber complex that dates back to the 14th century and was once the residence of a Japanese royal family. The building is a mixture of Japanese and Chinese styles. It was destroyed during WW2 but has been wonderfully restored. We enjoyed looking round the rooms and halls that contained very little furniture except the main hall which had a throne. There are walkways outside that pass through trees and gardens. We heard some calm music but couldn't locate its source until we discovered it was coming from speakers concealed inside small concrete posts.

The views over the city and beyond are outstanding.

Back on the monorail and this time we sat at the back and watched the graceful tracks unfolding as well as admiring the views of the city.

The main street in Naha is vibrant and colourful with palm trees, shops and restaurants all huddled together on either side making it a photographic gem. We had 1160 yen left and we were hungry. We found a nice little place and remarkably we were able to eat for exactly 1160 yen. We had a delicious veggie meal complete with chopsticks.

Local children in full colour outfits gathered on the quayside to give us a send-off with a tambourine and dance performance.

I have now learned the names of our Iranian friends; Raza and Atty, Mahmoo and Feriba. They are really nice people.

Another performance from the String Idols but they were let down by the electrics on their violins which made the high notes sound screechy. But apart from that I enjoyed their show.

Cruising to Keelung, Taiwan.

SUNDAY 27 MARCH. East China Sea. Hazy sun, cool, slightly choppy.

While I was photographing the magnificent and sumptuous Easter Egg display in the atrium the librarian was sharing my enthusiasm, especially when I told her about the massive chocolate free for all we had on the Queen Victoria when you could eat as much as you liked - before going on statins!

Terry Waite filled the theatre for his lecture about the dreadful things that happened to him in captivity; the interrogations, the blindfolds, the waiting, the fear. He was chained and they beat his feet with cable. He decided the only way he could cope with his trauma was to refuse to feel self-pity and refuse to be angry.

How kind of Cunard to deliver two chocolate bunnies to our room. But I suspect they'll go to children in Vietnam.

Kept our lunch date in the Golden Lion with Tony and Sandy (Nobby's Beach.) Tony is a retired estate agent. They're good conversationalists and among other things we talked about the stress we suffered during our working lives. I could easily befriend this couple and what welcome companions they'd make on our dinner table.

The passenger talent show was more like a comedy performance. Two Japanese girls, one of whom was pretty hopeless, opened up with a song. Two dancers next who seemed ok then another Japanese lady danced solo while another sang "You Raise Me Up" and went off key. There was a small choir which was less than ordinary. A guy sang the Tennessee Waltz which was good. Then finally another Japanese disaster in the form of a guy who simply could not sing, and to make matters worse he forgot his words. My conclusion is easy, I think these Japanese should stick to making cars!

Sat with the Mc Donald Brothers for a while in the Lido. They're a very friendly pair and I told them Cunard would do well to book more acts like them rather than ten a penny vocalists.

Captain's announcement "While new cases of the norovirus have decreased it's too early to relax restrictions"

Excellent piano practice. Played the middle of "I'm in the mood for love" to work some fluency into my fingering. I also played "Autumn Memories" and "Embraceable You." - I'm getting used to my big flashy Yamaha Grand!

David looked like a clown in his big wide red cummerbund. I was talking about guides on shore excursions and how they can babble and be a hindrance. He totally disagreed and said he often asks questions. There is something about the man I dislike. His wife Susie is ok though but perhaps a little twee.

We exited the theatre after two numbers from "Hollywood Nights" because we were fearful of the Cunard singers giving us dreadful nightmares.

The internet was painfully slow and took 40 painful minutes to send an e-mail to Jay.

Keelung tomorrow.

MONDAY 28 MARCH. Maiden Call. Keelung, Keelung Harbour Taiwan. Sunny and warm.

Keelung is known as the rainy city because it gets about 200 days of rain per year. It's a busy port in the north of the island of Taiwan which is separated from China by the Taiwan Strait.

Surprisingly there was no welcoming entertainment even though it was Elizabeth's maiden call.

I stood on deck 9 and looked out on an Aladdin's cave. The city and harbour looked ripe for exploring as did the shrines, and hill top pagodas. The city seems like a mixture of old and new but it's always the old that attracts us.

After we found the bus station, an Australian couple asked if they could join us saying they'd feel safer with other people; we didn't mind.

They introduced themselves as Marilyn and Kelvin. The 102 bus took us to Heping Island Park. The journey was interesting with many run-down apartment blocks, houses and shops.

The park borders the sea and before we headed towards it we saw a woman in a little shrine chanting to recorded music and further on was a small Buddhist Temple. An interesting pathway led upwards to an open hexagonal concrete shelter with a viewing area overlooking the sea. The uneven rocky shore line and a single mountain out at sea made interesting scenery.

The most fascinating aspect of the location however, was the vast area of rocks and the effect that nature has upon them. Centuries of wind rain and sea have carved some pretty weird sculptures and abstract shapes that would be the pride of any art gallery. Big mushrooms, human heads, animals, faces, figures and strange ornaments abounded and worked the imagination. A pleasant cliff path then took us to the exit.

Whilst waiting for the bus we wandered off a little and came across a beautiful small temple, amazingly colourful and full of gorgeous ornaments with statues and candles surrounded by the sweet aroma of incense.

Our new friends had proved good company with Kelvin smoking one minute and injecting insulin the next!

When we arrived back at the bus station our new friends opted to go back to the ship while Val and I explored the side streets. What we saw would have been condemned back home.

Everywhere was a tangle of shops, eateries and street kitchens often with masses of electricity cables linking properties on both sides of the road. A complete jumble, but that's its charm and much more photogenic than pristine modern areas. Many people were eating, some just wandered by, others had the odd hand cart and some wore face masks. Scooters seem to be the main form of transport with multitudes of them parked up.

Thanks to our zoom lenses we were able to catch folk unawares as they were eating their food with chop sticks. The whole area is big on food with most places selling it for consumption both indoors and out. We decided to go for indoors. Herbie Denton, pianist, just happened to walk in and was happy to join us. We had a tasty two course without losing the knack of using chop sticks.

We chanced on a magnificent temple and went in to look around. The dominant colour was red with masses of intricate carvings of strange shapes and animals, many figurines and candles. A man approached us who explained that the temple was Taoist and the biggest in Taiwan.

A big sign at one eatery advertised "Pork, large intestines, salted vegetables and pig's blood soup." Ah well, if you like that sort of food! Our cameras were in a frenzy as we walked around the vibrant area of cluttered streets and pavements. We came away feeling the experience had been so worthwhile with a wealth of photos to boot.

To round off a very enjoyable day we bought two large bottles of beer and found a picnic bench surrounded by plants just outside the terminal. A local man with a rusty old bicycle approached us but we couldn't understand a word he was saying, but we knew he was trying to get us to try some spirit he'd got in a bottle. After he went away a Japanese student asked if he could talk to us, presumably to practice his English. The old man reappeared and we never quite knew what his motives were but he seemed quite harmless.

As we were approaching the gangway I got talking to the classical guitarist from Rouge. She told me Julian Bream no longer performs because of health reasons. She also said she'd met John Williams a few times but never performed for him and she thinks Ana Vidovic is a bit wooden.

I stood on deck 9 for the sail away and watched the city fade in the evening light. The street running at right angles away from the harbour was a mass of tail lights from cars as they moved through the canyon of buildings. Windows turned into gold rectangles. The huge white statue of the Buddhist God of Mercy flanked by two models of mythical creatures in gold leaf stood on a hilltop along with a beautiful temple. Twilight took over, changing the skies into orange with pylons and the power station chimneys not unattractively silhouetted. Three layers of mountain ranges in deep shades of grey topped with an orange and yellow sky presented a sight indeed to savour.

Saw Caroline. I felt a little embarrassed because I've neglected her but I explained we'd been busy with Japan. She was fine about it. I arranged to give her some music at one of her late performances.

We told our table companions that we'd be leaving early to catch Jazz 'Under the Stars'. David and I don't seem to say much to each other.
As always we enjoyed the jazz group tremendously. They included two great numbers; "Chicago" and "Do you know what it means to miss New Orleans" it was 45 minutes of bliss and Boddingtons!

The pick pocket act in the theatre had great promise but he turned out to be a flop.

Cruising to Hong Kong.

TUESDAY MARCH 29. South China Sea. Sunshine in cabin 6:30 am.

I met an elderly couple at breakfast who were clearly not enjoying their cruise because they claimed they were not given the cabin of their choice and besides they were not happy about being at the front of the ship. She was so upset she started crying. I asked if they'd complained and they said they had but it was all in vain. They certainly had my sympathy.

Cool out on the decks with a calm sea and a hazy horizon.

Terry Waite was sat on his own waiting to start his lecture. So I seized the opportunity and approached him. I asked him if he minded me saying hello, he said not at all. I told him I bought one of his signed books in Durham Cathedral a number of years ago and how much I enjoyed reading it. He asked me if I was enjoying the cruise. I told him I was and mentioned our world cruise on two ships. Afterwards he went to shake my hand but then remembered "OH we're not supposed to do that." He was referring of course to the norovirus.

His lecture was captivating and he talked at length about his time in solitary confinement and how he coped with the trauma. As a young man he read Carl Jung which was a great help to him. Terry learned to live in the "now" and to capture the moment. His imagination was his saviour and engaged in self - analysis. He wrote a book in his head entitled Taken on Trust. He then told us he was previously hopeless at mental arithmetic but practiced it to help keep his mind active. Once he was given a book by one of the guards called Great Escapes which he thought was hilarious.

His only means of communicating with the other prisoners was by tapping on the wall and at one time he was quite ill with bronchial problems. After 5 years he was eventually released with the others. At the end of his lecture he won a standing ovation.

A couple we met on Miyajima Island invited us to sit with them at lunch. He is an outspoken retired primary school teacher who sounds gay. He makes holiday scrap books using photos and memorabilia etc. She enjoys painting in watercolours and both do work for the church. They were both keen to know about our lives. Interesting people, who would be good to have around on Saturday nights in our pub.

The classical matinee nearly didn't go ahead because the lovely flautist had been ill in her cabin for the past four days. I suspect it was the norovirus.

Anyhow they filled the ballroom with a discerning audience eager to listen to the history of the tango; a four movement piece portraying four distinct ages of the dance. There were other virtuoso pieces ending with Tico Tico. The concert was a flawless recitation of sheer tuneful and rhythmic mastery where both were completely at one with their instruments.

184

I'm always conscious of being disturbed during my piano practice. I can guarantee that someone will enter the room but I'm learning more and more to play on regardless. I wasn't really motivated but I did manage to improve a few elusive bars of Georgia. I gave my last 15 minutes to Nancy and enjoyed listening to her playing Eric Satie.

Actually managed 8/20 at the quiz. Some double this and like to think they have achieved something great but forget there may be four or five in their group.

The Iranians brought a small bottle of spirit to share with us. They are genuinely nice people and I sincerely hope they're not involved in the uranium enrichment programme!

Sacha, the nice bald guy was welcoming people into the theatre and was telling me how some folk are still irresponsibly coughing and sneezing and then touching the hand rails.

The McDonald brothers again. They sang the Beach Boys, Simon and Garfunkel and played Irish reels. The audience love them.

Listened to Caroline for the last ten minutes. Although she's talented she sometimes sounds like a dirge. She played "The A Train" which sounded good, it's an unusual piece for the harp. I gave her some photo copied music and she said she'd still like a get together for a practice session.

Hong Kong tomorrow.

WEDNESDAY MARCH 30. Ocean Terminal, Victoria harbour, Hong Kong. Warm, clear.

The staff were wearing masks at the entrance to the Garden Lounge. Presumably a sanitising process was underway. Someone said that as a result, embarkations could be delayed by up to 2 hours.

Terry Waite was in the lift and I managed a few words with him. He was very friendly and I asked if he'd got a busy schedule he said he had and would be in Belfast tomorrow. I also asked if he'd got a lot of stamina. He said he had. He asked me what deck my cabin was on before wishing me well.

Many people on cruise ships have fascinated me but none so amazingly as an Asian man on the Lido Pool Deck attempting to fly a rather large red kite. He had winding gear strapped to his chest and after many attempts with the help of his wife he eventually got the thing airborne. "Big red bird flies over Queen Elizabeth." He then produced a contraption to hold his mobile phone which he attached to the line. He then manoeuvred the thing upwards by releasing more line. Well, that's a novel way of photographing or filming the top of the ship!

We set out on one of Cunard's tours called Lantau Island Uncovered. Our first call was the exhibition centre for Tsing Ma, the world's longest single span road and rail suspension bridge. We were able to look at photos, diagrams and a few artefacts relating to the bridges' construction which Britain had a hand in. The main cables are 1.1 meters in diameter. A viewing platform gives full length views of the bridge, and it was quite an experience driving across it to get to our next destination.

The Tai O fishing village is interesting because it's built on stilts on the river. As we walked across a small bridge we were able to get close to the action. It was like a shanty town where the stilts supporting the homes were actually sloping and you felt as though some structures were on the verge of collapsing. I zoomed in on one lady who was eating her noodles with chop sticks. The area has retained some of its history and is a glimpse of how Hong Kong used to be. An ancient street is lined with shops selling lots of strange seafood and we came upon a colourful Taoist temple. We broke away from the guide to enable us to take photos from slightly further afield.

The main attraction in Lantau is the Po Lin Monastery which contains three magnificent Buddhas and the largest outdoor Buddha in Asia measuring 85 feet. It's made of bronze and stands or rather sits on a hill top. A circular walk way at the base of the Buddha provides a 360 degree view over the island, the most impressive being the monastery complex.

A descent of 268 steps took us to the monastery grounds where we saw the Mountain Gate. A huge stone structure with three arches containing beautiful carvings. A three tier shallow circular platform was interesting which is known as the Di Tan, meaning "alter of earth," and is used for functions and ceremonies.

A vegetarian lunch was laid on for us in the monastery dining room but I had to refrain because the food appeared to be drenched in olive oil, but I did enjoy the coke! Soon afterwards I had to make a dash to the loo.

Oh dear, it all gushed out. The big D. Had I got the norovirus? I was forced to make two more visits and began to think I might not be able to go to Nha Trang on Friday. I managed to stabilise a little and tried not to let he problem affect my enjoyment of the complex.

Many people were praying with lighted incense which gave off a delightful fragrance. A group Buddhists monks stood nearby and a couple of children posed for us on the temple steps. And for sheer beauty, opulence and colour, the Hall of the Ten Thousand Buddhas did not fail to impress us.

It was time then to take the cable car back to the mainland. The ride is 5.7 kms. long and lasts 25 minutes, an enormous feat of engineering. The journey was a thrilling experience, and I felt like birdman of Lantau as I looked down on the forested hills and back at the great Buddha. As we descended over Tung Chung Bay we saw the airport and clusters of sky scrapers.

We changed the last of our money and were able to buy 4 cans of Heineken before taking in the final 30 minutes of Hong Kong.

When I reached the cabin I had another Big D in the toilet and then felt so bad I hit the sheets at 5.30 pm. We both slept until 8.40 pm and decided to remain in bed. What a state to get into after a wonderful day. Of course we missed dinner.

Cruising to Nah Trang.

THURSDAY MARCH 31. South China Sea. Sunny and warm. I have never spent as long in bed for a long time. At 8:00 am I eventually got up feeling a little better. It was well that it was a sea day, hopefully it would allow me to recover in time for Vietnam tomorrow. I waived my customary deck walk. Val and I actually had breakfast together before relaxing on the Lido Pool Deck with a brew. Val was pretty sure I hadn't got the norovirus.

Excellent speaker in the Royal Court called Malcolm Nelson, a retired customs officer who gave us an entertaining lecture entitled "Customs Officers' Battle against Smuggling." These included drugs, pets, counterfeit goods, cigarettes and paedophiles.

Took a book out from the library. "The expert's guide to 100 things everyone should learn how to do, with subjects as diverse as how to iron a shirt to how to have a conversation.

The matinee concert featured the Zeitgeist duo who we saw on the Aurora. They played the three movements of summer from Vivaldi's Four Seasons. Wonderful music but Val wasn't happy with the electronic pick up on the violin. She thought it made the instrument sound screechy.

Back to the library for some internet. Our bonus minutes have been confirmed. Jay said Neil has suggested we put on a concert at the Burn Naze at the end of May. That's something to look forward to and maybe I'll be able to take a step backwards when I get home. We were surprised to see Adam who is now in charge of the computers. We first met him on the Queen Victoria. He seemed happy to talk to us and I love his broad American accent.

Zeitgeist were in the Lido Pool in their bikinis frolicking with two guys, probably a welcome contrast to performing classical concerts.

Good piano practice with more attention to detail especially with "Georgia." The great thing is that I won't be out of practice when I get home.

David and Susie asked us to join them for the quiz but we declined preferring our own company. He became tense about a particular answer and stood up waving his finger about. The quiz master told him to calm down. Anyhow we clocked up 8/20.

At dinner we made some effort with him to prove we're not totally alien. He likes to flaunt his knowledge and likes to contradict. Susie is ok though but a little bit "girlie."

Raza said we would be welcome to visit them in Tehran. Jolly nice of him.

Listened to Caroline for the last 15 minutes. She's looked at my music and liked it. She has suggested we wait a few days before we get together. I don't know what Cunard's policy is for passenger musicians to jam with the ship's professionals.

Nha Trang tomorrow.

FRIDAY 1 APRIL. At anchor. Nha Trang. Nha Trang Bay. South China Sea, Vietnam. Sunny, hot.

Nha Trang is a coastal city on the South Central Coast of Vietnam. Its beautiful bay is amongst the world's best.
At 8:00 am the theatre was packed with groups waiting to join their tours and by 8:30 am there'd been no movement. We became

impatient and wondered what was happening. Eventually the captain announced that The Vietnamese authorities would not give us clearance to disembark but negotiations were in progress. Naturally we suspected the norovirus was to blame. By 10:00 am we were given the all clear and made our way to the tender.

When we arrived at the pier, Vietnamese officials in masks were asking us to sanitise our hands. Easy, it was the norovirus that had caused the delay but why hadn't the captain been honest with us?

We met our tour bus and guide to be taken to villages and country side. No changes since our last visit 3 years ago. Still the same road, side shops and shacks and the beautiful long promenade. Hordes of people in masks were riding scooters. Often mum and dad and two small children occupied one scooter and it was fascinating to see all the different goods being transported on two wheels. We also saw lots of modern hotels.

We arrived at a village and watched some local women weaving mats before we began walking down a dusty track to reach the Loc Tho Pagoda. This is actually a place of worship. The pagoda is 7 stories high and has beautiful gold leaf murals. There's also a Buddhist temple. Nearby is a school for orphans and under privileged children.

Many children were having lunch in the dining room. They were immaculately dressed and were happy to smile with us. Some of their hairstyles were unusual with the back and top of their heads shaved leaving a long fringe. We spoke to some students from Tokyo who were there to teach English. We then moved on to a classroom and could have handed out pens and chocolates but we'd left them on the coach not realising we would be visiting a school. When we were leaving, someone followed us back to the coach to pick up the goods but we would have preferred to have personally handed them out to the children.

It was very hot as we watched folk going about their daily lives in quite an undeveloped area.

We journeyed on to a typical Vietnamese country house built in the Chinese Yin style. The houses are handed down from generation to generation. We glimpsed the small living room and kitchen which is quite spartan by our standards.

The same limbless beggar turned up at two destinations and it was obvious he was being shunted around by his mates on a money making expedition. I couldn't resist a donation though.

Vinh Thai Village was the next stop to see a communal house. This is where the locals worship their village gods.

Time for a bite at a country side resort. We crossed over a curved wooden bridge and then saw a row of four poster beds lining the river embankment. The beds had mattresses and mosquito nets. We were given a plate of fruit but I declined the coconut milk because of the saturated fat. Two women were playing plucked instruments while a guy was playing a bamboo flute. He let me have a go and I was able to make a sound.

A long area of rice had been spread along the roadway to dry and no one seemed to mind when motorcycles ran over it.

We saw water buffalos and men working near a paddy field demonstrating their skills at tilling the land with picks and shovels.

The final stop was an embroidery work shop, but we had other plans with two more objectives to meet. We told our guide we'd make our own way back. We had no choice but to jump in a taxi to show us where the shuttle bus stop was located. Once this had been established we made our way to the beach for a swim in the South China Sea, or rather to leap about in the waves. We had mountains and palm trees for company and we saw Queen Elizabeth at anchor in the distance. My ecstasy lasted 45 minutes but Val got out a little earlier.

Our final ecstasy was sipping cans of Carlsberg under an umbrella at a friendly corner bar while watching the locals and the traffic going by. We both agreed on our love for Vietnam and had a superb day out.

David was talking endlessly at dinner, happily flaunting his knowledge. He claimed that some kind of bribery was involved between Cunard and the Vietnamese which allowed us to enter Nha Trang. WHAT!! If that was the case and there was a leak, then Cunard would indeed be in deep water - no pun intended!

Again we left the table early for "Jazz under the stars." We heard some good numbers but generally they were a little disjointed.

Saw a brilliant comedy act called Goronwy Thom. A funny juggler who took the rip out of people by directing them to certain seats and he used juggling balls to do clever impressions. He also invited folk onto the stage to help with some of his hilarious routines. During his finale he rode a tall unicycle and created an uproar. A very talented performer indeed and of course we were buzzing when we left the theatre.

Cruising to Singapore.

SATURDAY 2 APRIL. South China Sea. Hot, clear and choppy.

The Phuket Port talk was interesting but no trips thank you, we've decided to spend a day on a beach.

Chanced on Raza who shook my hand, and when I said "We shouldn't be doing this"
He said, "John I love you so much I'm prepared to risk the infection." What a lovely guy."

Sat with Ivor, ex primary school teacher, although Val said he was a headmaster. He was certainly having a go at some of Cunard's negatives. It's frustrating when you meet interesting people only for them to disembark before you get to know them.

Matinee with the Zeitgeist duo. The violinist seldom makes eye contact with the audience and there's a certain smugness about her. Nancy thinks the woman is weird but there's no doubt about her virtuosity.

During my writing and people watching routine in the Garden Lounge I saw an officer and approached him about yesterday's delay into Nha Trang. I asked if it was because of the norovirus but he couldn't or wouldn't say, but denied bribery was involved. He said ship's berthings are arranged 3 years in advance.

Captain's announcement…New cases of the norovirus have decreased and therefore restrictions will soon be lifted.

Managed 11/20 at the quiz. An exceptional result.

The Iranians were pleased with their post cards. We exchanged e-mail addresses as they are disembarking on Monday and we may not see them tomorrow, but I know they'll be eager to hear from us. Mahmoo told us there's a serious problem with pollution in Tehran with the consequent health troubles especially caused by smog. Lots of hugs all round. We enjoyed their company immensely and I think they enjoyed ours.

The Troubadours at the Royal Court. Four guys sang Bridge over Troubled Water a cappella with good harmonies but I wasn't keen on the rest of their songs.

Singapore tomorrow.

SUNDAY 3 APRIL. Singapore. Marina Bay Cruise Terminal. Hot.

Singapore is a rich tiny Island Republic founded by Sir Stamford Raffles in 1819 as a trading station. 76% of the population are Chinese.

After breakfast I was having a cup of tea on the Lido Pool Deck while watching the deck stewards preparing the towels and positioning the sun beds. The occasional person was emerging from the pool. All very calm, until I began contemplating some of my negatives which include judging people without first getting to know them. A bad habit I should work with.

The captain announced that we were traversing the Singapore Strait which is one of the busiest shipping lanes in the world. When you look out over the sea you realise why.

Around 2:00 pm Elizabeth berthed at Marina Bay Cruise Terminal and we were off the ship at 3:00 pm. We took the covered foot path part way to our first objective, Super Tree Grove which resembles something out of science fiction. Strange looking artificial trees 25 and 50 meters high stand in a cluster with an aerial walkway between the two tallest. A restaurant tops one of the tallest trees. Admission was closed as lightening was expected but we were able to explore the area after we'd had a bout of rain.

The Sky Park over shadows everything in Singapore. Another amazing icon with three tall hotels supporting a huge long curved boat like structure. There'll be more about it in the next chapter.

We saw a most unusual sight; a huge white sculpture of a baby boy that seemed to be floating on the bushes. The sculptor is Marc Quinn, the man behind the limbless and naked Alison Lapper creation that was exhibited on the fourth plinth in Trafalgar square.

We came by a giant conservatory called Cloud Forrest and decided to give it a try. Another magnificent experience.
Its glass dome houses a man made 35 meter tall mountain covered in mist and vegetation with the world's tallest waterfall. You take the lift to the top and weave your way down along exciting walkways. There are wooden sculptures and numerous tropical plants and flowers to enjoy looking at, all very absorbing. Shame about the noisy children though.

As we made our way to marina bay we caught the sunset over the lily pond and by the time we reached the bay the sky scrapers were lit and reflecting onto the water. We had a pint costing $ 12.00 US but we waived the food because of the saturated fat levels. The water and light show however was magical. I'm not sure how it works but it seems that mist clouds are created with laser images beaming onto them. The images were both real and abstract. Water fountains flowed in parallel. A truly magnificent sight.

We sauntered round the marina through gorgeous palm trees and passed by the Merlion. This is an 8 meter high white statue, half fish and half lion that cascades huge volumes of water from its mouth. Another impressive sight was the huge ferris wheel which was lit up in purple and white with the lotus shaped museum next to it which was also lit up. The water captured their beautiful reflections.

We looked in at the Fullerton Bay Hotel. Modern luxury, with a shiny marble floor capturing arty reflections. The chandelier is awesome, and the views across the bay are magnificent.

We thought it would be fun to be taken back to the ship on a tuk tuk cycle but at $50.00 US we said no thank you. Instead we got an immaculate Mercedes taxi for $12.00 US.

It was 9:40 pm when we hit the Lido for a meal and a pint. The show was unappealing and when we got into bed we felt a pleasant relief after all the walking we'd done. There is no doubt that keeping fit helps one to get the most out of a cruise.

MONDAY 4 APRIL. Singapore day 2. Hot.

The covered walkway took us most of the way to the M.R.T. This stands for the Mass Rapid Transit station. It's Singapore's underground railway. The stations are palatial with marble floors.

Once we'd figured out how to buy a ticket we were on our way to Chinatown. The carriages are modern, spacious and very clean.

As expected Chinatown was colourful and vibrant. We were surprised to see Marilyn and Kelvin who joined us for a coke. The area is decked out with red and yellow paper lanterns, awnings fronting souvenir shops, the odd massage parlour, and tattoo boutiques, clothing outlets, stalls selling puppets, and many restaurants and eateries. Val found a photographic shop where she bought a filter. In the near distance the skyscrapers added to the scene as they gazed down on us as did a high rise apartment block where horizontal poles are used for pegging out the washing. Again you have to be a little intrusive to get the best photos but we've learned to do this in a very cautious manner, we wouldn't want a confrontation in a foreign country.
We found a pleasant corner eatery with inexpensive menus. The fried rice and sea food was delicious and so was the Tiger beer. Unfortunately Val could not hack the chopsticks!

Underground again this time for Little India. Not as compact and as intimate as Chinatown but worth seeing. Another shoppers and photographers delight. The shops and buildings are full of bold colours and it was fun watching everyone going about their work.

Another corner spot for a sit down and a coke. It was 4:00 pm and we debated whether to go back to the ship, but we decided instead to take the underground to try for the Sky Park which actually became the highlight of our day.

The elevator took us 200 meters to the sky terrace which resembles a long curved boat supported by three hotel towers. The terrace is home to a restaurant, tropical plants and trees, a huge observation deck and a 150 meter long infinity swimming pool with a vanishing edge. We had no access to it but we could look at it and take photos.

The evening gave us excellent visibility and we could see for miles. Here's what we saw; The Cloud Forrest Dome, The Flower

Dome, commercial shipping out at sea, Marina Park with Super Trees, parks, high rise housing, big wheel, flyovers, sky scrapers, floating football pitch, helix Bridge, Lotus Museum, Raffles Hotel, Fullerton Hotel, Marina bay, The Merlion and the cathedral. All the sights of Singapore in the palms of our hands. A truly wonderful experience.

Back on the ship for a beautiful sunset.

David and Susie were absent from dinner. Four newbies joined the table. Eddie and his wife Irene and their two friends, Jean and Pat. What followed were some amazing coincidences. Eddie went to Revoe School where my dad and my children were educated. Eddie also lived in Meadow Crescent Carleton and previously Reads Ave Blackpool. He took up the piano after retiring 20 years ago. He said he's got his grade 7. Well, what a great start to the proceedings. They now live in Chorley.

A guy called Tian Jiang, International Virtuoso Pianist was our entertainment in the theatre. He opened with Mozart's Alla Turka. It was fast and laser sharp and played with brilliant virtuosity with backing from the band. From then on I thought it all went into decline but the audience seemed to enjoy it. It was a performance of crash bang. Even the beautiful Love Story was played as though he had weights on his fingers. And the cheek to continue with O Sole Mio, My Way and Nessa Dorma. These have been done to death and are mere musical clichés. Insult followed injury and what we got was a painful clatter. The piano was never made for that. It was hard to believe that he was educated at the Julliard School of Music in New York.
Cruising to Penang Malaysia.

TUESDAY 5 APRIL. Strait of Malacca. Dull, clear, very warm, calm sea.
We were advised that hygiene restrictions would be lifted but we were still waiting. There is another epidemic on the ship…obesity.

Watching women getting in and out of the pool is bad enough but you get the best sagging cellulite of all time!

The Japanese are conspicuous by their absence. We're used to seeing them wandering round in groups, keeping themselves to themselves and it's so true they photograph everything in their path. It's interesting that the majority of them are oddly shaped and physically quite small.

I wonder if Melvin King, ex-governor of the bank of England filled the theatre because of his lecture or because of who he is. I was so looking forward to his talk about the financial crisis but the poor man seemed incapable of using simple language. He was so full of jargon I gave up on him. Other people felt the same.

On the other hand, Malcom Nelson's lecture was just the opposite. The ex-customs officer talked about catching drug smugglers. He said "Dogs who sniff into bags for cash are usually bitches." Ah Ah!

We seldom see David and Susie out and about but today was an exception. We saw them on the Lido Deck and they were keen to find out about our new table mates. Could David and I be making an effort with each other?

Progressive piano practice on the grand. A couple of dancers were there who probably resented my presence because one was teaching the other. I stuck to my guns and played on regardless. These are the pieces I practiced; Gypsy Tango, Yesterday, In My Solitude, Autumn Memories and I'm In the Mood for Love.

The sea was another mill pond.
Only six turned up to see the Tiffany String Quartet - music that's never been bettered. There's something very special about evening classical recitals in the Garden Lounge.
Penang tomorrow.

WEDNESDAY 6 APRIL. Penang, Malaysia. Swettenham Cruise Terminal, Malacca Strait. Hot.

Penang is a Malaysian state comprising the tiny island of Penang and Seberang Perai on the mainland. It's multi-cultural where the various religions live in harmony. Georgetown is the capital.

I was talking with a lady passenger I met some weeks ago and asked how she enjoyed visiting the Great Wall of China. Of course she was delighted to talk about it and was also happy to tell me about the electric bicycles her and her husband would be taking off the ship into Penang. A rather pleasant lady with one huge fault; Not once did she ask about my travels. How unfortunate some folk never learn to communicate because they're totally wrapped up in themselves with zero awareness. I immediately decided therefore to have no further dealings with her for the rest of the voyage.

We walked to the bus station in the heat amid the old buildings, overhead power cables and traffic. We chanced on Marilyn and Kelvin who tagged along with us on the bus to Penang Hill. This is Penang's highest mountain standing 2000 ft. above sea level. We took the funicular to the summit. Luckily we were seated at the back and were able to watch the spectacular views of Georgetown unfold.
The top resembles a small village with beautiful flowers everywhere both in and out of pots. There's a mosque, Buddhist and Hindu temples as well as the usual eateries and souvenir shops. We even saw an owl museum with live owls. The governors' house is interesting to explore with its spacious rooms and verandahs but is now disused. In its heyday it must have been very impressive and cooler to live in than at street level.

We shared a 20 minute buggy ride to take us off the beaten track and we were advised not to get too friendly with the monkeys as they can be little horrors.

We were lucky a second time and had the front seat in the funicular for our descent and at one stage I thought I was on "the Big One"

Interesting bus journey back. Lots of high rise apartment blocks with every available space on the balconies used for drying washing.

Marilyn and Kelvin decided to return to the ship. Kelvin is a diabetic and felt uncomfortable in the heat.

Our next stop was another education. An easy walk from the bus station took us to The Chinese Stilt Village. This is part of Penang's heritage and history. The village is known as the Clan Jetties. There are 6 of them and were built in the late 19th century by Chinese immigrants who looked for a better way of life. The piers are built on stilts and project into the sea. Each pier is named after a clan with the Chew clan being the most popular. The dwellings and walkways are made of timber and almost beckoned you in to explore. We sampled three of them. Streams of red paper lanterns hung from above with pots of flowers everywhere. Often you could see into living rooms but we felt it was courtesy to be as unobtrusive as possible without actually spoiling our visit. The dwellings are colourfully painted with shrines at the front of some of them. Folk were either sat outside relaxing while others were going about their work. Val thought the occupants in one of the dwellings were breeding dogs because there were cages.
There are tiny outlets selling cooked food, souvenirs and art. We paced up and down and had carte blanche with no one bothering us as we put our cameras into overdrive. We also took photos of the adjacent piers. Everywhere resembled an up market shanty town and a classic case of seeing how the other half live. We even came across a tiny bar with big parasols. Three of the bar stools consisted of sawn off Honda 50's which were bolted to the floor with just the back wheel and seat remaining. A good example of lateral thinking! Of course we had a heavenly beer each while having a few laughs with the owner.

Finally we rounded off a delightful day with a late lunch at the Chew Jetty Cafe at the entrance to the Chew Clan pier. Eating with the residents has always been our idea of enjoying some culture allowing us to make connections with the locals. The prawn fried rice was very tasty. The food seems to be cooked from a barrow on the outside pavement, and despite the no smoking sign we were served two beers by a China man with a fag hanging out of his mouth! Bravo! It was then time to saunter back to the ship.

I have a problem with my flute. The F# notes down to low C have become mute, I cannot make them sound. Does it mean I have to spend the rest of my voyage without my flute, a very depressing thought indeed?

We sat in the Golden Lion and Listened to Herbie crucify everything he sang. Even more painful was having to listen to our table mates babbling on compulsively.

On a positive note Danny Elliot starred in the Royal Court. A multi-instrumentalist from Australia we'd previously seen on the Queen Victoria. He opened up with Caravan on the clarinet then played various pieces on the flute, bagpipes, Irish whistle, guitar, didgeridoo, panpipes, mouth organ and piano. He also has a great voice. A genius performer who sent us to bed on a high.

Phuket tomorrow.

THURSDAY 7 APRIL. At Anchor Phuket, Andaman Sea. Thailand. Hot.

Phuket is situated at the southwest of Thailand and is the country's largest island - a tourists' gem.

The sun was streaming into our cabin at 7:00 am and with good views of Patong beach from our anchor point we felt a day of dipping in and out of the sea and relaxing would be our mission.

At 9:45 am the tender was still not operating and we were told that the swell had made it necessary to transfer operations from one side of the ship to the other. Porkies? We were eventually taken to the landing area by a vessel belonging to the Phuket authorities. The vessel held 300 passengers but we still wondered why the ships tenders were not being used.

We didn't need a map because we knew where the beach was situated. We hired a bed each and canopy with a difference. The base of the bed was actually piled up compacted sand with a type of li-lo across the top. A little primitive perhaps but for $10.00 US who could complain? You could spot the Cunarders simply by the tell-tale towels they'd brought along.

The beach is crescent shaped, about two and a half miles long with soft white sand. The backdrop presented a variety of trees and lowish shops and apartments with mountains in the distance to our right. Throughout the day I had five sessions in the lovely warm sea. The moderate swell allows you to make gentle leaps upwards which is more exciting than just swimming.

The parasailers were out in force and were fascinating to watch as they flew like birds over the sea. If you're looking to have a go then you'll be accompanied by an operator who is unharnessed and appears to be just sitting and holding on to the wires. Very daring indeed.

We were constantly being approached by hawkers and had to politely say "no." They weren't really a problem. The people watching was excellent, nothing more entertaining than looking at the huge variety of human shapes.

An American woman came on the scene to ask if we could watch her belongings while she went for a swim. She told me in the most dramatic terms that I was the image of her brother in law back in America. I asked if he was intelligent and had a good personality. She said "indeed yes"! She continued to talk dramatically about other matters and I said "I love your accent." She joined Val for a swim in the sea.

While the tide was going out I exceeded the buoy line to get my depth. I then approached a black guy to test my communication skills with a stranger. He was born in the Cameroons and has worked in Paris for the past 25 years. I asked if he was daring enough to parasail. He said "no way."

We dined in primitive style after ordering a big chicken salad roll each from a hawker with coffee served from a flask. Very welcome indeed.

In between dips in the sea I would read and relax and I even wrote one full page of my journal. Luxuriating on the beach, had been well worth it.

It was then time for the inevitable beer to celebrate our enjoyable beach break before meeting the tender. We found a nice bar but they wouldn't accept American dollars. Fortunately there was a money changer nearby. We were then able to buy a beer each but the bill didn't match the advertised price, which was because of 7% VAT and a 10% service charge. The cheek! Anyhow it's always enjoyable to have a beer on a foreign shore especially when the weather is hot. We found another bar and had another beer and were able to spend the last of our baht. It was 6:00pm when we reached the pier for the tender.

I spoke to the nice John Cartlidge, chief of security and asked why the captain doesn't always tell us what is going on. The reply was that different captains communicate in different ways and that a new captain was now on board who might be better at keeping us informed. I also asked about the mornings tender problems and was told that the boat we used was on hire to Cunard as a service to the passengers. I couldn't help feeling the real reasons were being covered up.

I have given Herbie Denton a new name, "the executioner" because of the way he kills all his songs!

I have decided that David and Susie are compulsive babblers and maybe that's what put off the others from joining us for dinner.

I handed the atomic bomb leaflets to Graham, a passenger I first met in Singapore who said he'd like us to get together for a discussion.

Looks like some of deck 3 will be sealed off from Cochin to Dubai as enhanced security against the Somali Pirates. I wondered if it is really necessary or just a propaganda exercise to give the impression that Cunard are most definitely committed to the security and welfare of their passengers.

Looked in at the Cunard singers and dancers show which left me completely unmoved. Although the theatre was quite full only a small number were applauding which told me that that perhaps some people were there merely to kill time.

Cruising to Chennai, India.

FRIDAY 8 APRIL Anderman Sea and the Bay of Bengal. Hot. Clear with calm sea.

The Cochin port presentation had to be aborted because of a sound fault. Anyhow we'll be independent, and on a friends' suggestion we have planned to use tuk tuks to take us sightseeing.

I've taken to the Café Carinthia each morning after breakfast for about 30 minutes writing. The huge vases of flowers are good company as I take up my seat by an ocean window. But an elderly couple seem to resent my presence because I never buy a coffee. I overheard her saying "There are people in here who don't buy anything". She clearly doesn't want me there. Tough. I'm not buying a coffee when I can get it free from the Lido.

Took my book about the famous and infamous to the Garden Lounge for some peaceful study. The article about Nelson Mandela made good reading and I thought it was amazing that he was the only person outside the royal family to be on first name terms with the Queen. Caroline came by and I told her my flute was laid up but fortunately I'd brought my Irish whistle. She said we could probably work something out. Val was unusually nice to her.

The Captain's midday announcement included a story about the origins of "On the Fiddle." It refers to long ago. If a sailor could play a musical instrument especially a fiddle he would be excused certain chores while entertaining the other sailors. Of course for obvious reasons many new sailors often learned how to play a musical instruments before they ever set sail.

Another brilliant lecture from Malcolm Nelson. Drugs were often found hidden in coconuts and one woman hid them inside bananas with the skins sewn back together!

Matinee with the Zeitgeist duo. The brilliant violinist continues to give me the creeps through lack of eye contact. After the performance Val gave a hand bagging to two officials for failing to action the background noise.
Comfy chair in the shade on the Lido Pool Deck with my book. I read the chapter about John Profumo. Now there's a man who had a conscience, he eventually did charity work that won him the CBE.

I'm now resorting to my Irish whistle, it's a poor substitute for the flute but I'm having a go. I'm out of practice but I have the time to bounce back and hopefully my playing will sustain me until 10 May.

Two couples joined us for the quiz and how pathetic that 6 of us could only clock up 10/20. The young Scottish quizmaster seems to have an ego. He's pretty hopeless and should resign.

How unfortunate that Graham and his wife have a separate dinner table to ours, they'd be most welcome to join us. Arranging a get together isn't easy because he plays a lot of bridge. However we're meeting tomorrow afternoon in the Golden Lion. Seems a really nice guy.

I decided to draw full attention to myself at dinner by becoming unofficial quizmaster. It worked very well. Three of my questions were about Mandela the other three about Profumo. Then Eddie took over by asking ridiculous questions about flags. Afterward we talked about the piano and I was surprised that someone with grade 7 can neither memorise, improvise nor accompany a singer.

Gave Mike Doyle a miss because of his political incorrectness and sat in the Queens Ballroom instead to listen to the new band playing great numbers from the American Song Book. The bass player is superb.

An hour on the internet and replied to Jay's e-mail.
Cruising to Chennai.

SATURDAY 9 APRIL. Bay of Bengal. Hot. Calm with long graceful ripples splaying out from the bow.

The young waiter in Café Carinthia asked if I was writing a book and when I said yes he was very interested to know all about it. Then to the garden lounge for caffeine, creative writing and a critical assessment of human traffic.

Golden Lion to meet Graham. We had nearly an hour together with music being our first subject. He's semi - retired and has been playing the guitar for the past three years. He is a doctor who suffers from depression. When I asked if it affects patients with mental health conditions he said he listens to them without rushing to write a prescription. He cannot cope with going ashore in the heat and prefers to remain on board with a book. When it came to the atomic bomb my only contribution was that it was mass murder. It was an interesting meeting and he seems like a nice person who's well spoken. His wife is a Samaritan. One of the attractions of holidays like these is that they bring many interesting people in my direction. Graham is certainly one of them.

During my piano practice a professional dancer appeared and asked me if I'd got my practice time reserved and when I told him I had he promptly departed with his pupil! I continued to polish my numbers and the lady in white glasses told me I sound very pleasant.

At dinner Irene and I talked about singing and choirs but I couldn't help thinking she has an inflated opinion of her own abilities.

Danny Elliot was brilliant. He entered the theatre via an audience stairway while playing "Amazing Grace" on the bagpipes. Next it was the piccolo, the electric violin, tap dancing and singing. Just to repeat my previous assessment "One of the most talented performers I've ever seen." A musical genius with a great personality.

Chennai tomorrow.

SUNDAY 10 APRIL. Maiden Call. Chennai, WQ4 Berth Ambedkar Dock, Bay of Bengal, East India. Hot.

Chennai, formerly Madras is the capital of Tamil Nadu State and is the fourth largest city in India. It's situated on the shore of the Bay of Bengal. Contrary to what we might think, the name "Madras Curry" is not used in India but was invented by restaurants in Britain. Chennai is the gateway to the town of Mahabalipuran which is where we visited.

At breakfast I was sitting with a polite couple in their 70's from Chicago. She was telling me that as a young woman she was learning to play the violin. One day she received a phone call from her teacher to say a pupil had cancelled their lesson and would the woman like to come along. On her way along icy roads her car was involved in an accident and ever since she's been in a wheel chair. How sad.

We set off by coach for the 40 mile drive to Mahhabalipuran - Town of Temples. During our drive there were lots of scenes: Many tuk tuks, numerous run down shops and workshops, stalls selling fruit and vegetables, cooked food, women in saris sweeping up and people just lolling about. The litter and rubbish laying around wasn't a pretty sight and no-one seemed in a hurry to clear it. Overall though, it was a pleasant journey as we followed the Bay of Bengal Coast in a southerly direction.

Krishna's Butterball is a huge granite boulder which is perched precariously on a 35 degree rock slope. The boulder is smooth and the size of a bungalow. Its position seems to defy the laws of gravity, and you'd think the slightest touch would send it rolling. Not at all; there have been many failed attempts to move it. It seems it's been there for 1200 years.

Arjuna's Penance tells the mythical story in bas relief, of the River Ganges from its source in the Himalayas. Two huge rocks were selected to carve life size figures of elephants, other animals and mythical creatures. The work of art is possibly the biggest of its kind in the world dates back to the 7th century.

Next to this, again, carved out of solid rock is a small temple complete with pillars and chambers which you can enter.

There were women in saris selling food and drinks from barrows. It was fun capturing these scenes on our cameras because of the lovely colours.

Back on the coach to take us to the star of the show. The Five Rathas. Ratha means chariot but these small temples are nothing like chariots.

How did those amazing stonemasons work their genius out of solid rock? One can't imagine what sort of tools they had in the 7th century.

Monoliths of the first degree. As well as the small temples, the carvings of the life size elephant and sacred bull are awesome.

It didn't take long for Val to give a hand bagging to a guy who complained that his wife was being harassed by hawkers. For goodness sake, hawkers are part of the scene and you just have to accept them.

A group of teenage school girls were happy to talk to us and pose for our cameras.

Finally we were taken to the Shore Temples which were constructed out of blocks of granite in the 8th century - another awe inspiring scene and again you kept on wondering how on earth they did it. There are also many lions carved out of rock.

We looked through the wire netting to see the long beach. Crowds of locals were just standing there and I hardly saw anyone bathing. It was so hot I could easily have hopped over the netting and into the sea to cool off.

Before boarding the coach we had a look at the souvenir shops - they were actually huts - and there were women selling melons. The odd cow added to the picture.

When it was time to hand out the chocolates that we'd amassed over the weeks we were suddenly mobbed just like we were in manila. Frantic hands were reaching towards us to grasp what they could. One little girl got her hands on a small box of biscuits and then fled. Val thought the girl was a gypsy.

Once we'd boarded the coach we started eating from our 'lucky bags' but outside, the children were begging and looking at us so pitifully that I stepped off the coach and handed out most of our food.

Our journey back to Chennai took us past shops and shacks that were so run down you'd think you were in a third world country.

But we were in India - the world's second fastest growing economy!

It was disappointing that the ship didn't have a range of curries on the menu. Cunard are very good at themes but alas not on this occasion.

My curiosity has now been satisfied. Elizabeth's course is set for the south of Sri Lanka to reach Cochin because the strait between India and Sri Lanka is too shallow.

Spectacular sun set from deck 10. Managed some dramatic shots. It would have made a welcome change had the string quartet played for the sail away. Instead it was the inevitable Changez who were banging it out.

The recital of sitar and drums in the Royal Court was quite tedious. Sounded like a cat meowing.

Cruising to Cochin, India.

MONDAY 11 APRIL. Bay of Bengal. Hot. Clear blue skies calm sea.
Sat with the Chicago couple again at breakfast - they seem to enjoy my company.

Came upon Eddie and Irene who told me about their ordeal when they were robbed in Manhattan.

Matthew's port talk was about Dubai - not one of our favourite destinations but we are looking forward to the desert safari and perhaps a beach and the museum afterwards.

Another educational and partly humorous lecture from Malcolm Nelson entitled "Swallowers." People sometimes put drugs such as heroin into condoms and small balloons, swallow them and try to bring them into the country. They're often stopped because something doesn't look right. Why are they not carrying a suitcase? Even the way they are dressed can be a giveaway as can body language. Suspicion can also be aroused when certain flights are used. It has been known for some to die of an overdose when "bags" have split open. The drugs chairs are interesting - special toilets that suspects are required to use where their waste can be hygienically assessed. Charming!

One of the pieces the Zeitgeist Duo played was perhaps very appropriate because of the very hot weather - "Winter" from Vivaldi's Four Seasons. I always feel emotional whenever I hear it. Their final concert will be made up of requests for pieces they've previously played. I chose Schubert's Ave Maria.

While Val was getting ready I filled the cabin with Irish music on my whistle and felt the occupants on either side of our cabin were very fortunate indeed.

One of the questions at the quiz was what colour is the Golden Gate Bridge. Orange. Wrong, red. Nonsense. It's orange, I should know I've crossed it four times.

Looked in the Royal Court at Phil Brown, singer. When he started talking about his time as a bus driver we promptly departed having heard it all before. He sings old hat and he'd be better going back on the buses!

Cruising to Cochin.

TUESDAY 12 APRIL. Indian Ocean. Hot and sunny.

It's five days since the health restrictions were lifted and what relief it was to be able to serve yourself and not have to be specific about requirements from those who served us.

The nasty woman was absent from the Café Carinthia - I considered sitting where she normally sits to see how she would react if she appeared. I then started to think rationally - perhaps she's not at peace with herself, maybe she's suffering.

Malcolm Nelson had us enthralled with another lecture entitled "Lies and excuses. - what people say when they're stopped by the customs officers i.e. "Mamma packed the case"

Another lecture from Mervin King, ex-Governor of the bank of England. Although he filled the theatre he failed to impress. I was looking forward to learning more about the financial crisis but alas I don't think he knew the meaning of simplicity as most of it went over our heads.

Found my niche under a canopy on the Lido Pool Deck while reading some great life stories. I was surrounded by some people who like to babble, others who enjoy sitting quietly with a book and then there are those who pile on the sun cream and bake in the heat. The waitresses weave their way in and out serving beer and when not serving beer they're circulating with empty trays hoping that the situation will be rectified.

Something completely different in the Garden Lounge - Poetry and harp. Caroline alternated her harp music with poetry recitals given by Tommi, social host and Amanda Reid the cruise director. Very entertaining with a pint of Boddies to enhance the proceedings.

Only four of us at dinner, the Chorlyites were absent. David and Susie told us they both take statins and maybe think it's ok to eat cheese and puddings every night! And yes they like to babble. There's Imodium for physical diarrhoea - what about something similar for verbal diarrhoea!

I was looking forward to seeing the American ventriloquist, but he failed to hit the mark. Good voice though.

Cochin tomorrow.

WEDNESDAY 13 APRIL. Cochin, Ernakulam Wharf, Kerala, Willingdon Island, South West India, Arabian Sea. Hot.

Cochin is a major port on the South West coast of India. It is often referred to as the Queen of the Arabian Sea.

Our plan was to hire a tuk tuk to do our sightseeing but we decided on an air conditioned taxi instead. Our driver, Nadim, a Muslim, told us the different religions live peacefully side by side.

It was quite hectic with all the tuk tuks, and general traffic. Lots of run down shops and much litter despite there being a sign which read:
'Clean city my dream city'

After we agreed to do a river trip we eventually entered a track which brought us to some commercial tents and a mooring and after some haggling, we paid US $45.00 for one and a half hours in a small motorised vessel with a canopy.

Even with the hum of the boat's engine our experience was peaceful and relaxing and our man willingly slowed down whenever we wanted to take photos. The riversides are home to rich and poor with lots of shacks with washing on the lines and the odd posh house, and with palm trees everywhere we captured some interesting images with nice reflections, courtesy of the calm waters. Smaller versions of the Chinese fishing nets are fixed at certain points on the riverside and to add to our delights we saw kingfishers, egrets, a bird of prey and many others species. I wondered what the occupants of some of the shacks must have been thinking when we pointed our cameras in their direction, but they are probably used to it. Finally there were friendly folk who enjoyed waving to us from the odd vessel sauntering by.
Conclusion: An enjoyable far from the madding crowd experience.

Onward through the vibrant streets of Cochin where there are few if any traffic signs. On the way to the Chinese fishing nets we stopped at the Catholic Basilica Cathedral with its majestic white twin towers and an interior resembling a treasure chest. We found ourselves in the aftermath of a wedding where the bride and groom happily posed for Val's camera and so did the women in saris, unwittingly!

Next stop was the area of the Chinese fishing nets. These are a series of massive contraptions set up by the Chinese 1000 years ago and are still in use today. Huge partly conical shaped nets are lowered into the water from primitive booms made from long slender tree trunks spliced together for length with rope. There are ropes and pulleys which are counter balanced with bundles of large stones which are tied to the ropes.

I was invited to haul in the 'catch,' which considering the size of the operation was considerably small - like using a sledge hammer to crack a nut. I took up a further invitation to walk along the planks to be near the nets. And then I knew what was coming. I was asked to make a donation of US $20.00. WHAT!! I gave a US $1.00.

We looked at another church, a museum and then a 'shop' for the driver to receive his commission, usually it's a petrol voucher for bringing in customers. But we only had a quick look round and then left.

As is customary on tours like these it was time for a beer and our driver took us to a pleasant al fresco bar overlooking the river and said he'd wait for us. We sat with a couple of Cunarders we hadn't met before - Sam and Karen. They were great company and we shared a few laughs over two and a half large Kingfisher beers each. Delectable. When the bill arrived they refused to let us pay. How kind.

Back to the ship along more interesting streets, more tuk tuks, colourful shops, colourful people, colourful everything!

Dr Graham told me him and his wife went ashore but he couldn't cope with the heat and wished a coconut would have fallen on his head and sent him unconscious! He said he has low self-esteem. I didn't like to ask if he was having treatment for his depression.

More jazz under the stars with the inevitable Boddingtons accompaniment.

Excellent singer at The Royal Court - Helen Wilding. Her tastes are identical to mine. She sang three Gershwin songs and one Cole Porter,
and as a complete contrast she gave us both Schubert's and Bach's Ave Maria. Bliss. How wonderful as well that there was no Abba or Lloyd Webber. Unfortunately though, her version of Over the Rainbow missed the mark. As always the band were superb.

Cruising to Dubai.

THURSDAY 14 APRIL. Arabian Sea. Hot. Choppy.

During my early morning brew on the Lido Deck, a woman asked me the date. She had a journal and very soon we struck up a conversation about writing which somehow led to immigration. We exchanged names, she's called Olwyn.

As I was about to enter the elevator a rather glamorous young woman approached me and asked if I'd like a haircut.
"What do you charge?"
"Twenty six dollars"
"HOW MUCH?"
"It's much cheaper at home, I do need a trim though"
"Yes we have noticed sir"
"Can I think about it?"
"Course you can sir"

The Malcolm Nelson lecture was a case study about a complicated drugs case where we were the judge and jury. Sad to say I lost the thread of the plot.

Usual Garden Lounge for caffeine and creative writing while I judged folk as they passed by. Yet I don't suppose for one minute folk don't judge me. I imagine them saying, "Look at that tatty long haired guy, always writing. No pride!

Lunch time Dixieland jazz in the Golden Lion pub with chicken tikka to boot. A feel good forty five minutes. How can anyone live without jazz? It's the ultimate musical expression. Spoke to Malcolm Nelson who agreed that Mervin King verged on the unintelligible.

It's quite comical watching rather large women on the pool deck with flesh bulging out of their swimming costumes, not to mention the old men with bare chests. Some people enjoy baking in the heat while others like sleeping.

More piano in the Yacht Club. Two dancers appeared probably expecting the place to themselves. Tough.

Jazz again, this time in the Garden Lounge. Superb. Afterwards I asked Victor if the soprano sax was easier to play than the flute. He just said all instruments have their peculiarities. He agreed to meet me tomorrow to look at my flute,

Full dinner table but no explanation from the Chorlyites as to why they were absent last night.

I don't particularly like Roy Walker as a person or as a comedian but he does know his craft and especially how to pause. His jokes are retro. I've heard them all before. On a funny note though, in terms of state benefits he referred to England as Treasure Island!

Had an hour on line to do my internet banking and to check my e-mails. Jay sent me the play list for May's Burn Naze concert. The songs are cheesy but the instrumentals are good.

Cruising to Dubai.

FRIDAY 15 APRIL. Arabian Sea. Very warm but Choppy. Val's birthday.

Olwyn joined me for breakfast. We talked about obesity and the amount of food some folk put on their plates. She said offending people should be put on a raft. She then said something quite unusual. She told me I'd got lovely eyes and that eyes were very important to her!

"Happy birthday Val." She rejected the watch I'd bought her and said that a present from one of the destinations would have been more acceptable. Oh dear!

Malcom Nelson's lecture was called "Trains and Boats and Planes" for concealing the importation of drugs. Informative and funny.

Met Victor, the band leader as arranged. He carried out a cigarette paper test on my flute. He closed the holes with cigarette paper between them and the pads and in two cases the paper could be easily removed which meant I'd got two leaks. "Thank you Victor, I now know it's not my embouchure that's causing the problem." So it's back to the Music Cellar when I get home.

Took out a book called Peace of Mind and started reading it under the canopy on the Lido Pool Deck. I copied out some of the entries - I thought the best one was, "Philosophy is common sense in a dress suit"

Good news! An entry in the daily programme; "For all those interested there will be a creative writing group starting tomorrow in the Yacht Club." I shall be the first there.

A very commendable 13/20 at the quiz.

Val was the centre of attention as she blow out the single candle on her cake surrounded by a group of waiters singing "happy birthday."

Arranged a meeting with Dr Graham for tomorrow at 4:00pm.

Variety show at the Royal Court Theatre. I'm fascinated how some performers think they're really talented when frankly they are not. Take the Cunard singers - they should have gargled before they went on stage. The ventriloquist was poor and I expected Helen Wilding to save the day. Alas, her previous performance was miles better but this time she seemed too intent on promoting her looks and personality. I gleaned something from it as usual, by focusing on the band.

Cruising to Dubai.

SATURDAY 16 April. Arabian Sea. Gulf of Oman. Very warm. Choppy.

Olwyn told me there is a compulsive talking know it all on her dinner table. I said she should come and meet David on ours. We then decided that these people should be sent to the ships' correction centre!

Heard that there will be 1200 disembarkations at Dubai tomorrow with about 1400 embarkations.

A fellow passenger took the creative writing group - Annie, a Scottish ex school teacher. There were eight of us, including a retired mathematician and a retired academic. Our first exercise was called bend and stretch. She gave us a list of ten words relating to childhood and we were given ten minutes to write a piece using ideas from the list. I wrote about my dislike of 30's music as a young boy to my love of playing it on my flute as an adult. I read it to the group who gave it a good reception. The next exercise was a little odd. She gave each of us a chocolate éclair and asked us to write about it under her supervision taking into account texture, the sound of unwrapping it, and the taste. My concluding sentence was "To sweeten my foul mouth." Again, most of the group enjoyed my efforts but not everyone was willing to share theirs. Creative writing on the high seas, what next!

At lunchtime I came upon the mathematician who introduced me to his wife Jenny, She's an interesting dramatic sort of woman who was at the Royal College of Music with Rick Wakeman and Andrew Lloyd Webber. How interesting. When I mentioned my piano slot she offered to come along and give me some tuition. How kind.

Very disappointed with Zeitgeist duo for not playing my request - Schubert's Ave Maria. Nevertheless, they played like maestros with other requests from their previous performances.

Another meeting with Dr Graham who said the amount of obesity and sun exposure on board was worrying. He told me the most widely prescribed drugs are for heart problems and that statins are certainly not prescribed to meet targets. As for music, he owns many guitars including a Hoffner Bass. He cannot play by ear.

As previously announced by the captain The Royal Navy's frigate, Defender passed by and circled our ship while carrying out manoeuvres with accompanying blasts from foghorns. Helicopters also appeared occasionally flying very low and of course the decks were full of folk eager to watch the drama.

Penny turned up at the Yacht Club as promised. She likes my piano technique and pointed out a few of my faults. We looked at 'Embraceable You' as an exercise. She advised me to keep my wrists in line with the backs of my hands while imagining a 50p piece balancing on each. I have to take care to give each note its correct value, and keep middle C opposite my navel. I'm very grateful to her. She said she would be willing to come again. Naturally I felt very honoured.

13/20 was a poor showing at the quiz considering there were six of us.
I don't suppose I'll ever shine at quizzes as I'm not really interested in trivia.

Variety show. The singers and dancers sang as bad as ever, but Paul Christopher's 'Foggy Day' was excellent. Roy Walker topped the bill with jokes out of the arc.

Tried to come up to date with my e-mails but the internet was so slow
I was forced to abort the operation.

Dubai tomorrow.

SUNDAY 17 APRIL. Port Rashid Cruise Terminal, Dubai, Persian Gulf. Hot.

Dubai is situated on the South East coast of the Persian Gulf. It's now famous for space age sky scrapers, deserts, beaches, mosques and *shopping malls. It also has the world's tallest building.*

As I previously stated, Dubai is not one of our favourite places but today has changed all that.

Our 4WD jeep was waiting for us on the quay side ready to take us on a desert safari. Another couple joined us and then we were away out of town while marvelling at the glittering skyscrapers. It took about an hour on good quality roads through the desert before we reached the dunes.

The tyres needed to be deflated a little to improve the traction, and whilst this was going on we climbed one of the dunes which was heavy going. The view from the top was magnificent - miles of desert with big smooth sand dunes.

We boarded the jeep and then the fun started. Jaffa drove us up and down the dunes swirling this way and that giving us a thrilling experience. He was frantically turning the steering wheel to counter all the sliding about. Clouds of sand were being churned up at the sides of the jeep and showered the windscreen a few times - not for the claustrophobic. We would then descend into the valleys ready to ride the dunes again. The best word to describe it was WOW!! We tried to take photos but it was physically impossible. When we got out we did manage to bag some pictures of the other two vehicles.

The safari continued to a camel farm where these fabulous animals are bred for racing, there was about a hundred of them in a large enclosure. Some were roaming freely but I noticed their front legs were tethered. I love the serenity of camels.

Last on our list was an Arabian camp, which is sheltered between the dunes with open wicker huts forming a circle and a large flat board at the centre which was the 'stage.'

We started with a camel ride. The only item between us and the camel was a blanket which provided a lovely intimate feeling, unlike our experience in the Gambia where we had to sit in a frame.

Coffee and dates next in an open wicker hut. But we waived the hookah water pipe!

Only two of us tried the sandboarding, myself and a 78 year old man who was brilliant. It was a struggle to carry the sand board to the top of the dune because of the heat. They got my feet into the foot locks and after a briefing I eased my way to the edge and then let go. I was zooming down at some speed but eventually lost my balance and tumbled down while everyone cheered. Fortunately I was cushioned by the sand. Undeterred I went back for seconds, and this time I was able to go a greater distance. The thrill of sand boarding! I could take it up, and wondered if I was a 'natural.'

We would never have a henna tattoo, but because it was part of our package, we decided to give it a try. A young Muslim woman drew an Islamic design onto our arms with henna which was being squeezed from something similar to an icing bag. The drying time is thirty minutes and it lasts a week.

The last chapter was a barbeque buffet lunch which was one of the best I've ever tasted. No shortage of vegetable curry, chicken, ham, salad and a coke. We ate in an open wicker dining hut with low tables and huge cushions - a feast fit for a sheik!

A group of women including Val stepped onto the "board" and started dancing and letting their hair down while I was videoing them.

As we drove back to the ship, once again we enjoyed the drive on the long roads through the desert while feeling quite pleased with ourselves.

The shuttle bus took us to the Dubai Mall which is the largest in the world. An enormous palatial building with marble floors, state of the art ceilings with 1200 retail outlets. It's luxury shopping on a grand scale. Add to this, cinemas, an ice skating rink, posh eateries and restaurants and you have it all. The towering indoor waterfall with many life size silver sculptures of men swimming with the downward flow is spectacular.

As we left the mall the first thing to impress us was the Burj Khalifa, the world's tallest building which we were able to see at close quarters. It stands at 2716 ft. high and looked as though it was penetrating the sky. There is an observation deck on the 124th floor.

Many items in the area kept our cameras clicking: a lake, walkways, palm trees, flower beds, water features, lawns, small bridges, skyscrapers and a sunset. I suppose many people would have been wondering how long their memory cards were going to last!

One sight that really stood out was four young women graduates in their purple gowns and hats excitedly taking selfies. I kept my distance and captured some good portraits with my zoom lens and as I walked off feeling quite pleased with my catch one of them chased after me. She was quite aggressive and told me I had no right to take their photos and half threatened me with the police. When she demanded my camera I apologised and promptly deleted the images. I
have to admit that the incident left me feeling quite uncomfortable but when I caught up with Val I felt better for having told her about it.

We stayed for the fountain show - a dramatic spectacle of numerous high powered water jets surging many meters in all directions in spectacular patterns synchronised with music and lights to boot.

We had a couple of beers in the Golden Lion and had Paul Christopher, the ballroom singer for company. A nice interesting guy aged 67 but doesn't look it. He was easy to gel with - he sings the American Songbook and loves Ella Fitzgerald. We have a lot in common.

We ate in the Lido because it was too late for the restaurant. We'd have to wait until tomorrow night to meet our new table mates.

Not impressed with the Cunard singers and dancers or The Patriot Girls but we let that ride because of the brilliant day we had.

Cruising to Muscat.

MONDAY 18 APRIL. Gulf of Oman. Big swell. Hot.

Most of the stern on the promenade deck was sealed off to allow security to carry out their operations and scan the seas for the enemy.

Matthew's talk was about Aqaba with its main feature being the gateway to Petra which most people will probably be visiting. We've pre booked a trip to Wadi Rum.

We were surprised to see the Great Bill Miller who we've met on previous cruises. He was sat nearby and of course we approached him. Soon the conversation turned to English soaps which he loves. He'll be giving five lectures until Southampton then he boards the Queen Mary for New York. What a life, what a man, he's the best speaker I've ever heard.

As it was our final leg I cancelled my gratuities and renewed my complimentary internet time.

The creative writing group was made up of 18 people of various nationalities. I admire Annie for keeping a momentum and not allowing small talk to get in the way. She set two exercises similar to the last ones. I wrote about what Grange Park Council Estate has become but won't allow anyone to condemn it. My conclusion for the "sweet" exercise was that it's another route to tooth decay. I was one of a handful of people who read their pieces aloud and Annie assured me for someone who doesn't write descriptions I do pretty well.

Scored a rubbish 6/20 at the quiz.

Two new couples have joined our dinner table. Liz and Ron but I didn't catch the names of the other two. They all seem to be good conversationalists but no doubt I'll find some faults with them.

We looked in at the theatre and left almost immediately. Who wants to listen to a bloody soul singer? My sanity is sacred.

Muscat tomorrow.

TUESDAY APRIL 19. Muscat Oman. Port of Sultan Qaboos. Gulf of Oman. Hot.

Muscat is the Port capital of Oman and is surrounded by mountains and desert. It has an ancient history and it seems the government have banned the construction of high rise buildings.

Hazy sunrise streaming through the cabin window at 5:45am.

The sail in to the Muscat terminal is full of delightful features at close quarters. Jagged mountains, a cluster of white buildings, a huge white replica of a frankincense burner perched on a rocky hill top and two sixteenth century Portuguese forts.

The announcement said the shuttle bus would take 30 minutes to the Muttra Souk - it actually took 5 minutes.

Six of us boarded a taxi which included Nidge and Jeet, Olwyn and Ted. We drove to the Grand Mosque along modern roads that cut through barren mountainous landscapes with not a hint of traffic congestion. Happy motoring!

The mosque is supremely beautiful and modern with white and dark grey marble walls, enormous chandeliers and a spectacular dome. The Persian carpet in the main prayer hall is the second largest hand loomed carpet in the world. It took 600 women 4 years to weave. Happily, there were no restrictions on photography.

One of the guides invited us for coffee and dates and took us to a room where we met two clerics who made us very welcome. They answered our questions and even gave us an English copy of the Koran.

The surrounding mountains are volcanic and jagged and have an eerie beauty about them giving us a good idea of the lay of the land during a spectacular journey this time to a couple of 6 star hotels.

At the first one we were given a free rein to wander round the opulent interiors before going into the grounds and gazing down to the beach to see how the rich enjoy themselves.

At the next hotel, which was equally as luxurious we were given coffee and dates.

Our last stop was the rear of the Sultans palace and surroundings - more photographic gems especially as the flowers were in bloom.

We wandered round the Muttra Souk but most of it was closed until the evening when it suddenly bursts into life.

After a very enjoyable 30 minutes in a taverna with a long coke it was time to take the shuttle bus back to the ship. We were happy that the other two couples enjoyed both their day out and certainly our company.

As we were enjoying a pint on the Lido deck Val gave a handbagging to a couple of women for giving disapproving glances at her and Marilyn for talking loudly.

During the sail away I took to deck 10 for some people watching before capturing some evening sun shots on my camera.

More brilliant jazz in the Garden Lounge with the best bass player in the world with Victor banging it all out on his soprano sax.

During dinner we all talked excitedly about Muscat. David actually used my first name, a sure sign perhaps that relations between us could be thawing.

Looked in at Vanity Fair and when one of the female singers started howling out 'It Aint Necessarily So' it was our cue to leave or we would have suffered brain damage. We maintained our sanity by listening to the fabulous Queens Band with Paul Christopher singing jazz songs.

Cruising to Salalah.

WEDNESDAY 20 APRIL. Arabian Sea. Hot.

Another hazy sun rise from the cabin window at 5:45am.

A cup of tea after breakfast with Olwyn on the Lido Deck while trying to correct the world's faults.

We were required to take part in a security drill in case we met the enemy on the high seas - the Somalia Pirates. After the alarm sounded we were instructed to go to our cabins and sit outside until we heard the all clear signal.

I arrived early at the theatre to bag a good seat for Bill Miller's lecture and to say hello to him. As expected his "Floating Palaces" lecture was bliss. He's a gifted speaker who knows his subject well and moves his hands about to emphasise certain points. He's passionate and graphic and often changes his voice tone and intonation. These attributes add up to his genius - not to mention his sense of humour. Privately, he's an American in love with all things British including the Monarchy and soap operas!

During the afternoon I confined myself to the cabin as I felt quite ill. Fortunately I managed some sleep.

A miracle 13/20 at the quiz.

Full company on our dinner table. I like the fact that David seems to be responding favourably to me. I'm reserving judgment with the others until I get to know them.

Decided to give the Patriot Girls another go which paid off. I enjoyed their performance especially their Andrew Sisters songs. I forgive them and I'll be at their next performance!

Salalah tomorrow.

THURSDAY 21 APRIL. Industrial Port of Salalah, Arabian Sea. Hot.

Salalah is the second largest city in Oman and is situated on the south coast.

To mark the Queen's 90th birthday, a huge ugly bust of Her Majesty had been set up on a big oblong cake in the Atrium. Nothing like her, the sculptor should be fired. And yet many folk were taking photographs of the monstrosity. Why? So that folk can say, "Look what they've done to our Queen"

Our trip was called Salalah by 4x4 which we shared with Marilyn and Kelvin. I had the front seat and was surprised that Kelvin was happy to remain in the back. We were part of a cavalcade of 15 luxury jeeps. Our driver was called Abraham.

We motored through a couple of towns with masses of white buildings that appeared to be run down. And once again we witnessed the desolation of the desert with mile after mile of barren landscape with just an occasional white building or house.

First on the agenda gave us the opportunity to explore a flat rocky promontory with views of miles of beautiful turquoise sea backed by palm trees and white box like houses.

Next stop was the ancient ruins of what is believed to have been the palace of the Queen of Sheba. I actually regret not taking a picture but at the time I felt it wasn't really photogenic.

We continued on to Wadi Derbat which is supposed to be very green and lush in summer but not for us. The trees all appeared to be dead but I did enjoy watching the camels roaming about near the river bed.

Our last stop was Ain Razat. The springs from the mountains form channels that provide water for the garden area. We didn't expect to see so much colour in these parts. The cave was interesting to explore but hard work to reach in the searing heat.

On the return journey we stopped to look at a frankincense tree. But sadly I was none the wiser. What I did find interesting though was how Abraham reacted when Val told him she was a Buddhist. He asked me if I approved and he felt surprised that I did. He said "Muslim no problem, Christian no problem, Jew no problem but Buddhist - a problem." I think Val wanted me to change the subject.
Then he jokingly converted me to Islam which I thought was quite funny, but I was worried when he started calling me brother!

We noticed that the infamous bust of the Queen had been removed, probably because of complaints from both passengers and staff.

The sail away party marked the Queens' 90th birthday with flag waving, cocktails, Land of Hope and Glory, Rule Britannia, God Save the Queen and of course a royal toast.

Champagne was waiting on our dinner table for another toast to Her Majesty. God bless you ma'am and thank you Cunard!

Super entertainer, Jon Courtenay, accomplished pianist, singer and comedian wowed the audience with his great skills.

Cruising to Aqaba.

FRIDAY 22 APRIL. Gulf of Aden. Calm. Very warm

Port talk Istanbul.

The lecture entitled '40 years a soldier' by ex - General Lord Dannet sounded promising but was actually a flop. He shared the stage with his wife who was much more interesting. She talked about being married to a soldier and told us about her charity work.

By contrast, Bill Miller's lecture though was superb. He continued from his last lecture about Floating Palaces: 'Those Great Atlantic Liners.' I have to repeat he's a genius with language and paints big word pictures with every literary trick in the book. But his main attribute is the passion he shows for his subject.

During my deck walk I came by Caroline the harpist and joined her for a few minutes. She was using a lap top to write her journal which she referred to as personal reflections. She has two more contracts after she leaves Elizabeth: One again for Elizabeth and another for the Queen Mary.

Penny failed to show up at my piano practice but I tried to put into effect what she has already taught me.

The cabin steward knocked on our door to remind us of the blackout regulations and asked us to close our curtains to avoid being spotted by the enemy.

The Tiffany String Quartet gave a concert in the Garden Lounge. As ever it was bliss. My fix is always the lead violin or the cello. They played a piece called Plink Plank Plunk which was totally pizzicato.
A fun and catchy number to show off their finger plucking skills.

Clare Langan was an absolute joy on the flute. But what has she done to her hair? I don't like it up. I like it sweeping her shoulders. She seemed to play every note in the flutes' range and when she performed the Bach/Gounod Ave Maria with the pianist, the audience were mesmerized. She saw Val earlier and said she may be able to fix my flute. How kind.

Cruising to Aqaba.

SATURDAY 23 APRIL. Red Sea. Calm Sea. Hot

Why are there so many miserable faces in the Lido at breakfast?

Olwyn and Ted have booked the trip to Petra. I described some of it and told her she had much to look forward to. She then started talking about Ted and the heart attack he had 10 years ago. She's very concerned because he still smokes.

Port talk Piraeus for Athens. We're not sure where we'll be visiting but it won't be the Acropolis.

The Captain announced that blackouts and security restrictions on deck 3 have been lifted. Bravo. I can now resume my full wrap round walks.

Penny grabbed me in the Lido and apologised for missing my piano slot. She said she'll be there for my next one.

It was comfy under the awning on the Lido deck as I read some of my pros and cons book. One of the subjects for debate asked: Should the veil be banned? Is it a symbol of repression? Is it a walking prison? Should the wearer have freedom of choice? Belgium and France have banned it, should we?

A man took two separate items of food without using the tongs. When I challenged him he just walked away. Another passenger supported me. "Come on, let's all have another norovirus"!

All day I kept an eye out for Clare Langan but no luck. I wanted to ask her to look at my flute.
Even though I felt quite dreadful I managed to play some Irish and Scottish pieces on my whistle while looking out to sea, but the sight of the sea is much more appealing when I'm playing my flute.

More culture in the Garden lounge with a massive turnout. Tommi and Amanda Reid gave some Shakespeare recitations to mark 400 years since his death. An enjoyable performance but Tommi was way OTT! Caroline provided the music. The bards' language has never been bettered, that's why it still lives on.

Cruising to Aqaba

SUNDAY 24 APRIL. Red Sea. Hot.

I had a late breakfast at 9:15 am because I was feeling unwell. Then it was back to the cabin for a morning in bed.

Heard that the Queen Mary has the Norovirus and has been barred from berthing at Salalah. The question now is, will she be fit for Aqaba?

A little soup for lunch then back to bed.

Later, nothing could stop me from making it to the creative writing meeting. One woman wanted to babble, another wanted photos of the group and one wanted to give a talk! We were given three words and asked to use any of them. I wrote jokingly about our recent driver trying to convert me to Islam!
I only felt like 30 minutes on the piano and mainly worked on "Georgia." Penny failed to turn up.

From my window the sea was a mirror with a long column of blinding diamonds creating flickering reflections inside the cabin.

Bill Miller was in the lift and looked like a man of distinction in his black pin striped suit and red handkerchief. After I said he looked very dapper he thanked me for being sweet! He then asked my name.

Clocked up 6/20 at the quiz and at dinner I felt down because I was still feeling unwell.

Another show with Jon Courtenay, but compared to his first appearance it was unimpressive and besides, he really does have a large ego.

Aqaba tomorrow.

MONDAY 25 APRIL. Aqaba Port, Gulf of Aqaba. Jordan. Hot.

Aqaba is Jordan's only sea port and is located on the country's southernmost tip. It's the gateway to Petra and Wadi Rum - two of the most spectacular destinations in the Middle East.

Val said she'd seen Clare Langan at breakfast, so I dashed up to the Lido and found her. She was friendly and welcoming but told me she'd been ill. She asked if I enjoyed her Beatles medley. I said it was brilliant. She offered to look at my flute but I told her there wasn't time because we were about to start a trip. I thanked her and wished her well. She wished me the same in her lovely posh voice!

Our man was waiting on the quayside to take us to Wadi Rum, and as we drove out of town we enjoyed looking at some of the roads lined with palm trees and flowers. He was happy to educate us and said that Jordan is a peaceful nation and King Abdullah, who was educated in England, is well respected by his people. The country comprises 93% Muslim and 7% mainly Christian who all live in harmony.

We continued along straight roads through the desert with jagged mountains to marvel at before arriving at Sun City. This is actually a highly desirable camp with tent dining areas, a kitchen, a terrace and believe it or not wicker toilets with posh interiors.

Wadi Rum is a UNESCO world heritage site and is also known as the Valley of the Moon - Jordan's best and most magnificent desert landscape.

We transferred to a 4x4 truck with a canopy and bench seats to be taken on a long momentous journey by our Bedouin driver.

The desert scape is sensational and it's no surprise that many films were made there including Lawrence of Arabia and The Martians.

 Miles of copper and bronze sands brim with gigantic ornaments of granite and sandstone. These have been sculptured by centuries of wind and sand that have fashioned beautiful and eerie edifices. These majestic peaks come in ranges, clusters, or as single entities and are scattered all over the vast desert. The dazzling colours include ochres, ambers, beige and pale pinks to name a few. When you gaze at these awesome shapes there is a feeling of intimacy which is almost spiritual. Perhaps the most imposing of all however, are the fluted shapes of the Seven Pillars of Wisdom.

Sometime later it was time for a drink. Our driver stopped to collect some twigs to make a fire. He then produced a kettle of water, grating and tin wind break and very soon we were sipping tea with sage. Delicious.

We saw a Bedouin with a group of camels all saddled up presumably to take tourists on a ride but there was no one else around. We seemed to have the desert to ourselves.

We were taken to an area where Lawrence camped out in a cleft in a mountain which gave him permanent shade. A long tent nearby provided refreshments in quiet surroundings.

It was 91 degrees but at night it gets quite cold. We motored on through the undulating desert with a strong warm wind in our faces and a partial bumpy ride. Wadi Rum must surely be the stuff that National Geographic is made of!

As a little extra, our driver took us through his village where the houses are one storey and quite pleasant but there was rubbish and litter all around.

The king allows the Bedouins free water and electricity because the water is under ground and comes off their land.

Back at the camp for a delicious meal. We had chicken and rice with many individual bowls containing salads and other food. The hospitality was very impressive. We thanked our driver before picking up our other car for the lovely journey back to Aqaba.

We were surprised to find a liquor store in town and we were also surprised that the Jordanians are allowed to consume alcohol. Anyhow Val was able to restock with a few bottles of wine.

I was looking down from deck 3 at the waiters on the quayside as they were setting up a long row of tables with wine glasses and silver trays in readiness to give a tipple to those hundreds of passengers returning from Petra.

What could be better than savouring a beer under the stars on the Lido Deck while reflecting on a wonderfully enjoyable and educational day out with a shed full of photographs to prove it!

David and Susie were absent from dinner - a nice relief from their tongues. The others talked about Petra while we sang about Wadi rum.

Cruising to the Suez Canal.

TUESDAY 26 APRIL Gulf of Aqaba/Gulf of Suez. Cooler. Calm Sea.

Sun streaming into the cabin at 6:45am.

Saw a passenger in the Lido self-service wearing a shirt, tie and pullover. What was in his head?

Witnessed a rare sight indeed; A long line of dolphins leaping in and out of the sea. Big, black, loveable and dramatic, but the show only lasted about 30 seconds. I fumbled with my video camera but I was too late.

Another Bill Miller lecture. Again I was captivated by his use of the English Language. He is my role model and my inspiration.

The Queen Mary is ahead of us—a majestic sight but alas, we have heard it's full of the Norovirus. Could it be a floating hospital?

Another relaxing read under the canopy on the Lido Deck. My subject was the pros and cons of surrogate mothers. Maybe I should make pros and cons my daily bible - a great way to broaden ones' mind.

The creative writing group met in the Admirals Lounge with two of the women continually babbling. We were given more trigger words to kick start our ideas. It was a small group which gave the members confidence to read their compositions. My creation was about Wadi Rum, theirs was about Petra, but sadly no one mentioned its epiphany.

Another piano lesson from Penny. She's certainly helping me to develop my technique and also makes notes for me. I value her time. She left after 40 minutes while I played "Georgia" using the hand positions I have been taught.

The poetry presentation in the Garden Lounge was called Chimes, Hearts and Harps. These sessions should contain shorter poems, but Tommi, who is really very good, goes over the top with longer ones. The lovely Caroline played some nice harp but her songs verged on the dirge! Amanda read a funny piece by Pam Ayers entitled 'I wish I'd looked after my teeth'

Brett Sherwood gave an entertaining magic show. His disappearing cage was excellent but the rest of his show was a bit white bread. For me though, any magician is generally better than a male or female singer.

Elizabeth is at anchor awaiting her turn to transit the Suez. The Queen Mary was almost alongside and seeing her lit up at night was quite an experience.

Found out from the news on Google that the Queen Mary had a minor outbreak of the Norovirus with two reported cases. Nonsense. It's being played down. I also read there was a lot of unrest on the ship because passengers were unable to go to Petra. It is, however on its way to Limassol which is very poor compensation.

Awaiting transit of the Suez Canal.

WEDNESDAY 27 APRIL. Suez Canal. Coolish. But sunny.

The Suez Canal is an artificial sea level waterway connecting the Red Sea to the Mediterranean Sea. It was opened in 1869 and runs for 120 miles. Thousands lost their lives during its construction.

We entered Suez at 6:00am and ended at the Mediterranean at 4:00pm. A total of 10 hours transit.

Bill Miller was on deck 9. He looked impeccable in his jacket and tie but what about those red slippers! He was beaming at the sight of the Queen Mary 2 in the distance ahead of us and he said he couldn't wait until early evening for the two Queens to meet in the Med. We were both active with our cameras and talked about the 36 exposure roll film of yesteryear and how you'd worry in case they didn't turn out. We also touched on the Norovirus outbreak.

The private decks on the bow were opened to enable everyone to enjoy front views of the canal including those of the Queen Mary.

The transit was full of interesting sights: Limestone embankments, minarets, patchwork farmland, farm workers, palm trees, sheep, deserted villages, ferries, workers waving to us, small fishing boats, a railway, road construction, mosques, monuments and the

237

Mubarak Peace Bridge - a 2.4 mile long road bridge 60% of which was financed by the Japanese.

The Queen Mary looked majestic indeed as I gazed at her from the bow. And there was Penny waving to me from the deck below. I waved in return and she continued to wave and I felt quite honoured and I wondered why she kept it up. I then realised it wasn't me she was waving to but the web cam!

Chanced on Bill Miller in the Lido. When I told him about our mail run in New Zealand he was very interested and said he may include the story in one of his books. He enjoys engaging with people and sometimes uses their stories in his books. He keeps a journal to record his experiences. We talked about the ship being a microcosm - a haven for amateur psychologists!

During his lecture he told the story of when Rita Heyworth was a passenger on a cruise liner. One evening while she was at dinner, a member of the crew entered her suite and stole her toilet seat. He was a big fan and felt it was the only way he could get close to her. Unfortunately for him she never actually used the particular toilet containing that seat! Oh dear!

Our Diamond status allowed us a meal in the Verandah Restaurant - a posh number for fine dining specialising in French cuisine. Our food was served on silver platters with silver domed covers. It's how the rich do it. Add to this a table next to a window to look out onto the Suez Canal and we had it all - another memorable experience.

Not long after we entered the Mediterranean We cruised in tandem with the Queen Mary for about 3 miles. There was flag waving, cheering, fog horns and passengers from both ships waving to one another. It was quite an occasion but we felt sympathy for those with the Norovirus.

Necessity is the mother of invention, and because I'm missing my flute I tried a bit of jazz on my Irish whistle in the form of "Stormy

Weather." Hey presto, it worked but I need more practice. To hell with Irish traditional music!

Forty five minutes of bliss with the Tiffany String Quartet in the Garden Lounge, but why does the viola player continue to look as though she's sulking?

Our new dinner table companions, Liz and Ron are Cockneys and good company. Not so sure about Jane and Jeffrey.

The Polish violinist was generally good and looked ravishing in her evening gown. Although she was great to watch I wasn't overjoyed with her playlist and I thought the band were a bit heavy handed.

Cruising to Istanbul.

THURSDAY 28 April. Mediterranean Sea. Cool. Slightly rough sea.

I can't imagine a Cunard cruise without Bill Miller on board. Anyone interested in communicating, speaking, presentations or even creative writing would do well to attend one of his lectures. The morning presentation was about the 175 year history of Cunard ships, and the meeting of the three queens in Liverpool last year. He weaves his magic words and presents them to you as a gift.

Heard a heart breaking story of a couple in their 80's who took equity out of their home to pay for a suite on the full world cruise. Sadly the experience is not living up to their expectations and they are clearly not enjoying it. Also heard another story about a honeymoon couple who set sail on the world cruise which was funded by their parents. When the ship arrived at the Azores the couple sacrificed the rest of their voyage and flew home because they couldn't face any rough seas. Makes me wonder if there was anyone on the ship who could have reassured them. I'm also asking if there's a way round their insurance, would they be able to make a valid claim?

An irresistible chicken tikka in the Golden lion. Jeffrey came by and joined us. Alas the poor guy hasn't a grain of personality. My argument is simple. If you don't wish to have a personality, fine. If you want one then jolly well go and get one!

Annie asked us to brainstorm Suez then write a short piece about it. Two women, including the Asian lady told us they were bored with Suez. My composition asked questions about its construction and about the human labour that was involved. I also wrote about the interesting aspects that could be seen along its route.

I asked Nidge if there was a reason why he sometimes wore a white turban and sometimes a black one. He said there was no difference except the white one shows the dirt more easily!
A very reasonable 9/20 at the quiz.

As we were passing the Queens Ball room we noticed that the captains' reception that was just finishing was for platinum and diamond guests and wondered why we had not been invited. We saw Sasha and queried it with him. He said he would find out why we were not invited. In the meantime he gave us an ample glass of wine each.

I'm still trying to make an effort with David. We talked about gratuities and he said he was unaware that they would be charged on a daily basis to his account. He said he would cancel them tomorrow.

Cruising to Istanbul.

FRIDAY 29 APRIL Aegean Sea. The Dardanelles. Sea of
Marmara. Sunny. Calm

Here is a poem I wrote about an experience I had in the Lido just
after breakfast:

WHAT WILL IT TAKE TO MAKE ME WISE

What will it take to make me wise?
How many times have I said to myself,
"Don't leave the cabin without your camera"
The early sun was lurking behind the broken clouds
Projecting a fan of a dozen big bold beams onto the sea
With the rose horizon vying for attention.
A rare spectacle was touching me.
But no camera.
I hurried to the cabin for it
Then bounded onto the promenade deck
But the masterpiece had gone.
Slipped away.
Leaving me mournful
And feeling my sin of omission
Was tantamount to sacrilege.

The little plump black waitress in the Café Carinthia said "Hi John,
how's the book coming along?"- Cunard are fortunate to have
someone like her with a massive personality to make the guests
feel special.

Found out that last nights' reception in the Queen's Ballroom was
for passengers who boarded at Dubai. So we were actually
undeserving of the wine!

Port Talk Valencia. We've been before on the Oceana and know
what to expect. But the second time around won't go amiss
because it'll pin things down. So that is the last of the port
presentations. Matthew is good at his job and I like his voice but he

would do well to slow down a little. He should also spend more time on independent travel.

Ron and Liz joined us in the Garden lounge. Some years ago Liz broke her back in a cycling accident in Hawaii and is now fully recovered. She never felt discouraged about riding again in fact her and Ron have booked an electric bicycle tour for Athens. Good on them! They're a lovely couple.

It was interesting to see some of the Greek Islands in the Aegean but I couldn't put a name to any.

At my request, we looked at mind maps at the creative writing meeting. Annie sometimes uses them as an alternative to standard brainstorming. I didn't particularly learn anything as I've been using them for years. Our subject was Petra and the Asian lady, who loves the conch was moaning about feeling paralysed by the overwhelming number of writing opportunities she was having and not being able to fulfil them all. I suggested she got on with it and put at least something down on paper or she'd need counselling! Barbara and I have decided not to attend the creative writing session which will be presented by a member who's only been once. I don't like the idea of someone taking over. We're comfy with Annie and prefer to keep it that way.

We looked at the war memorials as we cruised through the Dardanelles. It was the scene of a failed campaign led by the British in WW1. We fought the Turks and lost at a cost of 260,000 troops. As a result, Churchill resigned.

Practiced "Stormy Weather" again on my whistle while gazing out to sea. Maybe the piece will lead to others and keep me jazzed up until we arrive at Southampton. However, the instrument is a mere toy compared to the flute.

Looked in at the Royal Court. It was Rietta Austin again. She makes us laugh when she goes on about her weight but makes us walk out when she starts to sing.

242

Internet PAINFULLY SLOW.

Istanbul tomorrow.

SATURDAY 30 APRIL. Istanbul, Salipazari Cruise Terminal, The Bosporus, Turkey. Sunny and Warm.

Istanbul is Turkey's most populous city and one of the world's beautiful destinations. It lies both in Asia and Europe which is separated by the Bosporus that links the Sea of Marmara to the Black Sea.

The view of the city from the ship rivals anything we've seen on the world cruise - an elevated skyline splendour of minarets, domes, towers and the harbour.

It was a day of Turkish Delights while working through Val's itinerary, first with an interesting walk to the Galata Tower. On route we came by a group of elderly men seated at a table with coffee and cigarettes seemingly putting the world to right. I felt they'd make a good triple portrait so I persuaded Val to get their permission. They reluctantly agreed and soon she had secured another one for her collection.

The area around the Galata Tower has a square, alfresco dining area, a few shops and a converted tram car serving coffee and snacks.

The Galata Tower looms upwards like a gigantic fat pencil. It was built of wood in 528 and used for fire watching. The current stone structure dates back to 1348. The lift took us to the top where we emerged into a delightful restaurant. The floor above gave us access to a narrow stone wrap round balcony, and it was there that we struck gold - a 360 degree panorama of the entire city. Majestic. The Blue Mosque, The Haghia Sophia, Topkapi Palace, various mosques and minarets, Galata Bridge, Golden Horn, The

Bosporus, sailing vessels, terracotta rooftops, and narrow streets and of course our ship, the Queen Elizabeth at berth.

We must have spent half an hour shuffling round the circumference capturing every square inch of a most beautiful and dazzling city skyline.

At street level we bought coffee from the converted tram car while exchanging a little humour with the two guys inside. They thought Val looked 35 while I looked 50 - nothing wrong with a bit of flattery - Turkish style!

As we weaved our way down a narrow street there was plenty to hold our attention especially when we came across a huge music shop selling every kind of stringed instrument imaginable. The guy inside seemed intent on trying to sell me an odd sort of wind instrument.

Next, a tram ride to the Dolmabahce Palace. A man stood up and offered his seat to Val. When I thanked him, he said "Sir I am a Muslim"

The Dolmabahce Palace was built in 1853 for the Sultan and his harem when they were moved from Topkapi Palace. The entrance is by way of the Sultan's Gate where formal gardens greet you with fountains, lily ponds, ornaments, lawns, flower beds, shrubs, trees and attractive pathways. Tall ornate railings and a huge gate separate the gardens and palace from the edge of the European side of the Bosporus. All very impressive but the best was yet to come. I've read that the palace is totally un-Turkish and is built in a variety of Western styles.

You wear plastic cover over shoes to protect the floors. Photography is forbidden. The main stair case contains crystal balustrades and is topped by one of many enormous chandeliers that hang throughout the palace. There are pillars, huge tapestries and fresco ceilings. The sumptuous and opulent halls have different names: The ceremonial Hall, Ambassador's Hall, The Pink Room and The Blue Room to name a few. There are 202 paintings on display and many bearskin rugs. Fourteen tonnes of gold was used to guild the ceilings. Oddly, we didn't see the bedroom or the kitchen and we would like to have visited the harem but because there was a 20 minute wait we decided to waive it because we had our itinerary to complete.

Another tram took us across the Galata Bridge and delivered us to the street entrance to the Topkapi Palace - not on our hit list.

A break from culture. The Le Safran restaurant across the road looked quite appealing, especially the al fresco area close to the pavement. We spent about an hour there in the shade. Our meal was partly Turkish and very tasty and so were the beers which were served in large pot beakers. Add some people watching and it made for a very pleasant and relaxing time indeed.

Last on the list was a stroll up hill to the Blue Mosque area. On the way we looked in through the café windows and watched the women rolling huge pieces of dough which are then baked and used in various Turkish recipes.
The 17th century Blue Mosque, probably the high spot of Istanbul, looks like a huge beautiful plant rising out of the ground surrounded by minarets, palm trees, fountains and flowers - a photographers dream. The inside is as magnificent as the outside.

Finally we took photos of the Haghia Sophia before looking at the hippodrome where the chariot races were held. We were down to our last 2 lira and I asked the roast chestnut man what he could do for us. He gave us one roast chestnut each!

We were so concerned about becoming dehydrated that we decided to walk back down to the Le Safran where they take American dollars. The beer was delectable.

We boarded the tram for another pleasant ride back and then a 15 minute walk to the ship feeling pleased with ourselves because we'd had a perfect day.

It was a spectacular sail away as the ship made her passage from the Bosporus to the Sea of Marmara. All those magnificent sights we'd seen earlier gently faded into the distance and a Turkish flag seemed to be proudly waving us off.

Poor Herbie, he played my two Cole Porter requests and murdered both of them.

I don't think Jane was very pleased when I told her that people don't always get out of the pool when they wanted to wee! David droned on again with his knowledge while Susie had cheese and biscuits for her afters and as usual managed to waste most of it.

Cruising to Piraeus.

SUNDAY 1 May. Dardanelles. Aegean Sea. Sunny, warm, calm Sea. Sunshine flooding the cabin at 6:45am.

Saw Barbara from the creative writing group. We've agreed to make a stand against the woman who'll be making a presentation later on about creative writing - we don't like imposters!

Cruised back along the Dardanelles and saw the Allied and the Turkish war memorials which were very clear in the morning light.

I broke my routine from the Promenade Deck and took to decks 9, 10 and 11 for my morning walk. A nice change with lots of ups and downs and ins and outs.

Lecture from Wayne Hemmingway which included his rise from rags to riches partly through helping the poor. I felt he was rather self-righteous and certainly self-promoting. Some funny bits but I decided I wouldn't be going to his next lecture.

We were given more trigger words for a piece of creative writing on Istanbul. When it came to my turn to recite I merely read out my notes, but I gave them my poem about the sunbeams. My efforts were well received and at the appointed time, three of us walked out as a protest against the new speaker.

When I started my piano practice, a dance instructor appeared and switched on some music to give a couple some tuition. When I asked him to turn it off, the situation became confrontational. I showed him my letter confirming my piano slot which he almost grabbed out of my hand. But I stood my ground and won, he then left in a huff and said he'd be back in an hour. The couple were very understanding when I explained things to them. During the rest of my slot I was very conscious of what Jenny had taught me.

When I chanced on the waitress from Rio, (Hi John how's the book?) I decided I wanted to make her feel good. I told her that Cunard should feel very fortunate to have someone like her working for them someone with a bubbly personality who can interact with the guests. She appeared to be overwhelmed but thanked me tremendously.
Another Rhymes, Chimes and Harps in the Garden Lounge. I think the pinnacle was Caroline's rendition of the Bach/Gounod Ave Maria. Delightful.

The Royal Court Theatre gave us a duo called "Ineffable." She has a brilliant figure and performs amazing feats of contortion especially on the high drapes.

Piraeus tomorrow.

MONDAY 2 MAY. Kanelos Pier, Piraeus Greece. Sunny and warm.

Piraeus is one of the largest cities in Greece. It's actually the port of Athens which is 7 miles away.

It took 50 minutes to walk to Piraeus Railway Station which was longer than we expected. Fortunately there were many items to grab our attention along the way especially the beautiful picturesque Agia Triada Cathedral and by complete contrast the Orthodox Church of St Nicholas.

Easy 15 minute train journey into Athens. And then the graffiti, it's everywhere.

We had the Acropolis for company all day - either we were gazing up to it or the Gods were gazing down! After we had a coffee Val talked me into a walk round the Agora. It was a good move.

The Agora was the centre of civic and commercial life in ancient Athens and the foundations of many of the buildings are still intact. They were used for political, educational, commercial, theatrical and athletic purposes as well as for assemblies. We were walking in the very area where democracy was born.

The best preserved monument on the site is the Temple of Hephaestus - the blacksmith god. Its elevated position among trees and lawns overlooks the whole of the Agora. You can enter the temple and marvel at its well preserved Doric pillars and roof. Just before we moved on I became fascinated by the sight of a solitary tortoise making its way across the grass. But it seems that tortoises are not uncommon in the grounds of the Agora.

We wandered round the rest of the site trying to take it all in with the help of information plaques as well as making the odd speculation. Val was amazed that I was showing so much interest. Socrates, the great philosopher would also wander round the area with his disciples which included Plato. Socrates was accused of corrupting the minds of young Athenians and sadly he was executed by being made to drink hemlock. Later, however, the authorities regretted their decision to execute their great philosopher. We stood on the exact spot where the execution took place - the foundations of the state prison. It felt quite strange to be standing at the very spot where one of the most famous figures in history had died.

The tiny Byzantine Church of the Holy Apostles is charming and has an impressive interior containing fresco figures which you can make out although they have faded over the centuries.

Finally the Stoa. This was a long colonnaded building used for shops. It has now been restored and houses a museum with many finds from the Agora including a child's potty seat!

I approached a museum attendant and asked if she enjoys her job. She said she did. And when I asked if the tourists were behaving themselves she told me she doesn't usually have problems with younger people, it's mainly the older ones, who can sometimes be very rude. She felt they hadn't mellowed! I thanked her for her time and she didn't mind me taking her photo for a souvenir.

It's interesting to note that the condition called Agoraphobia actually originates from the Greek agora meaning public open space used for assemblies and markets.

We found the perfect taverna with an al fresco seating area and a canopy. Pots of low shrubs separated our corner position from the pavement. We'd found an idyllic setting, especially for the views of the Acropolis and the Temple of Hephaestus. It was excellent for people watching too, as they drifted by in an almost continuous procession.
Our meal was partly made up of moussaka, and plenty of it. Delicious. And of course it was the inevitable two beers as well as being treated to unobtrusive Greek music from two guys playing guitar and bouzouki.

We spent one and a half hours in that gorgeous setting, and as a dining experience I would place it in my top ten of all time.

As we walked through the old town of the Plaka, the graffiti hits you. It's rife. A big blot on the district but it's strangely photogenic. Maybe these images are symbolic of unrest and unemployment.

Easy train back to Piraeus and because it was cooler we decided to walk back to the cruise terminal.

More self-indulgence - Dixieland jazz in the garden Lounge. It was the seven piece from the Queens ballroom, and unlike the theatre band, they don't use guitar and what a difference - much more clear cut. And the bass player - another life enhancing experience in its own right!

We heard that a couple are disembarking at Valetta and flying back to Southampton because they are afraid of the Bay of Biscay. What a pity. But once again I asked the same question "Did they seek advice or try to get reassurance from the staff?"

At dinner I suggested that each couple take it in turns to talk about their day in Athens - a more structured way of communicating which would avoid confusion and speech darting in all directions. The idea was for one couple to talk in turn and for the others to ask questions. But David condemned the idea in no uncertain terms. I responded in no uncertain terms by calling him a spoilsport. Later on I tried to be friendly by asking him what time he arrived back at the ship but Susie intervened and said it would be better if I didn't communicate with him. Lots of laughs with Ron and I think we've broken the ice with Jane and Jeffrey. They enjoy fell walking in the Lakes so there was lots to talk about.

The Royal Court Theatre gave us David Meyer who played the zylosynth, which is short for zylophonic synthesiser. He performed a mixed bag which included some classical music. His instrument was tilted forward to enable the audience to see it being played. He could also play it as a piano. His wife made two appearances and danced to his music. The band gave him superb backing.

Good news from Jay. Neil is becoming very keen on the American song book. I can see a quartet brewing – him, Jay, me and Enid.

Cruising to Valetta, Malta.

TUESDAY 3 MAY. Mediterranean Sea. Sunny and cool. Rough sea.

Ron had just joined me in the Garden Lounge when suddenly there was a massive down pour that felt like the sea was gushing down onto the glass roof, then there was a single flash of lightening. Minutes later the skies had cleared and the sun was out.

The morning lecture was good fun. A guy called Malcolm McFarlane presented a 60's singalong complete with memorabilia of the decade which included film clips, news items, sport etc. But he omitted four defining items: Good Vibrations, The Profumo Affair, The Cuban Missile Crisis and Sir Francis Chichester. Nevertheless full marks!

Lunch date in the Britannia restaurant with Marilyn and Kelvin - our lovely Australian friends. I took a risk with the mussel curry that paid off - delicious.

Classical concert in the Queens Room with "Travatori" which is Italian for wandering minstrels - a husband and wife duo who are classically trained singers who accompany themselves on guitars. Whilst their voices and harmonies were good, I would have liked a little more accomplished guitar playing, but they were fairly good.

The creative writing group unofficially met in the Commodore club because we were not advertised. Once again Annie gave us more trigger words to kick start a piece on Athens. My effort on the Agora was well liked. I am the sole male member but I don't mind - we're a friendly bunch.

Two other couples joined us at the quiz and the best we could achieve was a dismal 6/20. Heavens we're going into decline!

David and I are keeping our distance. I've probably burst his bubble. Let him sulk. I have a lifelong interest in people, they never fail to irritate me!

Darren Day in the Royal Court Theatre. Good Voice, rubbish songs.
I left after a few minutes because he was singing in an Elton John and then a Dave Bowie voice - a complete drone.

Valetta tomorrow.

WEDNESDAY 4 MAY. Valetta, Pinto Wharf, Grand Harbour, Malta. Sunny but cool.

The strategically placed tiny island of Malta with Valetta its capital lies in the Mediterranean, South of Sicily and east of Tunisia. Sunshine, good beaches and history make it a tourist magnet, but it's one of the most densely populated countries in the world.

Bill Miller asked if my happiness scored 9 out of 10. I said 8! I told him his last two lectures would be my two cherries on the cake.
"There you are Bill I'm trying to be as graphic as you are"
To which he replied "You'll be a speaker on Cunard soon"

This was our 4th visit to Malta and despite its size it has much to offer. And did you know it was the setting for about 114 feature films.

We hadn't planned to do a hop on hop off bus, but at 10 Euros each who could resist. But it took 3 hours which was longer than we expected. We only got off the bus once at Mosta to change to the blue line.

The Rotunda Church of St Mary at Mosta is famous mainly because a WW2 German bomb pierced the roof and landed on the floor while the congregation was listening to mass. Miraculously the bomb failed to explode and no one was injured. We saw a replica of the device in a side room. The Rotunda is very beautiful and has many arched alcoves containing small alters. The dome is spectacular and is the third largest unsupported dome in the world.

Our tour continued through landscapes that looked burnt out but the roundabouts are lawned and full of flowers. Generally the land is more fertile than it appears with many green patches and the occasional vineyard.

The Silent City of the Mdina looks magnificent from a distance - almost fairy tale like but when we arrived there we remained on the bus having previously visited it. We were on the top deck in the cool wind happily snapping away.

Golden Bay was as beautiful as we remembered, but we were too high up to fully appreciate it.

It seems there are many more cars on the island than when we were there last especially in Buggiba and the lovely bays on the way back to Valetta. The roads were so clogged up it has put me off going there again. Tragic.

As is our wont whenever we go ashore we like a drink and some lunch and what better venue than al fresco on Republic Street in Valetta in the shadow of the statue of Queen Victoria. The food was delicious, although I can't remember what we had. But what I do remember was having two succulent locally brewed pints. It was an adorable setting, full of atmosphere where it would have been fun sitting there until midnight slowly getting drunk!

The camera was made for Valetta and during our walk back to the ship we took lots of photos. There are many instances of paint peeling off doorways, balconies and window frames, but it adds character to a picture.

During the sail away I hatched the following poem entitled:

DEATH ON THE DECK

It was early evening
Elizabeth was saying goodbye to Valetta
The beguiling ochre skyline was receding
The sea was shimmering in the sunlight
A spectacle of calm
Spiritual
Almost holy
A setting for contemplation and reflection
Or just to be with the silence
But I kept my gaze with no analysis
Except for a feeling of joy and sadness.

Then the sail away party was ripe
For the enemy to strike
Killing these beautiful moments with their weapons
Of drums, bass guitar and amplifiers
Destruction
Death on the deck.
Amen.

My friend, Alun Williams would give up the harmonica after hearing Johnny Stafford play. He's ex Moreton Fraser Harmonica Rascals.
A virtuoso. He played classical as well as standards with gorgeous tones. He's very humorous too. As we were leaving the theatre we were flying high!

After dinner we were back in the theatre for the crew talent show. The Lovely young Asian woman who cleans the glass doors in the Garden
Lounge was the best act. She's an excellent singer. The rest were pretty average. Tommi, (poetry readings) was the mainstay in a sketch based in a doctor's surgery. He went completely off his head when he caught infections from all the other patients. Lastly the entertainment team performed a slapstick comedy act.

Cruising to Valencia.

THURSDAY 5 MAY. Mediterranean Sea. Sunny and mild. Calm sea.

I awoke very early and listened to jazz on my i-pod, completed my notes on the Agora and then read about reflective meditation. I often busy myself with items like these if I can't sleep.

Another Bill Miller lecture "Gateway to the World" which was about the great port of New York which included the skyscrapers. Again I was spellbound by his every word as he educated and entertained us. I can never praise him enough.

Took to the Canopy on the Lido Deck for some journal when I saw David approaching in what looked like an umpires hat and white jacket! Well it takes all sorts!

There was a diversion from our normal creative writing session. Freda was going to talk for 15 minutes with stories from her book, but instead she dominated the whole duration. Not my idea of a creative writing group. I would have preferred to do some exercises. Two other women agreed with me.

It seems the vast majority of folk on the ship are musically illiterate. The brilliant Tiffany String Quartet performed an early evening concert in the Garden Lounge with only a very small audience. Perhaps it would have been full if Abba and Elton John music had been playing. Each to their own! Anyhow I got the chance to hear "Plink Plank Plunk" again – probably the best lesson in pizzicato!

David and I are in deadlock. At dinner he sulked for most of the time.

Hilary O'Neal is enjoying a glittering career as a comedienne. Sorry Hilary for sleeping though most of your act!

Valencia tomorrow.

FRIDAY 6 MAY. Cruise Port, Valencia Spain. Our last port of call. Cloudy, warm.

Valencia is situated on the east coast of Spain and is the country's third largest city. Its history dates back over 2000 years - pure gold for sightseers.

Approached a woman in the Lido for not using tongs for the bread. She ignored me. I told her about the norovirus, she still ignored me.

A shortish day was ahead because of the mid-afternoon sail away. This resulted in many passengers eager to leave the ship with much queue jumping, but fortunately we made the first shuttle bus which enabled us to maximise our time.

We wandered round the old part of the city snapping everything in sight; towers, churches, plazas, ancient side streets and lots of graffiti.
But you need to be patient with the white vans or they'll clog up your photographs. Some of the trees however, are useful for framing images.

There are food markets and there are food markets but the Central Food Market in Valencia is a must see. Especially impressive is the huge intricate glass dome. There are 1000 stalls selling every delicacy imaginable surrounded by a riot of colour. We particularly enjoyed browsing round the fish stalls, I think every type of fish from the ocean was on display including stuff you've never heard of. The stallholders are immune to their wares being photographed and one imagines that there are more photos than fish sales.

Outside the market it was time for coffee under a canopy. (You must have guessed by now, we love canopies!) A busking guitarist providing some light entertainment.

We passed the Silk Exchange which was built in the 15th century. The interior is a treasure because of its many spiral pillars.

The grandest area we visited was Plaza de la Virgen which dates back to the 13th century. A beautiful square both for the culture vulture and the photographer. The Turia Fountain contains a statue of a man reclining on a slab which represents the Turia River but more interestingly are the eight statues of figures holding large jars with water gushing out of them.

The square also hosts three of Valencia's most important buildings:
the rear part of St Mary's Cathedral with its massive ornate arched doorway and adjacent bell tower. The church was consecrated in 1238 and contains numerous 15 century paintings.

The second is the 17th century blue domed Basilica de Virgen de Los Desamparados, and finally the Palau de Generalitat - a government building, which blends Gothic, Renaissance and Moorish styles of architecture.

The plaza was the perfect setting for lunch - al fresco of course, with the inevitable canopy! We discovered that paella originated in Valencia, so it was "Two paellas please and two pints" We didn't mind the forty minutes wait because not only did we have history to gaze at we had people as well, including a saxophone busker. Our paellas were served individually on cast iron dishes, and after adding another pint each for good measure it was bliss! - a great way to celebrate our last port of call.

Although the weather stayed dry but dull all day, the sun decided to appear just as we were leaving. Despite this we were well pleased with our short stay in Valencia.

Graham Wellard was sat close to us on the shuttle bus and I was immediately drawn to him through his personality and beaming smile. I told him I'd be at the commodore Club later to hear him play and I hinted how much I love "Embraceable You" He seemed like a good guy to talk to and has an enviable calm voice.

I would have preferred the string quartet to have been playing at the sail away party rather than Changez. Some classical music would have been a welcome break. But no it had to be Changez! Val mentioned it to Amanda to no avail. I know we like a whinge now and then but its minor compared to the overall enjoyment of such a wonderful cruise.

I was sitting in the Garden lounge with Ron and Liz while a few people came by to say hello including Barbara from the creative writing group. She said she likes my writing and has noticed it's philosophical - perhaps I'm the ships Socrates!

Bill Miller said he would be happy for me to video him before the end of the cruise. "Only for you," he said!

Val found out that a guy's wife on our deck flew home earlier because she's home sick. Odd. More like they've had a row. How tragic.

At dinner, David felt that sulking hurts so he decided to start communicating by flaunting his knowledge and his perfectionism. There were no words between us.

Graham Wellard is amazingly talented. His calm voice and clever piano accompaniment circulated the Commodore club like a warm breeze. He opened with "Embraceable You," probably because I'd mentioned it on the coach. He then played my two other requests- "Witchcraft" and "Stormy Weather" to perfection. The walking bass with his left hand was a dream. It was midnight when I walked back to the cabin full of the joys of the American Song Book! Jay would adore him.

Cruising to Southampton.

SATURDAY 7 MAY. Mediterranean Sea. Sunny but cool with average sea conditions.

The American and his invalid wife joined me at breakfast. Lovely people, very polite and I love their accents. He taught maths, statistics and computers studies at Illinois University before starting his own computer business. They are now retired.

Walking on decks 9/10/11 have now become my morning fix. One minute I'm walking up and down steps the next minute I'm walking by the covered tennis court and the bowling and croquet spaces and often by the Lido Pool.

I had an early immigration check to avoid queues later on. I'm amazed I've never been questioned because of the disparity between my passport photograph and my current image. My photo shows me without glasses and without beard. I now have both and there is a difference. It's been the same the world over, the authorities have never queried it.

While I was sitting in the Garden Lounge relaxing and bringing my journal up to date, Scottish Robert joined me. He said he'd like to read some of my entries and so we exchanged e-mail addresses for the purpose. A really nice guy who now lives in Newfoundland.

American Grace tried to give us some pointers for improving our creative writing skills. I'm sorry Grace you are just stating the obvious! Anyhow, I've become a popular member of the group and they liked my poem about leaving Valetta. Another meeting was arranged for later but I felt that one was enough.

Many passengers were on the decks to see the Rock of Gibraltar - a majestic sight especially because it's British. I was right when I thought David and Susie would be there with their cameras and as much as I don't particularly like David I felt it was right to give my good wishes to them as it was the day of their golden wedding anniversary. I approached them with a hug for Susie and a hand shake for David. The deed hath been done and I felt the better for it.

Half my piano practice time was reduced owing to a private function but I continued to practice what Penny has taught me.

Chanced on Kelvin and we talked about folk who are joined at the hip, who are inseparable. One can't go anywhere without the other. They follow each other round like lap dogs. Never any news to tell each other. How boring!

I'm happy to say that matters are a little more civilised at the dinner table because it seems that David and I are now relating. He and Susie had a good day with lunch in the Verandah Restaurant and a photo shoot with the ships photographers.

Then it was the chef's parade as they all tripped round the restaurant in a long procession to the Radetzky March accompanied by cheering, napkin waving and clicking cameras.

Graham Wellard took my fifteen Requests and played five of them. He liked my choices. Hopefully he'll play the rest over the next couple of nights. Herbie Dent was sat with me and I felt he'd do well to take a leaf out of Graham's book!

Cruising to Southampton.

SUNDAY 8 MAY. Atlantic Ocean. Sunny but cool and windy. Choppy swell.

Penultimate Day.

Olwyn's becoming the ship's whinge. She was complaining about having to grope about in the dark in her cabin for fear of waking Ted. She's not alone - I then joined in and had a whinge about certain folk.

E-mail from Paul. Jean and he were in tears because Annabel's dog, Roxy has died while she was being looked after. Paul recently won £800.00 net on a horse but has decided to give up gambling. I'm not holding my breath.

Bill Miller told me Cunard paid $45,000.00 to transit the Suez Canal.
Perhaps some of the money could be used to clean up Cairo.

The Royal Court Theatre featured Captain Aseem Hashmi being interviewed by Amanda. An interesting guy and quite funny. He lives in Coventry.

Malcolm McFarlane again with a Bing Crosby lecture which was very entertaining. It was about his life and his music and was sprinkled with singalong numbers. My parents would have loved it.

The creative writing group gave us a general discussion with Annie doing most of the discussion! She told us to try writing in the present tense. We then talked about the difficulties of writing descriptions and suggested we read John Steinbeck's Of Mice and Men to see how it's done. I chuckled at Annie's sign pointing to the Commodore club even though nothing had been officially arranged. Good on 'er!

Met Jenny as arranged and bought her a drink as a thank you for the piano tuition. We talked very little about music in favour of relationships. She's had many traumas. My listening skills helped us to connect as we discussed mental health with self-acceptance being a big issue. Then on a lighter note she told me two people on her dinner table are sending her over the edge. Well I could certainly relate to that! We exchanged contact numbers and a hug, and as she was leaving the lift she said" You're a lovely guy" What a compliment. Even at my age it's wonderful that certain people see me like that.

Took to the Promenade deck for an evening walk with intermittent emotion about the odyssey coming to an end. After all, I've been happily institutionalised for nearly four and a half months.

"Stormy Weather" is still my current fix. Never in my dreams did I expect to be playing jazz on an Irish whistle.

Bill Miller failed to turn up as arranged. Well, he is a celebrity and doubtless he had an unexpected engagement.

Jazz again in the Garden Lounge. It makes a difference when the leader has a good warm personality. It always makes it easier to connect to an audience. He announced that the band was going to compose a piece on the spot and Val was quick to notice it was a 12 bar blues jam which I've been doing for years!

Good dinner table. I'm happy for David and Susie. Best to end on a high note. The problem is Jane and Jeffrey. They're difficult to engage with despite the attention we've given them. They suffer from two things: unawareness and a deficiency of emotional intelligence. Quite sad.

Commodore Club again for some Graham Wellard therapy. I bought him a drink while he continued to play my requests. I told him about the "Rave-ons," (the band I was in when I was 18) my flute, and my improvisations. He said it was good that we'd met.

Fairly calm through the Bay of Biscay.

Cruising to Southampton.

MONDAY 9 MAY. The English Channel and the Solent. Sunny and cool with a calm sea.

The last day of the Odyssey indeed was emotional!
Olwyn was more upbeat at breakfast with no whinging. I should speak! But we did manage to mention a few irritating people! She

always calls me by my first name before and during a conversation.

Someone once said that your name is the sweetest thing you can ever hear but isn't it sad that some people are uncomfortable about using first names even if theirs is frequently mentioned.

A guy was using his hands to reach the bread rolls instead of using the food tongs. When I told him it was unhygienic he completely ignored me.

The lovely bubbling waitress in the Café Carinthia mentioned my book for the last time. Her name is Jamile. She was definitely worth a hug and a goodbye.

Saw Martin in the Garden Lounge. We both felt that a long cruise was a positive time for personal reflection, and in my case, whilst I've met some lovely folk I've been very critical and possibly too judgemental of others!

Malcolm McFarlane gave his last lecture - Frank Sinatra's life with a good compilation of singalongs and as expected it was interesting and entertaining with lots of people in fine voice. Most lectures and entertainment gel with me but I'd like to assign some to room 101.

I grabbed Bill miller before his lecture. He gave me a signed photo of himself and apologised for last night - he'd had an invitation to join the captain, so we arranged another meeting for the evening. He gave another lecture about the floating palaces and as ever he was as charismatic as I was captivated. The graphics just rolled off his lips. Good on ya Bill! A fitting climax to a brilliant cruise and good compensation for what we were to receive in the theatre later on.

Garden Lounge to bring my journal up to date. Scottish Robert appeared and was full of praises for it. We talked about nice and not so nice people on the ship. He and his wife would have been good company on our dinner table.

I circumnavigated the promenade deck a few times to the roar of the sea as Elizabeth ploughed through it. The wake of course was especially noisy.

The creative writers all know me as John - it's nice to be popular! It was an interesting last meeting even though it was cloned from Lodge Cottage back home! I made it clear that days ashore haven't got the monopoly on creative writing, it can be equally interesting writing about sea days. I proved my point by reciting my piece about Daisy May! I was never expecting to join a writers group at sea, and with Annie at the helm it's all been worthwhile - and then it was hugs and goodbyes.

Caroline was at the harp and I stayed to listen for a while. She said "Hello John." I told her I adored her recent Bach's Ave Maria - and then it was a hug and a goodbye. How unfortunate it was that we never had a proper jam.

Tommi, hospitality host appeared during my last piano slot and I told him I was feeling emotional I felt about leaving the ship tomorrow. He said that I wasn't alone, he too has felt the same.

Bravo! Bill Miller was waiting for me in the Garden Lounge. He said a few sentences while I filmed him with my cam corda. It was a good catch! He told me he'd journaled my story about our mail run in Akaroa N/Z. He's a lovely guy who knows how to connect. He gave me his new e-mail address and said he'd love to receive some of my journal entries. I felt honoured and came away buzzing.

The last quiz gave us our worst score to date, a depressing 3/20. But most people clocked up the same!

At dinner David and I were very wary of each other. I just listened while he flaunted his knowledge and talked self - assuredly with a perfectionist voice tone. Although I do not wish him ill I will not miss him. Susie though, is more down to earth and quite friendly.

264

It's my custom to film everyone at the end of a cruise but not on this occasion as I felt David might not co-operate. I handed my tips to the superb waiters and then it was hugs and handshakes all round.

Had one final pack before leaving our luggage in the passageway to be collected and then we were off to the Golden Lion to pay our respects to Herbie Dent and to take his photo.

So the final entertainment was the American Song Book in the Commodore Club. Thankyou Graham for playing most of my requests. Perhaps we'd have made it a nightly venue had the bar prices in the Commodore Club been less extortionate.

Southampton tomorrow morning.

TUESDAY 10 MAY. Southampton Water then Southampton Cruise Terminal. Dull but warm.

At 4:40 am I was wide awake thinking about the past 18 weeks and having to disembark the luxurious Queen Elizabeth in a few hours' time - how depressing! I then thought about playing flute number 2 when I get home - a blissful thought!

At 4:30 am, I donned Cunard's white dressing gown and headed to the Lido for two cups of tea. Two guys were already fully dressed. Chanced on Kelvin, also in his white dressing gown. He told me he's a poor sleeper and had just been for a smoke and a deck walk. I had my doubts about him and Marilyn at first but they became good friends.

Took Val her tea and then it was back to bed but I got up again at 6:30 for a last minute photo shoot for souvenirs.

Took a short walk on decks 10 and 11 more out of sentiment than for exercise and continued my photo shoot. The Great Queen Mary was at berth nearby and I thought about Bill Miller who would be boarding her for his voyage back home to New York. And it was quite a spectacle seeing thousands of Mini Cars and hundreds of JCB'S neatly parked on the quayside all awaiting export.

A couple in the lift were telling me they boarded the ship in Dubai and couldn't wait to get off. It was their first cruise and definitely their last. How sad! Perhaps they should have done some research first. Poor souls.

I heard that the Balmoral has the Norovirus.

The interior of the ship on deck two looked so different around the Queens Ballroom area because it had been transformed into a huge waiting room for disembarkation. More hugs, handshakes and emotions. But the biggest emotion was saying goodbye to The Queen Elizabeth.

Southampton to Sydney = 17,020 nautical miles
Sydney to Southampton = 24,232   "   "
Total   = 41,252   "   "

EPILOGUE

The party's over
The odyssey hath ended
It's all in the bag
I've got the photos
I've got the videos
I've got my journal
I'm special
I'm privileged
My experiences have put me on the rich list
As my mind becomes a treasure chest
Brimming with jewels
Brimming with lovely people.
Then back home when I'm asked
"How was your holiday?"
I can reply in one word-
"MOMENTOUS"

Printed in Great Britain
by Amazon

40409224R00156